A PARLIAMENT *of* SOULS

Companion to the Public Television Series

A Parliament of Souls

IN SEARCH OF GLOBAL SPIRITUALITY

Interviews with

28 Spiritual Leaders

from Around the World

Edited by

Michael Tobias
Jane Morrison
Bettina Gray

KQED
BOOKS
San Francisco

KQED President & CEO: Mary G. F. Bitterman

Educational and non-profit groups wishing to order this book at
attractive quantity discounts may contact KQED Books & Tapes,
2601 Mariposa St., San Francisco, CA 94110.

Grateful acknowledgment is given for reprints from various sources.
See page 284 for specific permissions.

Vice President for Publishing &
New Ventures:
    Mark K. Powelson
Publisher: Pamela Byers
Project Editor: Jan Johnson
Research Assistant:
    Steve Anderson
Editorial Assistance:
    Mark Woodworth
Project Assistant:
    Alex Lyon
Book and cover design:
    Sharon Smith
Production:
    Joan Olson
Interior Photographs:
    © Robert Radin
Cover Photograph:
    © David Wakely, 1995

On the cover:
    The Pantheon, Rome

A parliament of souls: in search of global spirituality: interviews
    with 28 spiritual leaders from around the world / edited by
    Michael Tobias, Jane Morrison, Bettina Gray.
                    p.   cm.
        "Companion to the Public Television series."
        Includes biliographical references and index.
        ISBN 0–912333–35–9
        1. Religions. 2. Spirituality—Comparative studies.
    3. Religious biography. I. Tobias, Michael. II. Morrison, Jane,
    1954– . III. Gray, Bettina, 1949–
    BL85.P36   1995
    291—dc20   95–10093
                                                                    CIP

ISBN 0–912333–35–9

Manufactured in the United States of America
10 9 8 7 6 5 4 3 2 1

Distributed to the trade by Publishers Group West

ACKNOWLEDGMENTS

Our thanks for the support, patience, and affection necessary to produce this series and book must go to Bettina Gray's husband, David, and her sons, Daniel and Walter. We would also like to thank the members of the board of the North American Interfaith Network for their invaluable assistance, including the Rev. Dr. Charles White, founder of Multifaith Resources, a tremendous resource of information, research, and support; Elizabeth Esperson, executive director of Thanks Giving Square in Dallas, Texas, and chair of the North American Interfaith Network; the Rev. Dr. Margaret Orr Thomas, chair of the Interfaith Working Group of the National Council of Churches; the Rev. Dr. John Berthrong, associate dean of Boston University and director of the Institute for Dialogue Among Religions; Dr. Elias Mallon, director of Graymoor Ecumenical Institute; Dr. Peter Lawrence, executive director, Office of Interfaith Programs of the National Council of Christians and Jews; Dr. Jamsheed Mavalwalla, president of the Zoroastrian Society of Canada; Dr. Suwanda Sugansiri, president of the Buddhist Council of Canada; Imam Yahya Abdullah and Marzuk Jaami, Al Islam; and Marks McAvity, World Interfaith Colleges Association. In addition the consultation from Dr. Diana Eck, professor of Hindu Studies at Harvard University and director of the Pluralism Project; from Kasumita Pedersen, executive director of the Project on Religion and Human Rights; and from Dr. Daniel Gómez-Ibáñez, executive director of the Council for a Parliament of the World's Religions was invaluable. Many thanks to the Presbyterian Church, USA, which contributed film crew and technical support; to Graymoor Ecumenical Institute and Sir John Templeton for their financial support; to Richard Landau and the film crew of Vision Television of Canada; to production assistant Carol Radin, and to Scott Forsyth; to the Blackstone Hotel, Max Abrams, Saito Oriental Antiques of Chicago, Alison Gibson, Bill Elias, Debra Wells of VISN Network in New York, and Peter Flemington of Vision Canada. Thanks goes also to: DeeHoward White, Peter Walker, William W. Gee, Mark J. Obradovich, Rinchen Dharlo, Francis Paone and Lopon Claude d'Estree, Dennis Passaggio and Howard Wexler, Ronald C. Reph of 3M Corporation, and KORET of California, Inc., and to Danny McGuire and the staff at KTEH-TV, San Jose, California.

A Parliament of Souls
A series of 26 half-hour episodes
Directed and produced by Michael Tobias
Interviewer/Host: Bettina Gray
Executive Producer: Danny McGuire
Co-Producers: Bettina Gray and Richard Landau
Associate Producers: Jane Gray Morrison and Robert Radin
Editors: Michael Tobias, Bettina Gray, and Jane Morrison
Filmed at the Presidential Suite, the Blackstone Hotel, Chicago
A Co-Production of JMT, KTEH, and Vision Network
of Canada

CONTENTS

Editor's Note: The chapters in this book are edited from transcripts of interviews. In all cases but one, Michael Tobias wrote the introduction to each of the interviewees. The material in the margins comes from various published sources. The source list is on page 281.

INTRODUCTION
by Michael Tobias

In my local phone book, situated between "chocolate" and "cigar & cigarette dealers," are listings for about 165 "churches" of various denominations. In addition to the variety of Christian churches one might typically expect, these include the Bahā'ī, the Chabad House Lubavitch, Eckankar, Manna Life Ministries, the Reconstructionist Federation, the Tradition of Tao, the U.S. Raelian Movement, and the World Metaphysical Society. The town in question is perhaps most widely noted for its liberal politics and contradictorily high number of homeless. It is not ordinarily construed as a bastion of religious types. Nor is it. But today's multiethnic America encompasses a wide ranging spiritual orientation that is, if anything, diverse. Such religious concentration is a challenge: can varied paths inspire, learn from, and enjoy each other? Can they intermingle and cross-fertilize in peace? Does diversity allow for, even hasten, unity? And is unity any kind of prerequisite for a harmony of human beings?

With over five thousand languages and dialects spoken in the world, 250 million indigenous peoples, and nearly two hundred countries culturally intermixing like never before, the late twentieth century offers unprecedented opportunities for a human community strengthened by dialogue and tolerance. The ethnic texture of America is an instructive microcosm of that dizzying array of religious and spiritual affiliations and beliefs worldwide.

A century ago, inspired by the possibilities for such dialogue, and in search of a common humanity, spiritual leaders and theologians convened at the first Parliament of World Religions in Chicago. Of the sixty-odd religious leaders on the stage in 1893 were two African-Americans, half-a-dozen women, several Asiatic monks (Zen, Jain, Vedanta, and Buddhist), and one Muslim, in addition to various Christian representatives. No known Jain or Zen monk had ever previously come to the United States. It was, for most, a first-time encounter with Shintos, Zoroastrians, and Confucians. Oxford University scholar F. Max Muller, editor of the 50-volume Sacred Books of the East, would describe it as "one of the most memorable events in the history of the world. . . ."

Subsequent to the 1893 Parliament, on an August day in 1914, members of the Church Peace Union (founded with money given by Andrew Carnegie) were meeting in Constance, Germany, with delegates of the so-called World Alliance for International Friendship, when the first World War broke out. Two such wars, the Shoah (Hebrew for Holocaust), Hiroshima and Nagasaki, and the countless other human and ecological tragedies of the last few generations have riveted the attention of the world's religions upon those questions which have tormented our species for its entire duration, but perhaps never with such burning relevancy. Who are we? From whence we came? Is there a purpose to our being? Is there truly free will? Is there life after death? Is there a God? Is human nature even equipped or inclined to act in accordance with its gift of a conscience? Might we yet ensure a harmonious human presence on Earth, and by what means?

Continuing dialogue to address these questions was the goal of the second Parliament of the World's Religions, held in August of 1993 in Chicago. And it is the driving force behind the present volume, as well. The contributors to this book all came to participate in one form or another at the Chicago conference, along with nearly eight thousand other individuals representing at least two hundred religious organizations. A multiplicity of perspectives, ideals, and questions emerged from the week-long event. But such queries do not invite facile answers, though plenty of resolutions and pledges towards the future did, in fact, emerge.

At the heart of the World Parliament was a distinctive tenor of concern, even alarm, that human violence and loss of faith are paralyzing our species' capacity to serve as ecological stewards, or to ensure human justice, happiness, and a spiritual existence on this earth. There is no question that our colossal crimes against nature—knowing and unknowing—have backfired, perpetrating a contagion of woes and a vast sea of individual suffering, highlighted by incessant "statistics" that can easily numb the stoutest heart. The soul rests in clear view of millions of crimes, dozens of small-scale wars, a billion malnourished children, tyrannized females, the indignity of unemployment, increasing poverty, disease, nuclear proliferation, burning rainforests, mangled coral reefs, polluted air, oceans, rivers, and soil, deforested mountain tops, and several billion other animals being cruelly and needlessly slaughtered each year by human beings. Truly, there is cause for angst and existential "nausea." In biological terms one might posit an incremental self-destruct mechanism at work in the human aggregate—the planet's intuitive strategy for dealing with a deadly species.

The soul also knows that there are alternatives to violence, discord, and disarray. There is, in the Creation, an overwhelming but explicable grace that touches all who seek. Its beneficence, truth, and beauty are generous to the point of profligacy, a facet of our existence repeatedly voiced by contributors to this volume. While religious differences have continued to sunder whole communities, from Egypt to Sri Lanka, individuals are often more malleable than masses. These persons are quietly willing to experiment with love, to boldly explore new avenues of empathy and nonviolence. Such themes and invitations are key to *A Parliament of Souls*.

Themes become questions, and questions, meditations. Contributors to this work address over and over such arenas as the existence and identity of God; revelatory access to God—through religious practice, prayer, meditation, and action; the question as to whether God, or any religious belief, is even crucial to ethical behavior. If there is a God, why is there evil in the world? What are our human responsibilities to ensure ethical behavior and the survival of the natural world, and of humanity? Does having a religion or spiritual practice mandate that we must become activists? How do we best serve the world? Within these broad areas, over the many hours of conversations, dozens of motifs spilled open: the fate of the Earth, the nature of morality, of virtue, and of evil; the relation of the sexes; the population explosion; the notion of rights, duties, and forgiveness. Some of our interviewees were particularly concerned with the role of science, of the political process, of ecological and economic sustainability, of animal rights activism, and of meditation. All were fascinated by the quest for spiritual identity: what does it mean? Is it relevant?

The approaches to such venerable queries, and the insights gained by reflection, are posed in lush and strikingly personal ways throughout *A Parliament of Souls*. It's the personal tone, and the sense of diversity within unity, that truly separates this volume from all others of which I am aware. Jacqueline Left Hand Bull Delahunt describes her Native American upbringing, her Christianity, and their integration with the teachings of the Bahā'ī faith. Robert Henderson focuses on collective heroism in the ghettoes, while Sister Jayanti summons a "billion moments of peace" from people around the world. Dr. A.T. Ariyaratne stares down a loaded gun, undeterred in his crusade to win economic dignity for the poor in his country. The Dalai Lama wisely compares the brilliant mind with the open heart in seeking solutions to environmental problems and human suffering. Thai Buddhist Dr. Chatsumarn Kabilsingh speaks of finding enlightenment in this life, now, through nonviolence, protest, faith, and commitment to something spiritual. Theodore Martin Hesburgh focuses upon civil rights, ecological issues, the threat of nuclear annihilation, and the redemptive benefits of service. Both Dr. Hans Küng and Robert Muller look optimistically at the capacity of religions to move people towards such service, while Charles Colson unearths the unexpected religious pathways and experiences that can, in turn, lead to true spiritual renewal. In his case, among other things, it was a quiet communion with a man who was condemned to be executed.

What became apparent during the filming, and subsequent editing, of these many voices and personalities was that there is indeed a profound unity in pluralism. Much has been made of the concept of religious pluralism. The word suggests a commonality of purpose. It implies that a society like America, so richly endowed with multicultural resources, can transmute that variability into a common good, rather than being polarized by it. Pluralism connotes an affirmative stance that acknowledges the universal truth of all traditions. It points to the combinatory genius of multiple histories, languages, cultural styles, and personalities and asserts that the story of humanity is nothing less than the full depiction of that diversity-within-unity. As Diana Eck of Harvard University says, "The whole issue of talking about and teaching about world religions wasn't in some other part of the world but in our own university community and in our own urban setting." She recognizes that "the old ways of what you might call exclusivism will not do for us anymore" because we are all together in this, aware of one another, and within shouting distance, if you will, of every religion, every belief system, every individual. And it is this encounter with other systems and faiths that can prove so liberating and instructive within one's own tradition.

This journey towards pluralism was not always so exuberantly embraced or envisioned. Consider the paradoxical nature of spiritual freedom in the United States. Although the Continental Congress of 1774 had first intoned the rights of native peoples, their subsequent decimation would scarcely touch America's heart. This country's denial of the intrinsic worth of her native people and African-Americans, and of their invaluable spiritual wisdom, extended to most "foreigners" as well. As Diana Eck has described in her important book *Encountering God—A Spiritual Journey from Bozeman to Banaras,* as early as 1882 immigration exclusion laws were targeted at the Chinese. A Montana newspaper described the "Chinaman" as "no more a citizen than a coyote." Soon, most other Asiatics were afflicted by this unabashed American racism.[1] Sikhs were labelled "rag-heads," and in 1923 the U.S. Supreme Court ruled that "Hindus" were ineligible for citizenship.[2]

Today, it must be recognized that we are all descendents of immigration, the precursors of an ethical melting pot that in a city like Los Angeles now translates into more than 140 anguage-speaking groups. Among them are four million Latinos, equivalent to Mexico City's population in the early 1950s. Over one million legal immigrants enter the U.S. every year. This tide—some of it expressly concerned with faith and religious freedom, but much of it not—scarcely begins to intimate the much greater wave of indigenous spiritual movement, revival, exploration, and cross-fertilization. For example, since 1934, nearly one mosque every month has been built in the United States. Soon, Islam will be the second most populous faith in this country. And as contributor Imam W. D. Mohammed, a leader of the Black Muslims, has said, "[African-Americans] should love America. We should love America passionately now that America has changed so drastically within a relatively short period of time."[3] In Chicago alone, there are 80,000 Hindus. And throughout the United States, there are over 50,000 Jains, and at least 5 million Buddhists.

Professor Martin Emil Marty, in describing his own understanding of Lutheranism, cites Martin Luther who believed that God also "works through people who aren't Christian." It is the quintessential avowal that all religions have an important message for our time, and that by working together we can convey that message in a manner that everyone will get. Quoting once again Imam W. D. Mohammed, he states, "Most of us are not so hung up on racial identity that we can't be comfortable with a member of another race and relate to them and enjoy their company." Both Sant Rajinder Singh and Sir John Templeton describe how science itself has begun to own up to that message of universal harmony—call it religious or spiritual—as underlying all other realities. Singh, as well as Zoroastrian Professor Kaikhosrov Irani, go on to prescribe a method for achieving harmony within oneself. It is no idle message, but a persuasive invitation to become a true human being in company with others.

But what is the distinguishing nature of spiritual reality? The question, in countless guises, surfaces throughout the interviews in this book. For His Holiness Sri Swami Chidananda Saraswati and for the eloquent Brother Wayne Teasdale, it is the possibility of a whole new civilization built upon love, compassion, and living in a sustainable kinship with earth. For Professor Rabbi Emil Fackenheim and Rabbi Irving Greenberg, it is the ability—in spite of the Holocaust—to forgive and to embrace life. Professor Susannah Heschel joins in with her heartfelt description of growing up female in a Jewish household and of her commitment to the rights of women to be themselves, to speak their minds, to experience the intimacy and full power of Jewish tradition without any interference. Similarly, Dr. Azizah Al-Hibri speaks authoritatively to the sources of Muslim tradition in defense of freedom of thought and spiritual equality between men and women.

Numerous religious leaders, like His Holiness the Dalai Lama, and Hopi Messenger Thomas Banyacya, Sufi leader Pir Vilayat, the remarkably erudite High Commissioner Dr. L. M. Singhvi, the late Acharya Sushil Kumar Ji Maharaj, and Taoist/Tai Ji master Chungliang Al Huang have all come forward during the past decades to lead the way in spiritual interfaith movements, ecological stewardship, sustainable community life, and political reconciliation, recognizing that all people—all species—desire liberation; that every Being has a soul that must be respected. Banyacya has gone to the United Nations to speak out against nuclear weapons, while Chungliang Al Huang has used his substantial gifts as an artist, musician, and choreographer to bring a philosophy of the harmony of life to thousands of fellow practitioners. The Jain Acharya Sushil Kumar, who passed away to another existence not long after his interview in this book, for most of his life walked throughout India spreading the message of non-violence.

Convinced of the paramount importance of belief, coupled with action, parishes in hundreds of communities are vanguarding local conservation efforts. And several U.S. religious groups—among them Jewish, Catholic, and Episcopalian—have sponsored a National Religious Partnership for the Environment. Countless ecological declarations and open letters by the world's religious leaders have been issued, including the "Statement by Religious Leaders at the Summit on Environment," in June, 1991. And since 1987, the United Nations has established an Environmental Sabbath, the first weekend in June each year, which has been adopted by churches, temples, synagogues, mosques, and other institutions. Contributor Hans Küng reflects these energies, the sense of a powerful harbinger, in the *Global Declaration* which he authored at the conclusion of the 1993 Parliament of the World's Religions.

The relativity of different religions and religious positions has been described by any number of poetic metaphors—numerous paths, infinite rays of light—each one leading towards some commonly perceived or understood divinity. And this abiding, all-accessible revelation has become synonymous with the very meaning of humanity, of what it takes to be a humane, caring person.

The potential for spiritual fellowship and religious tolerance is explored in this volume. We see that among Jains, for example, a crucial ethical concept is that of *parasparopagraho jivanam,* meaning all life is interdependent and mutually supportive. Brahma Baba, founder of the Brahma Kumaris of India, spoke frequently of a coming together of all religions. For the Bahā'ī, interfaith dialogue is critical to recognizing that all religions descend from the same God. Both Native American and Judeo-Christian traditions reiterate that the Creation is generous, involving one and all. For Buddhists, the notion of *pratitya-amutpada,* or "dependent origination," hinges upon recognition that cause-and-effect are both ecological and spiritual principles implicit to the biosphere. Similarly, Islam holds that "all natural phenomena are signs (ayat) of God, that nature shares in the Qur'ānic revelation, and that humans, as God's vicegerents (khalifahs) on earth, are responsible before God for not only themselves but all creatures with which they come into contact."[4] Similarly, in Hinduism, "an internal 'parliament of sub-traditions and sub-religions'," all fostering a singular Vedic tradition, has been commented upon.[5]

We invited many of those diverse delegates to be interviewed before cameras for a PBS television series. The idea was to engage these individuals away from the madding crowd of the Parliament itself, in a more tranquil and secluded place where they might feel at ease for an hour or two to reflect out loud on the many moral, philosophical, and practical issues that had absorbed them in their personal lives as theologians, spiritualists, and human beings. We found such a location when the Blackstone Hotel was kind enough to provide us full use of its famed Presidential Suite overlooking Lake Michigan, a mile or so away from the Parliament events. Throughout the week Bettina Gray interviewed our guests. This book represents a compilation of many of those edited transcripts.

Some are important "religious" figures, in the conventional sense. Others are, perhaps, better described as preeminent spiritual thinkers. However one tries, ineffectively, to encapsulate them, all are powerful hearts and minds, women and men of

wide-ranging backgrounds and nationalities who have felt and
thought deeply about the many crises and possibilities of our
age. They are not only members of a given spiritual tradition,
but in every case practitioners as well. We chose them according
to many internal criteria: we wanted a wide-ranging representation of faiths, nationalities, ethnic and traditional points of
view, as well as mainline religious traditions. We acknowledged
from the outset that it would be well-nigh impossible to encompass all traditions, or to even fairly represent any one tradition.
Nevertheless, we endeavored to sample from those attending the
Parliament a telling mirror of our spiritual age.

This work differs from most other works on world religions
for some very explicit reasons. First, it engages the reader on the
most intimate, personal, and experiential level. It is shorn of the
academia which pervades so much comparative religions. Because
this book is about the diversity of ideas, as experienced and re-
flected by so large an assemblage of individuals, the reader is
likely to find an extravagance of riches with regard to accessing
and truly appreciating the core of so much that might have
seemed abstruse or esoteric. In fact, my strongest sense of the
many participants was of their integrity and firm beliefs. It was,
and is, an exhilarating experience to encounter deep feelings conveyed so intimately and shared among friends who come from all
over the world, from remarkably different traditions, but who all
seem resolved to make this a better place to live.

Some of the diverse ideas in this book are mutually exclusive. And many are complementary in unexpected ways. But
what truly gives *A Parliament of Souls* its uniqueness is that it is
a book which introduces readers to a variety of religions, religious experience, and religious practice by people who are involved in those traditions at a very deep and trustworthy level.
In my encounter with other works on religious traditions, the
overwhelming sensation is one of an ivory tower, an encyclopedia, the arid halls of a library. One rarely has the sense of being
out there side by side with saints and sages. People who have
academically studied a tradition may be substantially different
from those who have experienced firsthand the spirituality and
religion of which they speak. But that is where this book lives.

I came away from my experience in Chicago uplifted by the
realization that religion—which so frequently has earned a bad

name—has more to offer our world than ever before. Humanity is struggling to achieve both physical and moral balance. It needs help, both information and wisdom. The "getting of wisdom" cannot be accomplished overnight. And what these diverse traditions and individual philosophers reveal is that the wellsprings of religious thought are ancient, recommended on the basis of much time and reflection. These faiths and insights—and their scintillating representatives whom we have presented here—are instructive, at times revelatory. Whether Hopi, Muslim, or Zoroastrian, Jewish or Jain, Taoist or Protestant, Lutheran, Buddhist, or Catholic, or any number of other traditions herein, there is a powerful and inspiring convergence of hope and goodwill that issues from seminal pathways through untouched gardens.

The ideas and personalities in this volume have not been arranged according to any "ulterior" sense of order. We have simply placed the spiritual traditions, and accompanying individuals, in alphabetical order. We have presented the twenty-eight contributors much in the manner that we met them. Their responses to questions, and the burning issues on their minds, are self-evident. All were straight-talkers, from the heart. Some were more "controversial" than others. But, in the lasting sense, I believe all were provocative and meaningful. Their collective compassion and insights form an invaluable moment in time.

NOTES

1. Eck, Boston: Beacon Press, 1993, p.35.
2. Eck, p.36.
3. *Los Angeles Times*, "The Imam's Next Move," by Judy Pasternak, Thursday, August 4, 1994, p.E1.
4. Seyyed Hossein Nasr, "Islam," in *Our Religions*, edited by Arvind Sharma, San Francisco: HarperCollins Publishers, 1993, p.529.
5. "A Portrait of Hinduism," by Dr. T. K. Venkateswaran, in *A Sourcebook for the Community of Religions*, edited by Joel Beversluis, Chicago: The Council for a Parliament of the World's Religions, 1993, p.64.

Symbols in order of appearance: Jainism, Christianity, Islam, Buddhism, Zoroastrianism, Jainism, Native American, Judaism, Hinduism, Taoism, Bahā'īsm.

PREFACE

by Bettina Gray

I found myself explaining to my two school-age children recently that while the discussion of and education about sex had
been the taboo subject in my generation, in their generation the
taboo subject seems to be religion. Sexuality, so vital to life experience, was at one time surrounded by a bizarre silence,
treated as taboo, and handled with kid gloves in any public
forum. Fortunately, this has changed dramatically. However, a
new taboo with equally bizarre implications has taken its place.
Religion, which defines cultures, explains much in human historical behavior, and is the wellspring of the traditions of
human rights, law, compassionate action, and a vast treasure of
art, has been missing from public education and, in general, the
media.

This is quite odd, for statistically, the people of the United
States are far more likely to profess a religious belief than the
populations of most other countries. Generally the material
available in the media is a narrow band of Christian evangelical
paid broadcasting or the brief news format coverage offered in
most newspapers and journals, which fosters misunderstanding

*Bettina Gray with His
Holiness The Dalai Lama*

by highlighting the conflicts and reporting the scandalous and the absurd in religion with stereotypes that trivialize, polarize, and perpetuate ignorance. We often hear of the worst of religion but seldom the best.

Meanwhile, as I write this, today's newspaper headline describes the murder of a five-year-old boy who was dropped out a fourteenth-floor window by two older children because he refused to steal candy for them. What is gut wrenching about this, besides the horror of children for whom life has little or no value, is that it is one story among an almost daily barrage. In the past, religious teaching, ceremony, and myth conveyed to the next generation the values and beliefs of a culture. Who now serves to pass on values, enlighten, encourage, redeem? Children serve as a mirror; they emulate what they see in the society around them. They learn our loyalties. As in some Grimm fairy tale the mirror on the wall is telling us who is *not* the fairest of them all.

Feminists often use the term *conspiracy of silence* to describe the way women's contributions are ignored and thereby trivialized. This could well be applied to the treatment of the broader subject of religion in the media and in education. The examination of religious belief and the discussion of the values most religions uphold is not trivial but vital. Our basic decisions about value systems, social and personal loyalties, and the way we implement these convictions will determine the shape of civilization (or the lack of it).

Religions have much to say to us of both the prophetic and the practical. There is surely a middle road between single viewpoint evangelism and the journalistic or scholarly "objective" observation (and all too often oversimplification) of religion that stands aloof from personal soul searching and from the broader examination of ethics, and value systems. Dr. Hans Küng, in a most eloquent and spontaneous comment at the end of our interview, said: "Are all these mosques and churches and synagogues built around a nothing? I don't think that is the truth. It is, of course, important to know that this ultimate reality we call God is precisely something absolutely different. You cannot prove this as you can prove in mathematics or in physics that it is. If it would be that, it would not be God. And so, it's a challenge. It's an indication for what I call a reasonable trust that there is an ultimate reality which sustains us, which is ahead of us, and which ultimately will save us."

In the past two decades, I have participated in dozens of interreligious dialogues on the local, regional, national, and international level and have watched the birth of a forum for interreligious communication, the North American Interfaith Network, as well as the growth of compassionate multifaith cooperation where once there had been suspicion, contention, and sometimes violence. Over the years, my personal motivation to continue in this arena could not have been sustained on the basis of intellectual curiosity, idealistic social convictions, or theological belief. It is, however, sustained by the discovery of and deep affection for those remarkable individuals from all of the traditions who continually give definition and incarnation to the highest aspirations of their traditions and of humanity: love, compassion, nonviolence, and unselfish generosity. The study of comparative religion, taught as it usually is from books and lectures, cannot begin to tell this story. For me the face-to-face encounter with those individuals who have sorted through their own tradition to discover and live out that which is vital, that which gives meaning and direction, that which offers hope for a humane future is a profound inspiration. These have been the most memorable conversations of my life.

I first encountered the existence of Jainism, for instance, when it was described to me as "those people who don't step on bugs, who won't kill a fly but allow thousands of people to starve around them." I was taught in those few words a contempt for a faith I have now discovered through living examples to have a tremendous resource for us in the understanding of nonviolence. *Jains* not only *believe* in nonviolence, they live nonviolently and judge all actions by that standard. I found my own standards and definitions of violence and nonviolence considerably expanded by my contact with Jains. This has had an influence on a number of my daily decisions and those of my children, who also reacted as I did to the friendly contacts we have made. It has increased the simple joy in life, the happiness and sense of well-being. We have in Jainism a tradition that represents at least four thousand years of the study of the meaning of nonviolence. And yet most people look at me blankly when I mention Jainism. My computer spell check doesn't even recognize the word. *Webster's Dictionary* gives inaccurate information about the dates of origin of Jainism.

I grew up on the idea that the Jewish tradition was one confined by law, ritual, and rules—inflexible and probably irrelevant to the contemporary world. It was represented to me as all law and no heart. These were blind misrepresentations, impressions that I picked up from the general environment of my small-town Kansas upbringing. I have found, instead, a tradition in which justice, fairness, and the law of Torah represent the deepest study and practice of compassion in action. "Love the Lord your God with all your heart, soul, strength, and mind and your neighbor as your self." The Jewish tradition represents a profound and personal encounter with that reality to which Küng refers and points to a source of strength that goes beyond human limitation and human tragedy. My discussions with Emil Fackenheim, Rabbi Greenberg, and Susannah Heschel about survival, hope, and transcendence in the face of the unimaginable atrocities of the Holocaust could not stand in more striking contrast with my original vague notion of Judaism.

Without neglecting the others, I can spare you my many misconceptions and unexamined assumptions that have been exploded. Honest encounter eventually means a surrender of misconceptions in the face of contradictory evidence, but much much more has been added than taken away. Honest encounter also makes us open, forthright, and able to suspend preconceived notions, at least for the moment of conversation. It means we take each other seriously and do not trivialize or minimize the importance of each other's beliefs. We do not need to suspend critical evaluation, and we should not become blind to the abuses and excesses of religion. However, no religion has an exclusive claim on authoritarian abuse, hypocrisy, the perpetuation of violence in the guise of religion, or the manipulation of religious belief to maintain the status quo. Knowing the worst is not a reason to avoid examining the best, and it is unreasonable to compare the worst of one tradition with the best of another.

More often than not, the setting of our first encounters with people very different from ourselves can shape the future of that exchange. My first conversations about religion began many

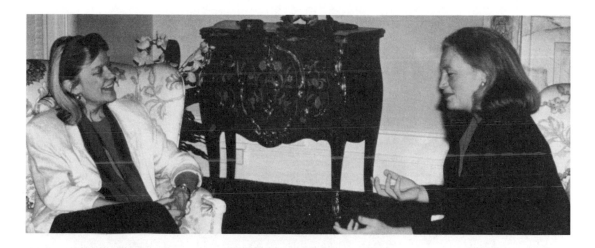

years ago around my kitchen table when I was a child. I would quiz any stranger who came into our home. I was eager, hungry to understand other beliefs, and hopeful to find anything that I could use. In a sense, my approach to the interviews in this series could still be called a "kitchen table" approach, for it is in our homes, around the kitchen table, face to face with immediate human need and concern, that we examine our lives and our values with friends to try to find out *what works*. It is at our kitchen tables where women, so often restricted in the formal rites and rituals of institutional religion, have reached out to one another to understand what is vital for the training of the next generation. This is where an honest examination of the basic questions often takes place. I hope that these interviews convey such an atmosphere and that readers and viewers who may never have met or ventured a conversation with a Hindu, a Buddhist, a Muslim, a Zoroastrian, a Jew or a Jain, a Bahā'ī or a Christian might very well have an opportunity to invite someone unfamiliar into their home, vicariously, through the medium of television and print, to begin to discover the treasures humanity has encoded in its religions and be encouraged by these representatives of the various faiths to find what works both individually and socially.

As we packed up our cameras to go home on a hot Chicago morning in the late summer of 1993, I stood in the empty Presidential Suite of the Blackstone Hotel, the original "smoke-filled room" where decisions that shaped this century were made and

Bettina Gray with Diana L. Eck

where we had just been privileged to glimpse and film a collective representation of human spiritual striving, inquiry, and faith. I had found in that room an assurance I had been seeking most of my life: Regardless of the worst in human nature, there is a "best" and it is alive and well all over the world in all shapes and cultures.

Did I learn anything from this extraordinary opportunity? That the basic truths are still simple, and that though they repeat themselves in a wide range of variations, they are centered in compassion. That spiritual awareness is something so simple and so direct but so challenging that we often attempt to obscure it in elaborate theologies, incarcerate it in insitituions, or argue it rather than accept the challenge and live it. In these people I saw the reality that truth knows no human boundary—that the Transcendent is alive and well with or without us and above and beyond our attempts to control it, and it continues to manifest itself throughout our world with surprise, joy, renewed hope, creative freedom, and, above all, compassion.

BAHA'I

BAHA'I

NATIVE WISDOM
Jacqueline Left Hand Bull Delahunt

Jacqueline Left Hand Bull Delahunt is a member of the Continental Board of Counsellors for the Protection and Propagation of the Bahā'ī Faith in the Americas. Appointed in 1988, she serves as a consultant and adviser to the forty-three National Spiritual Assemblies and to individual members of the Bahā'ī Faith in North, Central, and South America, including the Caribbean and Greenland. The seventeen members of this highest-ranking institution of the Faith in the western hemisphere are appointed by the supreme administrative body for the worldwide Bahā'ī community, the Universal House of Justice. Bahā'ī authoritative text refers to members of the Board of Counsellors as "the learned." There are five such Continental Boards of Counsellors in the world—one each for Africa, the Americas, Asia, Australia, and Europe—with a total membership of eighty-one Counsellors.

Born on the Rosebud Sioux Indian Reservation in 1943, Jacqueline Delahunt grew up in South Dakota. Both of her parents and all of her grandparents were members of the Lakota, or Sioux, nation. She was baptized, as were all the members of her extended family, in the Roman Catholic Church, the predominant Christian mission on her reservation. Nonetheless, members of her family were active in keeping alive the indigenous spiritual practices and sacred ceremonies of her Sicangu tribe of the Lakota nation. Delahunt participated in both religious traditions until, at age thirty-four, she became a member of the

Teachings of the Bahā'ī
World Faith

The Bahā'ī world faith ac-
cepts the writings of Bahā'
Ullāh (1819–1850) and
'Abdul-Baha (1844–1920)
as sacred texts. While the
Bahā'īs have no creed, they
have summarized their
teachings in the following
twelve principles:

1. *the oneness of hu-*
   mankind
2. *independent investiga-*
   tion of the truth
3. *the foundation of all*
   religions is one
4. *religion must be the*
   cause of unity
5. *religion must be in ac-*
   cord with science and
   reason
6. *equality between men*
   and women
7. *prejudice of all kinds*
   must be forgotten
8. *universal peace*
9. *universal education*
10. *spiritual solution of the*
    economic problem
11. *universal language*
12. *an international*
    tribunal

(Melton, *Creeds*)

Bahā'ī faith. She describes her acceptance of the Bahā'ī teachings as fulfillment of the promises of Christ and of indigenous
spiritual beliefs.

Delahunt earned her B.A. from The Evergreen State College
in 1974 and was a faculty member there in 1977. Later, she directed the Native American Education Program in Olympia,
Washington, and went on to serve as coordinator for minority
development for the National Spiritual Assembly of the Bahā'īs.
She subsequently guided the work of ninety-five regional committees and several national committees concerned with educational endeavors within the Bahā'ī faith.

For twelve years she was an active representative of the National Board for the Young Women's Christian Association of
the United States, which has, as its imperative, the goal of elim-
inating racism wherever it exists. She has been a member of the
Advisory Board for OHOYO, a national resource center for
professional Indian and Alaskan Native women, and chaired or
co-chaired various women's meetings throughout North America. Delahunt helped to found the National Coalition to Support Indian Treaties and was an early member of Citizens for
Indian Rights in Washington State. She was a founding member
of the Joyce Cheeka Memorial Scholarship Foundation, which
provides funds for American Indian students, and has chaired
the Indian Arts Committee of the Washington State Arts Commission.

HOW I BECAME A BAHĀ'Ī

Really being a Native American woman is how I came to be a
Bahā'ī. I began my life on a Rosebud reservation in South
Dakota in a very extended family. Seventeen of us lived in a
two-room cabin without electricity or running water. So we
were all intermingled in our lives. In the immediate household
was a spiritual healer—call him a medicine man, we call him
wachasuwa kah.

With that beginning, there was a definite orientation toward
the spiritual in life. And my family was syncretic, in that it combined an interest or an acceptance of the Roman Catholic
Church, which was on the reservation, along with full involve-

ment in the traditional spiritual base of the Lakota people—the pipe, the sweat ceremony, the sun dance (even though the sun dance at that time was outlawed). My life is very much wrapped up in these things.

When I was a teenager, I really began to doubt because I kept understanding that it was wrong for me to be involved in pagan things and things that weren't Christian. Well, maybe *pagan* isn't the right word—anything not of the Catholic Church. *Heathen* might be the right word.

We were told that we needed to get rid of these ways of worshiping and these awful things we believed in. Actually we were called superstitious. That was the word that I heard most often when it came to the traditional spiritual teachings of my family.

It was really confusing because I saw the power in the healing ceremonies. I saw the power of the prayer. And the people I loved most in the world—my grandparents, my aunt and my uncle, my mother—were praying in this way, and they meant it. To be told when I went to school that it was wrong was very difficult for me to try to sort it out.

I have some memories of being in a religion class when a classmate of mine asked why women couldn't be priests. And the priest said, "Because you're not spiritually equal to men. You can never be priests. Men are superior." Now this was one priest and his idea, his understanding.

That's when I began to allow myself to doubt their reality because I *knew*. And the doubts were awful because I also was being told that faith was a gift, and if I challenged that faith I was throwing it back in God's face. So there was turmoil.

I learned of Bahā' Ullāh's message and this concept of progressive revelation—which really said, "Well, yes, the White Buffalo Calf Woman and her teachings were right. And they were for you." She said that there would be a time in the future and that time does not deny the validity of all this but it carries it forward.

To begin with I remember, I opened up the newspaper, and I saw the name Bahā'ī, and it touched me. It was a spiritual experience that I can't explain. So I went looking to find out what is this Bahā'ī all about. I thought it was *Ba Hi* at the time. I finally found some people, and it took them a long time to tell me what it is about because we don't have clergy.

White Buffalo Calf Woman

A beautiful woman in white buckskin with a bundle on her back entered their camp, came to the lodge, and, with ritual attention to the directions, presented the sacred pipe to the chief. "With this pipe," she said, "you will walk upon the earth; for the earth is your Grandmother and Mother, and She is sacred." Thereafter, the pipe figured in their solemn rituals—the sign of their bond to one another and to the earth, their common source. After she had taught them the first of seven new rites, she walked away, turned into a red and brown buffalo calf, rolled over and became a white buffalo calf, and then a black one. White Buffalo Calf Woman, as she was called, had given the Sioux a ceremonial repertoire, with the sacred pipe at the center, for the expression of all their religious needs.

(Albanese)

My first challenge was that I asked, "Is this an organized religion?"

And they said, "Well, yes. It's very organized."

And I said, "Oh, well, that's too bad because I don't believe in organized religion."

And they said, "Why not?"

And I said, "For one thing I've never seen one that gives women credit for being as smart as men, and I know that I am."

INTEGRATING IDENTITIES

I think that my survival as an Indian woman and the survival of my people, the Lakota people, truly depend on the teachings of Bahā' Ullāh because they continue on. You see, I'm really to be a follower of the White Buffalo Calf Woman, which was where I began, and I really believe in Christ as well, now, but in a whole different way than it was presented to me. It's much more beautiful, and more deep than I heard it.

If I really listen to what White Buffalo woman said, she gave us teachings for the time. She gave us seven ceremonies. And she said there will be a time when I leave, but when I am gone you must remember me and you must never forget that I'm going to return. Always watch for my return. And these are the signs of my return.

So I believe that that time has come. I always thought it would be hundreds and hundreds of years in the future. But obviously, for me, and I have really examined it, it's for now. This is the day that she was speaking of. She has returned. Not in the same form that she came the first time but really in the teachings of Bahā' Ullāh.

Interestingly enough in the western hemisphere, the vast majority of Bahā'īs are Native people, indigenous people, because for all the various tribal groups there have been prophets and they have really pointed to the teachings of Bahā' Ullāh. So in my own reservation, among the Lakota people, there are hundreds and hundreds of people who immediately have accepted. Now the second part of acceptance is putting those teachings into daily life—and that's a little harder.

Two important principles in Bahā'ī scriptures emphasize:

Racial Unity
Racism retards the enfoldment of the boundless potentials of its victims, corrupts its perpetrators and blights human progress. Bahā' Ullāh's call that all humans accept and internalize the principle of the oneness of humanity is partly directed at destroying racist attitudes.

Emancipation of Women
The denial of equality to women perpetrates an injustice against one-half of the world's population and promotes in men harmful attitudes and habits that are carried from the family to the workplace, to political life, and ultimately to international relations. Even though he lived in the nineteenth-century Middle East, Bahā' Ullāh called for the equality of women and enunciated their full rights to education and work.

(SourceBook)

THE RESPONSIBILITIES OF BEING A COUNSELLOR

The seventeen on the Board of Counsellors for the Americas really serve primarily as a consultant body to forty-three national spiritual assemblies in the western hemisphere and also to the rank-and-file of Bahá'í, the individual followers of Bahá' Ulláh in those forty-three countries, in trying to help them apply the teaching of Bahá' Ulláh to their daily lives, to building Bahá'í communities, Bahá'í schools.

The supreme authoritative body in the Bahá'í faith at the world center is the Universal House of Justice. They make the appointments. It's not a mystery exactly, but we don't really know the precise criteria. It's people whom they think the faith needs to serve in this capacity.

I supervise the work of thirteen auxiliary board members in the Arctic of Canada and Alaska; throughout the state of Alaska, which is a separate national assembly; and the western provinces of Canada. I have some responsibility in Greenland, and some northern states in the Pacific Northwest in the United States. But because of my keen interest in indigenous populations, I also frequently travel into South America, and I've been visiting most of the tribes in the States and Canada. So the indigenous populations, in addition to geographical regions, are my particular area of interest.

I try to impart the skills needed to search the writings of Bahá' Ulláh to learn to apply them in daily life. It's like an international consultant agency to help the national assemblies and the Bahá'ís throughout the hemisphere, to learn how to apply the writings of Bahá' Ulláh.

Interviewer: Do you really think there would be less war if women were in power?

Delahunt: Absolutely, it's the only way there's going to be less war. On a very practical level, what woman would raise her children to send them off to war, raise her sons to send them off to be slaughtered?

ON BEING A WOMAN, A NATIVE AMERICAN, AND A BAHÁ'Í

When I was a fourth grader, probably nine years old, I remember walking down the street in Hot Springs, South Dakota, and somebody called me a little squaw. I didn't know what it meant but there was something in it. And I went home and asked

Sioux Puberty Rituals
for Girls

*The buffalo ceremony, the
puberty ritual for girls celebrated at first menstrua-
tion, placed young women
in the care of the sacred
buffalo and secured for
them a relationship with
White Buffalo Calf
Woman.*

(Albanese)

my mother, "What does *squaw* mean? That's an Indian word,
isn't it?"

She told me all these wonderful things about being a
woman. She said, "What it means is woman. What it really
means is that one day you are going to bear children that will be
the future of the Lakota people." And she told me these things.
She told me what a blessing it was and how women were honored. It was a beautiful thing to be a woman. She told how the
pipe had been brought to us by a woman and I, too, would be a
woman one day. And I was really looking forward to being this
wonderful thing, this woman.

When I was in high school, when I learned what they really
meant by squaw, that they really meant "whore," I thought my
mother was pretty dumb. I thought that she's awfully naive not
to know what they were really talking about.

Of course, it was later when I became a mother and I had
children and I knew exactly what she was doing and why she
did that. She was really trying to protect my esteem. I don't even
know if she would know what that word would mean, but to
protect the image of who I was and could be, so that it wouldn't
affect me too early in life. By the time I knew what it meant, I
could stand up straight and not think of myself in that way. She
did a good job, and I am grateful for that.

One of Bahā' Ullāh's teachings is the equality of men and
women. One of the things that they told me that really
impressed me was that if a couple had two children, a boy and a
girl, that they were obliged to educate them. If they had money
only to educate one, they had to educate the girl first because
the girl is the first teacher of the next generation and an educated woman makes a better mother. Especially a spiritually educated woman. This is also a Lakota belief.

When I was learning about the vision quest, when I was
coming into my teens, I said, "Why is it that it's only the boys
who get to do this?"

And my mother said, "Because the women already know
some things just from their life's journey; they understand
things. The men have to make this effort to come to know
them." So, in our seven sacred rites, it was only recently I realized this, the men have the vision quest but the women have the
coming of age ceremony and then they are co-equal.

RACISM AND BAHĀ'Ī

About the equality of all people, of all races, Bahā' Ullāh said, "I have made thee all from the same dust, why therefore do you exalt yourself above one another?"

All these teachings really speak to the equality of all people. His son and authorized interpreter, 'Abdul-Bahā, when he visited North America, pointed out what would be the most challenging issue in North America—racial prejudice. He said, in this next century, it will be the most challenging issue, and you must attend to dissolving it. That was in 1912.

I think that dealing with racism has to be a personal experience, not an intellectual one. I think it involves every individual in putting themselves into the situation, getting to know people on a personal level. I think that we can pass all the laws in the world, and obviously it hasn't done a whole lot of good. It really speaks to our inner reality and our personal actions that stem from that inner reality, to be involved, to know people. To socialize with people, to have genuine friendships with people different from whoever you are. If I'm Indian, it means I have to break out of this comfortable cocoon of friendships with Indian people and make friends with all kinds of other people.

Really, I think that there is a spiritual impulse in all of us, and then I think it runs up against tests. What makes you decide to go through that test is a spiritual conviction. I find that all the time in my life as an Indian woman.

I have a tremendous amount of rage. But I am also very optimistic. I'm perfectly convinced, with every ounce of certitude in my being, that we are at the end of a night and a spiritual springtime is dawning, and that we need the message. We need this Parliament of the World's Religions, but as a Bahā'ī, I feel personally that Bahā' Ullāh's teachings can lead us through this night, this mire we're in right now. Especially Indian people. I feel it's our future because it tells us where we stand. Bahā' Ullāh's teachings really tell Indian people where they stand in the world. They give an identity that no other people who have come to us have ever really given. Everybody wants to come and change us into something else.

One of the teachings of Bahā' Ullāh is this protection, this preservation of cultures because the flower garden of humanity

The International Bahā'ī Community

The international Bahā'ī community is estimated at about five million members spread out in 232 countries, containing within it 2,100 ethnic groups speaking more than 800 languages. In some nations, minority groups make up a substantial fraction of the Bahā'ī population; in the United States, for example, perhaps a third of the membership is African-American. Southeast Asians, Iranians, Hispanics, and Native Americans make up another 20 percent. Bahā'ī communities sponsor development projects, such as tree planting, agricultural improvement, vocational training, and rural health-care. The Bahā'ī international community is particularly active at the United Nations and works closely with many international development agencies.

—Dr. Robert Stockman
(SourceBook)

needs to be that flower garden. If it were all one kind of flower, it wouldn't be beautiful. You can't have unity in uniformity. The two words are close, but they conflict with one another, really. You have to have diversity in order to have unity. And unity is the fundamental teaching of Bahā' Ullāh.

Now in North America, there may be two million Indian people, maybe three, maybe less than two million. It depends whose census you're looking at and what criteria they use. When you see that we could fit all the Native people of North America in a little tiny corner of Bolivia, then you see a whole different possibility.

Yet, they are under attack, and I think it's the heart of it. It's the materialistic god, so to speak, that is attacking the people. Yet there is a reality.

I think one of the things I can say confidently about Indian people in North, Central, and South America, the Arctic, and Inuit people, too, is that we are people of God. I've yet to meet a person who's not living in the city—and even most Indians in the city—who, no matter what, isn't ready to talk about God at the drop of a, you know the word, to talk about spiritual things, to acknowledge this gift of life, this gift of this day, this place that we're in, the fact that we can talk together.

We are people of God. And that spiritual reality, for some reason, is still there. So despite this material onslaught that is decimating, has already more than decimated, the North American tribes, there is still this reality that even if it were down to the last few, I think that we would still have that integrity of spirit.

JUSTICE, FORGIVENESS, AND BAHĀ'Ī

When people are killed or their land is stolen, I wouldn't say forgive and move on. I would talk about justice, that we need to have justice. I would offer sympathy and help. Another thing is that Bahā' Ullāh said, "The best beloved of all things in my sight is justice, turn not away therefrom." And so we need to work toward that justice. But how then can we begin to take giant steps in our lives that make the difference so that justice can be?

Well, those steps are taken on a daily basis in getting involved and being involved in changing. There is so much to say, I'm trying to say it very quickly. The whole concept of unity means the personal involvement of the individual in every act, in every day. It means looking into what the possibilities of every situation are, offering not only consolation, but the pathways through education of all people to understanding.

For example, if you look at justice, you can't get immediately from here to the end result—justice. But if you think, what's going to happen to our systems when women are in places of power, equal with men? What's going to happen when people really understand about the differences of races, and the races are going to be represented in places of influence?

ON BLENDED RELIGIOUS IDENTITY

Blended religious activity is really a celebration of the past. It's taking what you want to take from it, acknowledging that not everything was perfect in it. You are taking those things that you think are beautiful. We don't know that we're always making the best judgments, but we can do our best, and take the good things.

You share that gift. But then you take as well, not so you change totally, but that's kind of what I've done. I think that serving on a seventeen-member body as a woman, as a Native woman off a Rosebud reservation, one of the things that happens to me is I see this responsibility and I think, well, can I go into the sweat lodge? Are people going to think that this is what Bahá'ís do, or what Bahá'ís are supposed to do? And if I don't, are they going to say, well, Bahá'ís aren't supposed to do that?

So everything you do is increasingly intentional when you carry a responsibility. But I see a lot of people who don't have the responsibility walking that path as well.

And I do go into the sweat lodge ceremonies. That's who I am. I don't need to change that part of me. And it's good, it's a gift. It's a celebration of the past. But it's present as well.

Unity in Diversity

The unity of the human race, as envisaged by Bahá' Ulláh, implies the establishment of a world commonwealth in which all nations, races, creeds, and classes are closely and permanently united, and in which the autonomy of its state members and the personal freedom and initiative of the individuals that compose them are definitely and completely safeguarded.

—Shoghi Effendi, (SourceBook)

BAHA'I

SOCIAL JUSTICE
Robert C. Henderson

Dr. Robert Henderson has been the Secretary-General of the National Spiritual Assembly of the Bahá'ís of the United States, the national governing body of the American Bahá'í community. His leadership in the Bahá'í faith is the culmination of many years of work toward furthering the goals of human justice. He says, "We must learn how to build true unity among America's races, ethnic and religious groups—eradication of racism is not enough."

From the nonviolent Civil Rights demonstrations of the 1960s to corporate America, Robert Henderson has been a champion for equality and social justice. He has spoken on ethnic equality nationwide to diverse audiences, from the Chairman's Diversity Action Committee of Amoco Oil and the Kellogg School of Business at Northwestern University to a keynote address at the Jimmy Carter Presidential Center at Emory University, a New York conference sponsored by Governor Mario Cuomo, and the Kentucky Governor's Conference on "The Vision of Racial Unity: An American Agenda."

Henderson is co-chair of the Religious Involvement Committee of the Martin Luther King Jr. Federal Holiday Commission, a member of the Committee of Visitors of the Marin Community Foundation of the Buck Trust, and a member of the North Shore Race Unity Task Force.

He earned a doctorate in Education from the University of Massachusetts (1976) and has worked with Fortune 500 companies to improve their performance and challenge corporate culture. He was a founding member of Air Atlanta, the first black-owned commercial jet airline, providing first-class service at coach rates. Managing Director of Tarkenton and Company, a management consulting firm, he has consulted for the HUD Fair Housing Commission, for the California Supreme Court, and for the Senate Foreign Relations Committee's Convention on Discrimination.

Henderson's initiation of the study "Models of Unity— Racial, Ethnic and Religious" resulted in a landmark analysis of intergroup unity in the Chicago metropolitan area. That model is being replicated in dozens of American cities. He has published several articles and books on management systems and training programs.

Bahá'í on World Religions

Consort with all religions with amity and concord, that they may inhale from you the sweet fragrance of God. Beware lest amidst men the flame of foolish ignorance overpower you. All things proceed from God and unto him they return. He is the source of all things and in him all things are ended.

—Kitab-i-aqdas 144

WHERE WE'VE COME FROM: WHERE WE'RE GOING

In some ways, we've come a long way because a hundred years ago, when the Parliament of Religions was originally convened, it represented a very small segment of the world's population. And significant parts of the American religious tradition, and religious traditions all over the world, were not only not represented, but were barred from participation.

The Bahá'í faith was first mentioned on the American continent one hundred years ago, at the first World Parliament of Religions. And significant changes have occurred in the world since then. Now we find that a very wide cross-section of the world's population is represented. But we have quite a bit to learn about how to talk to each other. One hundred years ago, for example, Frederick Douglass wanted to participate in the World Parliament and wasn't allowed to. He literally had to fight his way on stage in order to deliver a message about brotherhood and peace and the true purpose of religion—to unite and to harmonize and to liberate.

It's interesting and ironic that the purpose of all the manifestations of God, all of the messengers who established the great religions we know, was to make people happy, to foster unity and understanding, to educate, to build great civilizations. All these were based on timeless principles of social justice. What gets in the way of that is our small understanding and practice of these universal spiritual principles.

WHAT A WORLD PARLIAMENT OF RELIGIONS
ONE HUNDRED YEARS FROM NOW MIGHT LOOK LIKE

I think we'll see a vastly different world. First of all, I think that we will see a world that is struggling to give birth to global civilization. And I think that this will occur in the twenty-first century. I think that we will see a world where women have a much wider role, where the voices of people of color are heard, and they are active and in the forefront of participation in the important questions of the day.

I think that we will see a world where the institutions that serve humanity have been vastly reshaped. One of the Bahá'í teachings is that the call of Bahá' Ulláh is primarily directed against all forms of racialism, insularity, and prejudice. It goes on to say that if time-honored ideals or long-cherished institutions cease to minister to the needs of an ever evolving humanity, cease to benefit humankind, then they must be swept away and relegated to the limbo of obsolescent and forgotten doctrines. The law of life is evolution and change and growth and continual perfection and refinement.

I think what we are seeing now are the death pangs of modes of life and social institutions that no longer serve the best interests of humanity. And what we're also seeing and hearing are the birth pangs of new models of life, which will bring people into a much different association with one another and will change the organization of global society dramatically.

TRANSLATING PRINCIPLES INTO OUR DAILY LIFE

We have to make a beginning in the discussion, and that's why the Parliament of the World's Religions is so important. If there isn't discourse, we never find out what's ailing the body of humanity, what the significant issues of different races and religions are.

If it was all talk, we'd still be in the same position that we were in one hundred years ago. You see, there are two processes at work. And the Bahá'í faith describes these processes very clearly. One is a process of the collapse of obsolete forms of social organizations and institutions that don't work anymore.

And the other is the process of the beginning of a global organization where continents and nations and peoples and religions begin to talk to each other for the first time and begin to establish a common ground based on some kind of principle so that we can begin to take into consideration global needs and not just national or racial or cultural or religious needs of a specific population.

UNIVERSAL PEACE AND GLOBALISM

If we're to achieve peace as a human species, as a human family, it won't be the result of some negotiated political agreement or some new-found relationship among nations. It will be the result of the manifestation of an inner state of transformation. See, the essential is this—either human beings are incorrigibly selfish and aggressive and, therefore by definition, unable to build a peaceful world, or we are growing up on the job.

The whole expanse of history is the gradual evolution of the life of humanity, progressing from infancy to what might be described now as the turbulent adolescence of the development of humanity. So when we look at war and prejudice and exploitation and inequality, we can either see it as a symptom in the flaw in the makeup of human beings or we can see it as things we did when we were too young to know better.

The Baha'i view is that we are maturing. We're coming to what might be described as the confirmation of human evolution. And that will be marked by a universal peace, which is the result of individual spiritual transformation that expresses itself in the oneness of the human family, in the equality of men and women, in the equality of the races, in universal education, in the elimination of the disparity between rich and poor, and begins to create new institutions, new social organizations, and new patterns of life that give birth to what will gradually, in the fullness of time, become one human family.

I think that there is no difference between the purpose of religion as it was manifest in Hinduism, in Christianity, in Judaism, in Islam, in Buddhism, in Zoroastrianism, or in the Baha'i faith. The purpose of religion has always been the same and that is to know and to worship God and to carry on an

Bahá'í on World Peace

Acceptance of the oneness of mankind is the first fundamental prerequisite for reorganization and administration of the world as one country, the home of humankind. Universal acceptance of this spiritual principle is essential to any successful attempt to establish world peace. It should therefore be universally proclaimed, taught in schools, and constantly asserted in every nation as preparation for the organic change in the structure of society that it implies.

(*The Promise of World Peace*, SourceBook)

ever-advancing civilization expressed in acts of worship and service, to build a society that, ultimately, has been described as the kingdom of heaven on earth.

The Bahā'ī faith offers a different way of looking at the evolution of religion. If there is to be peace, it is clear that I can't tell you, if you're a Hindu, a Jew, a Christian, or a Muslim, that your religion is wrong. There has to be affirmation of the legitimacy of spiritual tradition. The Bahā'ī faith does that because it teaches the oneness of religion. We believe that all of these religions came from the same God with messages to humanity that were appropriate to that stage in humankind's development.

It has to be unity in diversity. It has to recognize the legitimacy of ethnic diversity, of religious diversity, of racial diversity, and so on. And it has to find the common ground of human experience.

The fundamental belief in the Bahā'ī faith is that the human family is one, that we are all the children of the same God. We are all equal. That's why there is no clergy, there is no individual authority. Our communities are administered by institutions that are elected by the body of the believers. And so it is very participatory, and all of our principles governing the patterns of behavior and the patterns of thought and the patterns of spirit are oriented to build unity, to build harmony and happiness, and to inspire service and the relief of suffering.

The World as One Family

When love is realized and the ideal spiritual bonds unite the hearts of all, the whole human race will be uplifted, the world will continually grow more spiritual and radiant, and the happiness and tranquility of mankind will be immeasurably increased. Warfare and strife will be uprooted, disagreement and dissension will pass away, and Universal Peace will unite the nations and the peoples of the world. All mankind will dwell together as one family, blend as the waves of the sea, shine as stars of one firmament, and appear as fruits of the same tree.

—'Abdu'l-Bahā

ONENESS AND THE HUMAN FAMILY

At a time when the spirit of religion has died out and social injustice has eclipsed social justice, God sends us a new messenger. Once his name was Moses or Abraham or Zoroaster, Buddha or Christ or Mohammed, and we believe that today it's Bahā' Ullāh. That is precisely why the Bahā'ī faith exists. That new messenger brings us two things. One, he brings us understanding of who we are and what our purpose is and how we relate to God and to each other. And the second, and indispensable, thing he brings us is the spirit of the new religion, which is the spirit that gradually begins to conquer the hearts of a larger and larger body of humankind. What Bahā'īs believe is that today is the day of the fulfillment of the prophecies of all the religions. And the object of the Bahā'ī faith is nothing less than the establishment of the oneness of the human family and the achievement of the kingdom of heaven on earth.

When you say the Bahā'ī faith, you say Christianity, and you say Judaism, and you say Islam, and you say Hindu. Because we regard this, all of these religions, as true and from the same God. It's like chapters in the same book. So you can't have fulfillment without the enabling steps that got you to the point of climax, and so the Bahā'ī faith, we believe, is the fulfillment of the promise of all of the religions of the past, but not separate, a continuation.

These are all the teachings of Bahā' Ullāh, who is the prophet founder of the Bahā'ī faith who emerged in the mid-nineteenth century in Persia.

ON RACISM

Racism is worse than you think. It's tearing the nation apart. It jeopardizes the internal order and national security of the American nation. But it is not just America. There are one hundred and sixty-nine wars going on in the world right now. The greatest percentage of those wars are interreligious and interracial conflicts. It's everywhere. And I think those are the death pangs of obsolete concepts of who's okay and who can be a part of our nation.

Now we have two choices. We can either settle it in venues like the Parliament of the World's Religions, where people with very different opinions get together and begin to talk it out, or, if we don't find solution in those venues, what will happen is, races will continue to clash on the battlefield and people will die and suffer needlessly.

I think a number of things can be done. We have to send different messages through the media. What the media can do is educate us to a different understanding of what's important about human beings. I think discussions like the one that we're having now are important. People begin to think to themselves, "I agree with that, I want that for my children. I want it for myself."

Right here in Chicago, where the school system is bankrupt, where 75 percent of the kids come to school hungry every day,

Bahā'īsm in America

The Bahā'ī faith was brought to America in 1892 by Ibrahim Kheirella, a Lebanese convert who founded the first American group of Bahā'īs in Chicago in 1893. The first U.S. convention was held in 1907. During 1912, 'Abdul-Bahā (1844–1921), son of Bahā'ī founder Baha' Ullah and the second major figure in the tradition, spent eight months in the United States and laid the cornerstone of the Bahā'ī House of Worship in Wilmette, Illinois. The temple took forty years to complete and was dedicated in 1953. Estimates in 1992 indicated that there were approximately 110,000 Bahā'īs and 1,700 local spiritual assemblies in the United States. The United States is the principal stronghold of the faith outside Iran.

(Melton, *Creeds*; Crim)

67 percent of the black children (which is almost the whole population of the school system), members of the underclass, come into kindergarten not knowing their last names. They don't know their last names! In that environment, which is so desperate, that's where we're trying to find out who you are and feed you, where we ought be able to just educate you and recognize that you are a wonderful and unique human being. What we have to do is to begin to tell new stories. We have to begin to tell stories of individual and collective heroism.

We did a study called "Models of Unity—Racial, Ethnic and Religious" because every year the commissioner of human relations in Chicago publishes a hate crimes report. And what it says is there is more hate in Chicago than there was last year. And so I raise the questions: Who is building bridges of understanding? Who's solving the problem?

Finding out that there is more hate isn't the answer. Finding out where there is more love and understanding is the answer. So we organized an effort to systematically survey three of Chicago's largest and very different kinds of neighborhoods, plus the twenty-two North Shore communities that are contiguous to Chicago.

We found that two things are true. One, hate's everywhere. And that story is being told. But love is everywhere, too. And that story is *not* being told. We found incredible stories of people, all races, all faiths, all religions, doing the kinds of things that when you hear about it, it would make you cry.

In a gang-ridden neighborhood, black, white, and brown people don't talk to each other, hide in their houses for fear of violence, drugs, and crime. Children are getting killed by the spread of gang violence. Emergency 911 doesn't work; the mayor's gang intervention program doesn't work. So the parents do the unthinkable. They start to work together to figure out how to save their children from being killed. They decide to take back the playground where the gangs congregate. And this is what they did. They painted a stripe around the playground. They repaired the backboards, and they planted flowers and repaired the lights. And they cleaned up all the drug paraphernalia and all the signs of violence. They organized a chaperon system so that their children could proceed to and from the playground and play safely. They drove the gangs out of the neighborhood. That's the power of unity. They were so successful that they took their efforts to schools and into churches and a variety of other things and began to find that, working together, they could do anything.

Why aren't we telling more of these stories? If we begin to tell these stories, it fosters hope and it tells us that without government money and without the backing of a federal program or new entitlement or a law, there are lots of folks who believe that this is the right thing to do simply because it's right. We need to understand how they are solving the problems that vex the rest of us.

WHAT PREVENTS PEOPLE FROM DOING GOOD THINGS?

The simple answer is that people chicken out. The more complicated answer is that when institutions fail and people stop believing in things, they stop believing in the power of religion. They fall away from God, cities break down, law doesn't work, violence spreads. What it spawns is a sense of hopelessness. People begin to believe that it doesn't matter what I do, because nothing works anyway. The whole spark of moral courage begins to die out, because people are only audacious when they're selling stuff. They are not audacious when they are taking the high road of principle or trying to champion the downtrodden or save the day for somebody for a good purpose.

When we went out and talked to these folks who were doing all these interesting things, they told us, one after the other, "I was just doing it because it was in my heart and I thought it was the right thing to do, but I didn't think anybody would care. And so I just did it because I thought it was right."

We have to show models of love because when hopelessness and despair conquer the hearts of a whole population, love is the proof that hope is not lost. And service is the proof of love. So we begin to look for spiritual communities and associations and individuals who believe in love, who believe in commitment to the service of other human beings and begin to tell those stories, begin to figure out how it is that they are building bridges of trust and cooperation.

In the Bahā'ī community, for example, we are, more probably than not, the most diverse religious community in the world. Bahā'ī communities are open to all races, all religious backgrounds, all classes and cultures and creeds. People come into the Bahā'ī to the community and there is unending diversity. So we have to figure it out. And we use a process of consultation as the central integrating principle of the Bahā'ī life. We regard it as a spiritual law of our faith.

Bahā'ī and Nature

Nature is God's will and is its expression in and through the contingent world. It is a dispensation of Providence ordained by the Ordainer, the All-Wise. The earth is but one country, and mankind its citizens.

Look not upon the creatures of God except with the eye of kindliness and of mercy, for Our loving providence hath pervaded all created things, and Our grace encompassed the earth and the heavens. . . . it is not only their fellow human beings that the beloved of God must treat with mercy and compassion, rather must they show forth the utmost loving-kindness to every living creature.

(SourceBook)

THE BASIC PRINCIPLES OF BAHĀ'Ī

The teachings of Bahā' Ullāh are the fundamental principles of the Bahā'ī faith. There is one God, religion is one, and humankind is one—there is one human family. The basic principles are the agreement of science and religion, the equality of the sexes, the elimination of prejudice and the equality of the races, the need to eliminate the extreme disparities of wealth and poverty, the imperative of universal education and the gradual establishment of one global civilization that doesn't obliterate national distinctions but brings nations into a higher harmony and a higher arena. This brings nations into a higher allegiance, that allegiance being the safeguarding and protecting of the entire world's population, the preservation of unity, and peace among all the nations.

Bahā' Ullāh is the first of all of the great prophets to teach the equality of men and women and to say that the achievement of full participation in the world's activities by women would be one of the assurances of peace in the world.

All of these principles have got to be the cornerstones of this age of fulfillment. This isn't some pipe dream where people run around like placid zombies in some euphoric state. This kingdom of heaven on earth, this age of peace, will be the result of human struggle over the vastness of life on the planet. And what we will learn from this is that how we organize our spirits and train them, how we improvise a spiritual life and how that is expressed in social, political, and economic institutions and philosophies and patterns of life in interaction, are interconnected, that you cannot divorce my view of you as a human being from how our organizations and institutions bring us together and afford us both equal access to happiness, to the essentials to lead happy and dignified lives.

BRAHMA KUMARIS

BRAHMA KUMARIS

YOGA

SISTER JAYANTI

For more than thirty years, Sister Jayanti has been an emissary for world peace. She follows the spiritual practice of the modern Brahma Kumaris, founded by Brahma Baba, a distinct melding of Yoga and Hindu teachings and practices. She is director of the London branch of the Brahma Kumaris World Spiritual University, and BKWSU's Non-Governmental Organization representative to the United Nations in Geneva. As well as assisting with the overall coordination of the activities of the Brahma Kumaris in more than sixty countries outside of India, her day-to-day work involves spiritual counseling, teaching, and translating, as well as overseeing the administration of Brahma Kumaris centers in twenty European countries.

Born in India and raised in England, Sister Jayanti has been at the forefront of global women's issues. She has participated in many UN conferences and projects in connection with women, development and the environment, and the role of spiritual values in positive world change.

One of Sister Jayanti's major projects involved many thousands of people around the globe. During "The Million Minutes of Peace Appeal," created especially for the UN International Year of Peace, people in more than eighty countries contributed their prayers, meditations, and positive thoughts toward peace in the world, with a final total of 1.34 billion minutes. The Appeal was something that everyone, young or old, educated or uneducated, could take part in. Indeed, the most minutes were collected from developing countries. Peace songs rang out at Manila railway stations, hot air balloons went up in London's Hyde Park, and Hong Kong traffic wardens refrained from issuing tickets when the Appeal was launched in September 1986. The project unleashed a wave of change.

Consistent with her global efforts toward unity and hope, Sister Jayanti has worked actively within the interfaith movement for more than two decades. She is an adviser to the Council for a Parliament of the World's Religions, a member of the Executive Committee of the World Congress of Faiths, and a member of the Advisory Body of the International Interfaith Centre.

In the role of spiritual leader and teacher, she says that it is practice, not theory, that is of paramount importance. She firmly believes that we cannot expect to change others or the world around us unless we are prepared to change ourselves, as she expressed in a recent seminar in Toronto on the challenge of change: "I am very well aware that any change within the world starts from something that is very small. It perhaps begins in the mind of one individual and is communicated one to ten and then one hundred and then to one thousand others. Within a short space of time you do not even know where that idea began. It seems as though it is coming to you from all directions. Not only do we influence the microcosm around us, but also together and individually we are responsible for the macrocosm as well."

CONNECTION WITH GOD

Ohm Shanti. First let me explain what it means to be a yogi because it doesn't even necessarily have to be anyone in a white *sari.* Yogi means to experience a union with God—a link with God. And yes, I feel I have that.

I think that it is a process and also a preparation in one's own development. I feel that it's an ongoing relationship. It is not something that happens in a flash and one arrives at the destination and that's the end of the journey. Rather it's like a human relationship that's been developed over a period of time. And through the time that we're developing that, there is a giving and a taking, an exchange, a benefit that we feel, something

---

The Brahma Kumari World Spiritual University

Dada Lekh Raj, a jeweler who experienced a number of spiritual awakenings that culminated in 1936 with a spiritual presence entering and possessing his body, identifying itself as Shiva, the Luminous Self, founded the Brahma Kumaris World Spiritual University in 1937. Following inner instruction, Lekh Raj entrusted the developing organization to single women and mothers (the Brahma Kumaris), the most distinguishing feature in the predominantly male-dominated world of Hinduism. It is the task of sisters, each of whom receive fourteen years of training, to bring forth the loving qualities of Shakti, the Hindu deity, to the world. Purity and celibacy is emphasized and the group is vegetarian.

(Melton, *Creeds*; Crim)

that we learn from each other. Translate that into that level of relationship of the soul with God, the Supreme. The way I understand and experience God today is very different from the first experience I had twenty-something years ago.

I think there is an awareness of a constant connection, in which there isn't a demand or an expectation anymore. But rather there is a warmth and a security that is an abiding one. I know what I should be doing to honor that responsibility and that relationship. And I also know what there is in store for me. Being a yogi wasn't a sort of flash, it's been a process of development.

YOGA IS NOT A SET OF POSTURES

I haven't been trained to do any postures, and I don't think it's the path that I'm going to travel on at this point in time. I understand where the idea has come from. If I may take you back a little, a few thousand years ago, when people experimented with different systems and disciplines to be able to try to reach within the mind, then if we can come to discipline the body, then perhaps through that we can arrive at the state so we can discipline the mind.

I don't think that it works quite like that. Someone who has amazing powers of mastery over body through hatha yoga, through gymnastics, or whatever else, doesn't necessarily have training for disciplining the mind. Yogi has come to mean someone who has mastery over the body. But the idea behind mastery over body had been trying to obtain mastery over mind. Then, when I want to sit in God's remembrance, my mind doesn't go in a thousand different directions. I am able to channel my mind and experience the focusing of that energy on God, which is what yoga actually is.

Again, it's akin to the human relationships. If I'm interested in you and I'm interested in our conversation, all sorts of things can be happening, but my mind will stay focused and my mind will be in yoga, in union, in communion with you, and communication brings results. If my mind is scattered and distracted, there isn't communication, there isn't communion, there isn't union, there isn't yoga. Apply that to union with God, and it applies to that state where my mind is interested in focusing on the

Raja Yoga

The program of the Brahma Kumaris is centered upon the practice of raja yoga, a special form of meditation that does not make use of mantras, breathing exercises, or hatha yoga postures. Rather, the student is taught to understand the mind and harness its power. The method is taught individually or in groups. The personal aspect of Shiva is worshipped.

(Melton, *Creeds*)

awareness of the beauty and truth that God is. If I'm experiencing God's love, God's truth, then I know.

The way I've understood God and experienced God is as a being of light. I came to that understanding first through being able to view the self. When I see you, I see myself. The first image, of course, is of the physical form. But within this physical form there is a being of light that is in the center of the forehead. And if you let yourself sit quietly, you can feel that source of life, that source of energy within.

When I practice this awareness of detaching myself from this physical form and coming back to the awareness of my true identity, then I am able to have that perception of the Supreme as a being of light, without needing to put on any other images or forms connected with it. When I think of myself in this human form, as a physical being, I need human things, I need physical forms to hold on to, and they'll always be artificial. But in the awareness of the soul, I can understand God being just light. And I am able to make that connection. Yes, love is the most powerful experience, but also peace, purity, power—this is God.

Spirituality means communion, to be able to explore a relationship with One and that is the Supreme. And so, even by definitions of these words, you don't have many supremes, you have one who is the Supreme. I see all souls, human souls, going through a variety of different changes, at times in a state of impurity, at times in a state of purity and greatness and divinity. My own feeling is that it's possible for the human soul to come to its state of perfection, its state of divinity. But God, the Supreme, is beyond all the changes and fluctuations and God the Supreme is the one with whom we connect.

THE ATTRIBUTES OF GOD

There isn't a masculine form or a feminine form. I think all these things have blocked us from having a relationship with God. God is a form that has, in a sense, all perfect attributes of love, of compassion, but also of power, of authority and strength. And so in human language, we would then say that this is the mother role, or this is the father role. I do experience God in those relationships, and that God is the Supreme

---

Types of Yoga

Yoga is a set of theories and techniques for doing meditation, unique in South Asia from ancient times to the present. The purpose of classical yoga was to provide a practical method for the isolation of the essential self. Although the word yoga can also be used for Buddhist or Jain meditation, it is most often used in Hindu contexts. Yogi is simply a name for any serious follower of one of the many schools of yoga, including

- *Jñāna Yoga, a reflective meditation on the discipline of knowledge, seeking to discriminate between unchanging consciousness and the changing patterns of awareness of one's body*
- *Karma Yoga, meditation on the discipline of action (karma), on how to act well without becoming attached to the fruits of one's action*
- *Bhakti Yoga, meditation on the discipline of devotion, aiming to realize union with Lord Krishna*
- *Mantra Yoga, meditation on the repetition of sacred sounds or utterances (mantras) derived from letters of the Sanskrit alphabet to attain knowledge*

Mother, the Supreme Parent, the Supreme Father, the Supreme
Teacher, the Supreme Guide. If you say we are God's children,
that is the very basic factor in my life. Whatever other factors of
color, race, culture, gender, different thinking, the relationship
is the eternal one of soul to soul.

The interesting thing for me here is that, although I the soul
am in a female body—so that the role that I am playing is a role
of a woman, which is wonderful, I enjoy it greatly—the human
soul is actually neither masculine nor feminine. What has happened throughout history, but especially in recent times, is that
we have become very fixed in those roles that we've been given
to play. It is important to step away from that so that I can develop the full potential that there is within me.

For instance, a person like Mahatma Gandhi, here is a man,
very much a man, who had tremendous courage and authority
and a pioneering spirit, with which so much could be achieved.
But equally there was a very gentle side, in which there was a
love, mercy, compassion, and purity. He was able to bring a
synthesis of these within his personality. It then is not masculine
image that comes across but the greatness of the spirit.

So again for every woman there is a wonderful sense of the
spirit of the feminine. And what the world definitely needs is
more of the feminine principle in terms of compassion, mercy,
and love. But equally, if I look at the negative of the feminine aspect, there is dependency, there is fear, there is attachment, there
is jealousy. These are the things that come up if I just lock my
self ito a female role in a woman. But I, the soul, can be detached from that. I can develop the positive feminine attributes
but equally the positive masculine attributes.

- *Laya Yoga, meditation on the disciple of disso-lution (laya), to become absorbed in the various manifestations of primal materiality*
- *Hatha Yoga, meditation on the discipline of exer-tion, a rigorous pro-gram of bodily discipline, deep breath-ing, and dietary control to purify the body*
- *Raja Yoga, a complex integration of various yogas*

(Crim)

RELIGION AS THE STUFF OF DAILY LIFE

I've been very aware that if there is anything constructive and
useful that I can do out there in the world, it has to be if I can
pull my act together within myself first. Often we term something service or giving or concern, but it is actually either feeding my own ego or satisfying my own inner needs. Instead of
finding a method whereby I can replenish my own inner being,
I'm actually taking things from outside. This is why you have
the situation where a person is trying to serve, but they come to

a state of "burnout," because they haven't been able to fill themselves first and then use that spiritual energy to serve.

I was very young when my mother came into contact with the Brahma Kumaris and Raj Yoga. I tagged along and was interested and loved the people. I was growing up in England, not the most conducive atmosphere for spiritual development in the 1960s.

At that point in my life I felt that religion would come, maybe when I was old and gray, but it had nothing to do with my life at that time. Except something that was very quiet and deep was happening inside of me. And that was a search to be able to find principles as an anchor in my own life. Yet the permissive society was leading in one direction. Some of my friends were pulling me in that direction. Then there was a very traditional, orthodox Hindu, Indian path that came from my parents. Then there was the more traditional Western style that was also an influence from some good friends in an older generation.

I needed to have something that I could relate to comfortably within my own heart and my own conscience. I didn't realize that religion had anything to do with these things that I was going through.

I suppose that religion has come to be associated with ritual, with scripture, with the written word or whatever was said a few thousand years ago. Today we divorce religion and spirituality. But, in fact, the essence of religion is to lead me—if I take that word *religio*, "ligament, to join together, to unite." Religion should lead me back to that original state of inner experience and enable me to experience that unity, that link, that union with God. When I discovered that finding a quiet time for myself, experiencing that inner being, making that link with God, was part of religion, or should be a part of religion, then I knew that this was what I wanted, that this was the foundation for life.

THE BRAHMA KUMARIS AND THE UNITED NATIONS

For the International Year of Peace in 1986, we ran a project called "The Million Minutes of Peace Appeal." When we first thought about a million minutes, it sounded huge. But what ended up, as pledges from people, in the space of a month, was a billion minutes of peace.

What we said to people was, is there something you perceive to contribute to world peace? The leaders are going to have their conferences; the UN is going to try and do what it can. Different people are going to be doing different things, but what can *I* do?

We asked people to give time, not money, time. And we asked them, "Can you give some minutes of your day just for the space of a month, one day, once a week, any day, whatever?" Give a few minutes of your time either in meditation or in prayer, or even, just simply, in positive thoughts for a better world, for peace in the world. People in eighty-eight countries responded and gave us a billion minutes of peace.

Well, that was really a superficial thing, scratching the surface. But it was a very good way to get people interested and involved. We wanted to take that a little bit deeper and have them thinking.

They invited us to do a follow-up project. We decided we'd do "Global Cooperation for a Better World." In this project, we asked people to think about their vision of the future and what it is they would like to see in their better world. This project ran from 1988 through to 1990, about three years. We collected millions of visions.

The amazing thing was that it confirmed something that I understood from a spiritual perspective—whether you are in California or I'm in London or in India, our hopes, our aspirations, our fears, our dreams, all of these are very similar, because we are human beings. Global Cooperation gave us the research and facts that validated this. It became the largest research project ever undertaken by a nongovernmental organization. It reached 129 countries. Kings and presidents and princes and prime ministers gave their visions. But equally, a leper colony in the Philippines, shoe shine boys in Brazil, aboriginal natives in India also participated and shared their visions. And their visions were very, very similar.

I'll give you an example. A person in Argentina said, "The color of our skin is different, but the color of our blood, sweat, and tears is the same all over. So why can't there be justice for all equally?" A person in Africa wrote, "Let me live simply, so

Brahma Kumaris on One Human Family

Respect, understanding, and tolerance enable us to celebrate life in all its diversity. Living by these values develops a deeper spirituality in our vision toward each other. Sharing these values establishes the common ground on which we all live as one human family.

—The Mt. Abu Declaration, Brahma Kumaris, 1989

Brahma Kumaris in the
United States

*The first Brahma Kumaris
Raja Yoga Center in the
United States was founded
in 1977 in San Antonio,
Texas. Each center has
three or more teaching sisters who guide it adminis-
tratively. In 1985 there
were ten centers.*

(Melton, *Creeds*)

that others can simply live." A shoe shine boy and a king both
said something like there should be love, there should be respect.

The thing about the project was that people weren't saying
that they wanted to have Rolls Royces. They didn't see that in
their better world. They weren't saying, "I want to have a swim-
ming pool in my better world." The things that they were all describing were things of value, spiritual values: love, respect,
truth, honesty. These were the things that people said that they
wanted to see in their better world. When we began this project
we had no idea that this was what was going to be coming out.
After these things started to come in, it came to us so clearly,
that this is what is at the heart of everything.

People have now come to a point where they realize that
there have to be values in our lives, and only then can there be a
better world.

If today people say, "We want to have a better world," then
it's not going to happen because somebody up there, not even
God [*laughing*], not even God can say, "Let there be a better
world," and it will happen. But it is when I say, "I need to have
a better world, but what can I do about it now? Let me start
making a difference in my life."

We have a slogan that says, "When I change, the world will
change also."

IDDHIST BRAHMA KUMARIS JEWISH
AIN NATIVE AMERICAN SUFI HINDU
IRISTIAN ROMAN CATHOLIC

BUDDHIST

KH BAHA'I JEWISH ZUROASTRIAN
OMAN CATHOLIC TAO ZUROASTRIAN
ROASTRIAN PROTESTANT CHRISTIAN
NDU MUSLIM JAIN ROMAN CATHOLIC
AOIST BAHA'I BUDDHIST SIKH SUFI
ATIVE AMERICAN BRAHMA KUMARIS
WISH PROTESTANT CHRISTIAN TAOIST
IDDHIST HINDU ZUROASTRIAN JAIN
OMAN CATHOLIC BAHA'I PROTESTANT
AOIST HINDU SUFI NATIVE AMERICAN
USLIM BRAHMA KUMARIS BUDDHIST
KH SUFI JEWISH MUSLIM TAOIST
ROASTRIAN CHRISTIAN BAHA'I HINDU

BUDDHIST

SPIRITUAL ACTIVISM
Dr. A. T. Ariyaratne

Dr. A. T. Ariyaratne, a Buddhist social activist from Sri Lanka, who trained as a school teacher and was inspired by Gandhi, began the Sarvodaya movement many years ago. As a high school teacher at the Nalanda College in Colombo, he took his students to work in a remote and destitute village to—as he describes it—"understand and experience the true state of affairs that prevailed in the rural and poor urban areas . . . (and) to develop a love for their people and utilize the education they received to find ways of building a more just and happier life for them." The movement helps the poorest of villages in his coun try develop economically and ecologically sound methods of self-sustainability. With this effort, he has set an international example of Buddhist environmentalism, self-empowerment, and compassion.

Sarvodaya involves the concept of *shramadana* (from *shrama*, meaning "labor or human energy," and *dana*, meaning "to give"). Today, Sarvodaya is embraced by over 30,000 villages throughout South Asia. Ariyaratne went on to study from the Bhoodan-Gramdan campaign, initiated by the scholar Vinoba Bhave, who walked all over India imparting the methods of Gandhi. In 1968, Ariyaratne initiated the Hundred Villages Development Scheme throughout the poorest of Sri Lanka's villages. Within five years, the movement had spread to four thousand such villages. By the 1980s the movement was huge.

"Lord Buddha's admonition to us was [to serve] by helping those who suffer physically to overcome physical suffering, those who are in fear to overcome fear, those who suffer mentally to overcome mental suffering. Be of service to all living beings.

—A.T. Ariyaratne

Theravada Buddhism

*Of the many formulations
of early Buddhism, the
only one to survive subsequent foreign invasions
was the Buddhism (later
called Theravada) that
came to Sri Lanka in the
third century B.C.E. The
Theravada Buddhists of Sri
Lanka are conscious of
having the special role of
preserving the original
teachings of the Buddha—
they consider themselves to
be the longest surviving
continuous tradition of
Buddhism in the world.
From Sri Lanka, Ther-
avada spread to Southeast
Asia, where it predomi-
nates to the present in
Burma (Myanmar), Thai-
land, Laos, and Cambodia*

(Kampuchea).

Ariyaratne decentralized its power base and created a series of structural innovations to empower local people, to provide homes for abandoned children, to lower prices of goods available to poor villagers, and to reconcile political opponents to each other in a country torn by such opposition. If Ariyaratne were to run for political office (which he has refused to do), it is estimated that about a third of all residents of Sri Lanka would cast their vote for him.

What most uniquely characterizes Ariyaratne's achievement is his emphasis on listening to local people and his insistence that they listen to one another in order to formulate sustainable and joyous pathways in this life. Those rural folk—who account for more than 50 percent of the human population, and nearly 80 percent in Third World countries—are, he insists, the experts. Local families and communities must judiciously come together to assist themselves, to be independent of urban power bases, and to do what is right for all sentient beings. This is the true spirit of both Buddhism and modern-day environmentalism.

Nearly assassinated on occasion by those failing to grasp the humility and humanity of his message and frightened by the egalitarian nature of that message, Ariyaratne has been compared to Mahatma Gandhi. Author of several books, he recently received the ninth Niwano Peace Prize.

THE SARVODAYA MOVEMENT

Sarvodaya means the awakening of all. This is a word coined from two Sanskrit words, meaning "awakening all," by Mahatma Gandhi. Mahatma Gandhi was a Hindu and a Buddhist, but this word is the same in our language.

I have to begin with myself. My personality awakening should be foremost for me, then the awakening of my family, then my community, then my nation, the country, and my world—the awakening of all from the individual to the world.

When I was a schoolboy, I was very impressed with the attitude my parents had toward our community, the village people. We were not very rich people, neither were we very poor, we were a middle-class family, but my mother and my father helped everybody in the community, so I got used to social service. Then when I started life as a teacher, I was wondering what we were doing in the classroom, teaching these children chemistry, botany, zoology, mathematics, languages, everything except for them to become human beings, to be of service to others. So I thought we must take education outside of the classroom, textbooks, examinations, without disturbing that part of it.

I had been to a lot of really backward villages in Sri Lanka with a friend of mine, and I used to bring the stories of how people lived to my children in the classroom. They said then why don't we go to a village during vacations and weekends and work with the village people constructing roads, toilets, houses, school buildings, irrigation canals, water, reservoirs.

Later hundreds of other schools joined, so it became a national movement where we gifted our thought, our time, our effort for the well-being of other people. Now we are working in over 23,000 villages in Sri Lanka. Plus, we are working in 8,600 places now, in Sinhalese, in Tamil—in Muslim, Buddhist, Christian, Hindu areas.

At the time, we were under foreign rule, and there were certain scholars who came to Sri Lanka and found Buddhism. And they wanted to separate the contemplative side of Buddhism from social action, because that was the way they could continue with the colonial rule. Buddha's teachings are more for this life, the family. Of course the individual awakening is very important. But the individual cannot awaken unless the environment is conducive to such awakening.

Then so many started asking questions. Why are you doing this? What is the educational foundation for this? So we used to say that here we are awakening or helping the student to awaken his personality by learning to respect all life. You respect your caste, race, religion, even respect nature.

We called it *shramadana*, sharing of labor. And then people started asking questions. What's the meaning of this? What is the philosophy behind this? So we had to tell them, we are learning principles to awaken all personality: first to respect all life, second to translate that lovingkindness into compassionate action—so what we call development and social welfare is compassionate action, then we learn to get the joy of living at that very moment. When we do this we have joy in living at that very moment.

Every moment we should be happy. For us to be happy, we should feel that we are of service to other people.

Statistics on Buddhism

Buddhism is the dominant faith in Southeast, Central, and East Asia. It is estimated that there are more than 300 million Buddhists worldwide. In the United States alone there are about five million adherents following as many as 75 different forms of Buddhism.

Mahayana Buddhist countries (approximately 50 percent of all Buddhists): *China, Taiwan, Japan, South Korea, Mongolia, Tibet, Nepal, Bhutan, Vietnam*

Theravada Buddhist countries (approximately 38 percent of all Buddhists): *Sri Lanka, Burma (Myanmar), Thailand, Cambodia (Kampuchea), Laos*

THE IMPERMANENCE OF LIFE

In 1952, a gangster was asked to kill me. I was innocently trying
to be of service to the students in our communities who were in
need. And some people's financial or other interests were threatened, so they gave a contract killer some money. I heard about
it. I went to him, and I told him, "This is what I am doing. If
you want to kill me, do it now, not in my school or with my students," because those places will have a bad name after them.

I didn't want other people's blood to be shed. So, at that
time, and even now, I have that courage. To let others live, if
necessary, you sacrifice. I mean, you are not foolish to throw
away your life like that.

It is a spiritual motivation, because every moment we are
born, we exist, and we pass away. Every moment. In our mind,
or body, is there anything that is permanent for two seconds?
Without our knowledge it's changing. Impermanence is a law.
And when you understand that, when you practice it, you get a
lot of courage. And even in death you see life.

So, he was so good, not only did he say, "Oh, what a crime I
would have done." And one lesson he taught me: "Against our
conscience, we don't kill. I was told that you are a very bad person, misleading students. Because we didn't have teachers like
you, we became criminals." And that man changed from that
day. Of course one of his colleagues killed him.

I had a number of experiences like that. But this is the risk
you have to take when you decide to work on an idea. For me it
is nothing. Only in giving, you receive. As Christ said, "Lose
thyself to find thyself." Buddha has advocated that. All religious
leaders have.

THE THIRD WORLD AND SOCIAL JUSTICE

You see, the Third World is not only there. It's right here, in
Chicago. Similarly, the First World is there in Colombo, in my
country, not only here. No matter where you go in the world, in
the poorest country in the world there will be a group of people
who have all the affluence in the world with them. True, when you
take the countries as a whole, a country like Sri Lanka, with a very
small per capita income, is called the Third World. Now what is

---

The Eightfold Path

*The practical discipline, the
eightfold path was taught
by the Buddha as a way
from ignorance to knowl-
edge, from suffering to
nirvana—the goal of Bud-
dhism, described as a perfectly peaceful and
enlightened state of transformed consciousness.*

1. **Right understanding—**
*holding a correct view of
the nature of reality*
2. **Right thought**—*thoughts
free from sensuous desire,
from ill-will, and from cruelty; nonviolent thoughts
(ahimsa)*
3. **Right speech**—*that is,
one's speech must not be
false or harsh, or involve
slander or gossip*
4. **Right action**—*nonviolent behavior (ahimsa) toward all living creatures;
refraining from stealing;
avoidance of wrong con-
duct in matters of bodily
pleasures; avoidance of intoxicants and gambling*

common to the affluent and the poor is the one objective of be-coming an affluent person or an affluent society. This we reject.

We have to reject poverty. We have to reject affluence. No poverty, no affluence will protect the environment, and also there will be social justice in the world. These are conscious decisions we have to make if we are to survive as a planet.

Because of the power to communicate, the affluent people, through all kinds of advertisements and various things, show the poor people this is the good life. But the poor people are not told how grief-stricken they are. Even the richest man is suffering because suffering is not only physical, it is something to do with the mind. So what we do is, we tell the poor people, "Let us fight poverty and powerlessness both by getting ourselves organized on self-reliance and community participation, and by having a scientific plan of action."

We have programs for preschool children. Thousands of preschool children are looked after in our Sarvodaya nurseries—their psychosocial development, their health care and nutrition—by specially trained volunteers. School-age children are encouraged to go to school, and if they lack anything, we try to provide them with that. Youths are helped to learn both community leadership skills and certain basic vocational skills.

Farmers are assisted and helped to give up using chemicals or pesticides or herbicides and use natural methods. And craftsmen are encouraged not to allow their craft to die out in the world because of artificial, mechanical things that come in to the scene. If you carve something, you are not only making a piece of art, your personality is also all the time changing and you are a happy man. And to give up that way of living is mad.

5. Right livelihood—avoidance of occupations that involve killing (hunting, fishing); monks and nuns must live solely on alms or food grown by themselves
6. Right effort—that is, avoiding and overcoming unwholesome states of mind, developing and maintaining wholesome ones
7. Right mindfulness—thoughtful contemplation of the body, of feelings, of the mind and its activity, and of hindrances of lust, anger, sloth, restlessness, and doubt
8. Right concentration—unification of the mind through right contemplation and effort

THE POWER OF VILLAGES TO CHANGE THE WORLD

Globally they can do it because human beings have so much of goodness. Look at the criminal who was asked to kill me. How much of goodness he had. He fell at my feet and said, "Forgive me for thinking of killing you." So there is goodness in every person. We should harness goodness. Sarvodaya is harnessing the goodness in all.

When the Roman Empire was about to fall, this same thing happened. This rural to urban migration is a sign that the wrong

kind of civilization we are building based on cities is soon coming to an end. It can't be sustained.

So there are, I would say, three or four things to be done.
One is to preserve, wherever you are, in the United States or in
my country or Canada, the individual, the family, and the
community living close to one another. Preserve it. Build on it,
globally.

Two, prevent that kind of community from getting influenced by the wrong things that may come from cities—the
wrong kind of lifestyles, unsustainable lifestyles, high use of energy resources, all that. How much energy is being used to
maintain an affluent style of life?

The third thing is tell the people who are controlling our society, the dominant group, "This is all wrong, you can't bring
affluence to all. The world doesn't have resources to do that.
Even if you create artificial resources like plastics, the kind of
technology you use will pollute your environment. So please, get
back to a simple lifestyle."

And the fourth thing is break this affluent and poverty-
stricken barrier. Think of humanity as a whole where we can get
linked up. A community here, who are very affluent, say fifty
families, can get linked up in the so-called Third World, the
poor world, with, say, some village community.

We need the United Peoples because most governments
don't represent their people. And this could be done using modern technology.

Imagine a beautiful tank, a huge water reservoir, built across
two hills, not very high, but without disturbing nature because
our civilization is a kind civilization. Irrigation canals, beautiful
environment. There you come and implant a five star hotel, in a
place where in history we never put up buildings on water
catchment areas. So we had a protest. Fifty thousand of us participated, and for three hours we meditated. That's all we did.
Seven thousand armed policemen were there. So that's a nonviolent direct kind of action.

Coral reefs in the country, you know, they are being torn
apart to make cement, a kind of lime. This is not done officially;
government prohibits it. This is done by powerful politicians
who give protection to poor people who make it their livelihood. For generations it was whatever broke and came down to
the shore that was collected. But that's not the way it is done

now. So very little consideration is given to the protection of nature. This is part and parcel of the modern free market economy that is being introduced into our country by the World Bank and the International Monetary Fund. They tell the government what to do and call for privatization of everything, but call it "peoplization."

What we say is there should be three sectors having equal importance and equal legality: One is the government elected by the people; two, the private sector—the companies and all that; three, a people's sector. We should have the same equality under the law. We should have the same access to bank loans, for example, if we do the same thing.

There are still some families left. Begin with them. New families will emerge. Tell them, "We must reconstruct our society based on our family." It's the family that teaches us sharing, pleasant language, constructive activity, and equality in association.

I would say that is the only solution to the global problem. Modern technology, communication technology is so developed, I can stay in my own country in a village, you can stay here, and we can still communicate about what is happening in our part of the country and talk about how your country is also responsible for this damage, say for clearing five thousand acres of virgin land where there was so much biodiversity. Now five thousand acres will be planted to pineapple. Never again can you have those plants and those species of animals and plants in that area. In five years, you will leave our country with your investment, with your profit, and you have destroyed something hereditary to the world. But ordinary people have no say in it because the area in which they live, that particular ecosystem, is no longer under their control.

That is why I say the future of the world is the individual, the family, and the community.

*Do not decry other sects,
do not deprecate others,
but rather honor whatever
in them is worthy of honor.*

—Asoka's Edicts

HOW WE CAN BECOME NONVIOLENT

There are different levels of violence: personal violence, structural violence, cultural violence, and so on. This new violence comes as a result of craving great desires, and you can satisfy them. Envy is created, and it ends up in a fight.

Concrete Suggestions for
Implementing Nonviolent
Economics

- *Our caring for others
  should lead us to insist
  on nothing short of full
  economic justice—leav-
  ing behind traditional
  "charity" and handouts.*
- *Gandhi and Tolstoy
  urge us all to do some
  necessary manual work,
  to commune with all
  those who are con-
  demned to especially
  alienating and harsh
  forms of manual work.*
- *Practice frugality and a
  simple lifestyle—pursue
  intentional simplicity as
  part of a strategy to
  achieve fairer distribution of available re-
  sources.*

When human beings don't have peace within their minds,
then of course, all this external violence also begins. So peace-
lessness of people in their own mind is the result of increased
craving leading to envy and ignorance and using any kind of
cultural or linguistic or religious difference as an excuse to start
violence.

We have in the world today personal violence, cultural violence, and the most dangerous is the structural violence. Structural violence is high concentration of political power in the
hands of a few, or high concentration of economic power in
the hands of a few. And then the rich start becoming richer, and
the poor start becoming poorer. But they are given the image of
a good life based on affluence, so they try to find money in all
kinds of immoral, antisocial ways. So we've got a tension between the extreme affluence in the hands of a few and the extreme poverty in the hands of the majority. That is one.

The other is spiritual decadence, spiritual degeneration. You
try to learn everything about others without learning anything
about yourself, how your body and mind work. Violence is on
the increase everywhere in the world. Not only violence to
human beings but also to nature. In Sri Lanka, we were doing
everything possible to prevent what is happening there today.
Even now we are struggling to put a stop to this bloody civil
war that is going on.

Of course a lot of people are benefiting from this civil war,
those who import arms and get benefit from that. Politicians can
say we have a civil war going on, so we can't devote time to do
developmental activities and instead spend all the money there
like that.

We are opposed to injustice. Injustice and violence go hand
in hand. Justice and nonviolence also go hand in hand. Therefore, it's not enough, you see, to have instruments of the government like the police or the military to crush these things.

But there should be other means you use to remove the real
causes that can lead to violence. So there we are active. We had
quite a number of what we called meditational peace marches
with Tamil, Muslim, Buddhist, Christian, Hindu—everybody
walking together, a hundred and twenty thousand at one time,
through the most dangerous areas where there was violence.

It makes a tremendous difference because here you are going

through an environment where you can get killed, so you know it because extremist violent people don't like any piece of it. So you make a decision, which needs courage.

Going through that, you only do two things. You are mindful of your breath, your movement of your legs and your arms in complete silence. And all the time you think, when you hear a noise, "Let that bird or animal or human being, let that person be well and happy in mind and body."

Radiating lovingkindness and improving your own mindfulness—that is a social action; that is what people see. And as we do it, there are some types of transformation taking place.

This is called equanimity. You have two sides of a river. You think that there is no connection between this side and that side because there is water. But actually it is connected under the water. So when you look at it in depth, name and blame, success and failure, abuse and praise, all these things are two sides of the same coin. So learn to accept them with equanimity.

- *Work. Especially, give the right to work to the weak, the poor, and the disenfranchised so that they might achieve greater autonomy and self-sufficiency.*
- *Learn to share, to give, to practice generosity on a daily basis.*
- *To whatever extent is feasible, practice local or regional self-sufficiency; support local agriculture and manufacture; practice economic and political decentralization.*
- *Support cooperative approaches to work and economic problems. Gandhi's plea was to avoid and denounce the practices of exploitive capitalism. (Excerpted from* How May I Help? *by Dr. Guy de Mallac)*

(SourceBook)

BUDDHIST

COMPASSION

His Holiness the Dalai Lama (Tenzin Gyatso)

Tenzin Gyatso, His Holiness the fourteenth Dalai Lama, is the spiritual and temporal leader of the six million Tibetan people. Born on July 6, 1935, in a small village in northeastern Tibet, he was recognized at the age of two, in accordance with Tibetan tradition, as the reincarnation of his predecessor the thirteenth Dalai Lama and, thus, an incarnation of Avalokiteśvara, the Buddha of Compassion.

The Dalai Lama completed his Doctorate of Buddhist Philosophy at the age of twenty-five, passing his examinations with honors. The exam was conducted publicly, before 20,000 monk scholars.

Ten years earlier, while still a teenager, His Holiness had already assumed full political responsibility as a head of state at a time when Tibet's existence was threatened by the Chinese. At age nineteen, he went to Beijing to hold peace talks with Mao Tse-tung, Chou En-lai, and Deng Xiaoping. His efforts to peacefully resolve Sino-Tibetan agitation were thwarted. A popular uprising resulted inside Tibet and on March 10, 1959, Lhasa, the capital of Tibet, exploded with a massive demonstration calling for Tibet's full independence.

As His Holiness was forced into exile in India by the authorities in Beijing, eighty thousand Tibetan refugees followed him. Since 1960, His Holiness has resided in the town of Dharamsala in northern India. From there, the Dalai Lama has traveled throughout the world drawing attention to the plight of the

Tibetans, 120,000 of whom are also in exile, and trying desperately to perpetuate the Tibetan language, culture, and identity. Due largely to his efforts, today there are more than eighty Tibetan schools, a Tibetan University, and the Tibetan Institute of Performing Arts in India and Nepal.

The Dalai Lama has on three occasions gotten the UN General Assembly to call upon China to respect the human rights of Tibetans and their right to self-determination. In his meetings with Czech President Václav Havel, with former President George Bush, and countless other heads of state, His Holiness has repeatedly stressed the issue of universal responsibility and interdependence. "Basically," he says, "universal responsibility is feeling for other people's suffering just as we feel our own. . . . Love and compassion are the moral fabric of world peace."

The Dalai Lama has had numerous and extensive meetings with Pope Paul VI, Pope John Paul II, the Archbishop of Canterbury, and many other world religious leaders. When eight rabbis and scholars from the United States visited him for discussions, His Holiness concluded, "When we became refugees, we knew that our struggle would not be easy. It would take a long time, generations. Very often we would refer to the Jewish people, how they kept their identity and faith despite such hardship and so much suffering. And, when external conditions were ripe, they were ready to rebuild their nation. So you see, there are many things to learn from our Jewish brothers and sisters. . . . Each religion," he says, "has certain unique ideas or techniques, and learning about them can only enrich one's own faith."

The recipient of innumerable honorary degrees and awards, His Holiness was awarded the Nobel Peace Prize in 1989. In his acceptance speech, he said, "The prize reaffirms our conviction that with truth, courage, and determination as our weapons, Tibet will be liberated. Our struggle must remain nonviolent and free of hatred." And in a statement that followed the Dalai Lama's acceptance of the Peace Prize, Norway's Prime Minister, Mrs. Gro Harlem Brundtland, stated, "This year's Peace Prize is a concrete support to all who strive for the increased awareness of individual responsibility for our common future."

Clad in basic robes, often seen with sunglasses, perpetually of good cheer, and prone to bouts of great boyish laughter, the

ever-vibrant Dalai Lama strikes an intoxicating presence. He
has been heard to say, "I am just a simple Buddhist monk—no
more, no less." He lives in a small cottage in the Himalayan
foothills, rises at 4 A.M. to meditate, and pursues a busy sched-
ule every day of administrative meetings, private audiences, religious teachings, and ceremonies. And he is fond of citing a
favorite verse, found in the writings of the eighth-century Buddhist saint Shantideva:

> For as long as space endures
> And for as long as living beings remain,
> Until then may I too abide
> To dispel the misery of the world.

HOPE FOR THE FUTURE OF TIBET

The main hope is Tibet eventually should be a zone of peace. I
think it would be a tremendous benefit not only for six million
Tibetan people, but also for India and China, the two most pop-
ulated nations.

Interviewer: Under what circumstances would you be able to
return to Tibet?

Dalai Lama: If we found genuine understanding with the
Chinese. Genuine understanding or agreement that is based on
mutual trust, mutual respect.

And of course, the situation inside Tibet, at present, is very,
very critical. First, this must stop. This must change. Then of
course, the Tibetan people, eventually, I think will really get
some kind of peace of mind. Or, when they develop some kind
of genuine hope or genuine trust, we can work with the Chinese.
At the moment, deep down, there is fear. This fear, I think it's
lasted for forty years.

So therefore, when such a situation has developed, then it is
the right time, you see, to think about my return. I try my best to
find some way to develop that. For that reason, I made maximum
concessions. But unfortunately, so far, in spite of my efforts, no
concrete response comes from Chinese government side.

Tibetan Buddhism

This form of Mahayana Buddhism seeks to develop the capacities of mind as well as the channeling of physical and emotional vitalities through discipline into the search for salvation. There are four major orders:

1. *Nyingmapa—the "ancient ones" or the "Red Hat" order, so called because of the distinctive headdress*
2. *Kargyupa—a school of oral tradition in which the secret mystical traditions are passed from teacher to pupil*
3. *Saskyapa—the first of the orders to establish the idea of a priestly monarchy*
4. *Gelugpa—the "merit system ones" or "Yellow Hats," a reform movement founded in the fifteenth century headed by the figure of the Dalai Lama, who assumes spiritual and temporal leadership*

THE HEART OF CHINESE/TIBETAN CONFLICT

I think there are many factors including historical factors. You know, in Chinese official documents they always say Tibet is a part of China since the thirteenth century. This is not true. An unbiased Chinese historian said they have a different opinion.

Then, from our side, in our literature or history, our relation to China is peace and pacifism. So this, of course, is one major factor.

Then, although I have some admiration about original Marxism, the most immediate main factor in their basic system is rule of terror since the Chinese communists so-called liberated Tibet. Of course, there is some progress here and there—in education, and in some other fields. We not only lost the fundamental human rights, but this brought a lot of destruction and human miseries. Therefore, those Tibetans who initially sided with good hope with this so-called liberation, now these people, as the time goes by, have completely lost their faith and their hope. Among this group are many communists, Tibetan communists.

Of course, all is likely to change, not from the government policy, rather I think due to economic development and also the communication with the outside world. I think, in the minds of the Chinese people, especially among the intellectuals, this is changing. Of course the desire of the democratic movement is now quite as strong in China as outside China. There is a quite thoughtful democratic movement. But the government side, regarding the Tibetan issue, is no change. No change.

It's time for elders to listen to the child's voice. You see, in the child's mind there is no demarcation of different nations, no demarcation of different social systems of ideology. Children know in their minds that all children are the same, all human beings are the same. So, from that viewpoint, their minds are more unbiased. When people get older, though, they start to say "our nation," "our religion," "our system." Once that demarcation occurs, then people don't bother much about what happens to others. It's easier to introduce social responsibility into a child's mind.

—The Dalai Lama

HOW CAN WE BEGIN TO CHANGE?

I think one good example, or, I think, inspiration, is the Palestinian and Israeli conflict. More than four decades, there is a lot of hatred and a lot of violence involved. But now they find some agreement in the spirit of reconciliation. This is, I think, a wonderful example.

So, basically, I'm always optimistic. With human determination, with more patience and if we make constant effort without losing hope, we will find, I'm quite sure within a few years' time, some proper way to solve this problem. And in the meantime, the international pressure or the international community support is very, very essential.

In the use of religion, religious faith or the emotional mental state utilized in a wrong way is also sometimes very harmful, a very negative force. I believe, in spite of different philosophies, all religions teach us to be a good person. Those human qualities such as patience, tolerance, forgiveness, mutual respect—these are the essence of religions. Various major religious traditions bring this message.

So if the politicians have a brilliant mind, with a more open heart, then things become much easier. And also I think it is very important to look to broaden the situation. After all, we all share in this same small planet. If we look from space, we hardly notice the national borders. These are mental creations.

I think, due to population and the world's natural resources and many other things—modern economies and also the environmental problem—now the reality is that we are very much interlinked with each other. But unfortunately, human mental attitudes remain behind.

If you look closely about our reality, then I think our common efforts now become of greater importance. Then little by little you see this agreement with one another.

ON THE CONNECTION BETWEEN SUFFERING, ATTACHMENT, AND LOVE

There are different levels of suffering, but, broadly speaking, suffering is a sort of conflict, even suffering due to the mental unrest. Usually I talk about negative emotion and positive emotion. These are very much linked with negative emotions such as hatred. Obviously, if you look at history and even today, you see many conflicts mainly due to hatred, such as Bosnia and also the Holocaust.

Hatred created a lot of suffering. That's clear. Compared to hatred, attachment is better. However, attachment sometimes creates hatred.

So, love and compassion. I believe that genuine compassion is more than love. It is not only the sense of close feeling toward the person or the community, but there is also the sense of responsibility or sense of commitment. Also genuine compassion is not based on personal good, something close to me, but rather on the other person or other community also has the same experience just like myself. They also want happiness and do not want suffering. On the basis of the realization of oneness as human brothers and sisters, we can develop genuine respect for their rights, genuine concern about their future. That is genuine compassion.

Basically I believe human nature is gentleness. Human nature is more compassionate. Of course, these negatives—anger, hatred, jealousy, doubt, fear—are also part of our mind, part of our life, but certainly not the dominant force. The dominant force, if you look from birth to death, the major factor for our life, even for good health, is human compassion, human affection. For example, if someone constantly develops fear or hatred, then that ruins the person's health. On the other hand, if the person keeps human affection, that creates automatically more inner calmness. It is very good for health.

So therefore, if you look at this level, then we can make a conclusion, "Oh, basic human nature is not so negative." This gives me hope in spite of many unpleasant events here and there. Still, there is potential.

And in any case, it is much better to remain with hope.

The Buddhist Faithful

- *As of 1989, there were an estimated 311 million Buddhists worldwide; of that number, approximately 50 percent are Mahayana Buddhists, 38 percent are Theravada Buddhists, and 6 percent are Tantrayana Buddhists.*
- *Approximately 5 million persons practice various kinds of Buddhism in the United States.*
- *There are approximately 100 organized churches in the Buddhist Churches of America.*

ON ENLIGHTENMENT, THE GOAL OF BUDDHISM

Although one has no experience with these deep, how do you say, the spiritual experience, one sees there is something. So continue investigation according to one's own inner experience. But then, you can feel, oh, if you put more energy on the development of mind, or spiritual development, there is definitely tremendous effect, transformation within ourselves.

Now, you know, in India, I utilize some of the ways of measurement. Not on the basis of day-to-day experience but, say, compare today with five years ago or ten years ago, twenty, thirty, forty years, then I see definitely a big difference.

Interviewer: *The diamond
sutra says that past mind
can't be grasped, present
mind can't be grasped, future mind can't be grasped,
with what mind are you
doing this interview?*

*His Holiness laughs, up-
roariously, along with the
interviewer, and, then, still
laughing, answers the question: Present mind.*

Enlightenment, according to Buddhist doctrine, is not done externally, but part of our own mind. So the achievement of enlightenment means self-serving never. There is the purpose of one's own interest, the purpose of Buddhist practice, certainly there is one's own interest also there, but this is a self-interest not clashing with other's interest.

Then of course, in Mahayana Buddhism, the interest of others always comes first. But then, in order to effectively serve others, first you yourself must have the quality or ability to serve properly. For that reason, the self-purification becomes very important.

PAST MIND, PRESENT MIND, FUTURE MIND

If you investigate more deeply, then we cannot find past mind or present mind or future mind. Now obviously, on the conventional level, everybody stays in time. It's very important. However, if we investigate based on external matter, if we investigate time, we cannot find present.

For example, today, 1993, in September, such and such hour, such and such minute, and further it goes to the second. So there's hardly any present—only past and future, no present. Without the present how can we define a path to the future? And then, if we investigate time on the basis of internal mind, no past and future. Just a momentary kind of feeling, that's the present.

So you see, if we investigate time then we cannot find. And also the self. This moment I'm talking with you. This self is a Tibetan, Buddhist monk. Definitely there is something. But if I investigate, besides this body, besides this mind, there's hardly anything left to identify as a self. In the meantime all the combination of body and mind, definitely there is self. But if we investigate, we cannot find.

MUST WE CHANGE OUR IDENTITY?

On the conventional level, these are reality. There is self, there is the human being, there is Tibetan self, American self, Chinese self, Indian self. On that basis if we develop compassion, if we develop harmony, without that then how do we develop harmony or compassion?

Simply the feeling of I or the feeling of self, or cherishing oneself—that's not negative. That is natural. I think in order to develop determination, or hope, we need a strong sense of self. Without that there will be no future. Self-confidence is very important. For that we need a strong sense of self. But then you see the problem, if the self-cherishing reaches such an extent of harming another in order to reach something for oneself, or for exploiting others. There are positive desires and negative desires.

We need the good strong sense of self and then strong will. With a strong will dedicate one's own future for the benefit of the other—a voluntary desire to take hardship in order to serve other people. So if it is necessary, even to sacrifice one's own privilege or interest. For that we need a strong sense of self.

Actually there is a lot of human negative or positive, or constructive or destructive, emotion in our daily life. Every emotion is combating. That is actually the practice of *dharma*. That is the meaning of the practice of *dharma*.

Dharma is religion—rather, I think, Buddhism. Or it is in many religious traditions to teach us the self-discipline. Self-discipline means one part of emotion wants certain activities or certain things. Then the other emotion knows, now, this is too much, this must stop. That brings self-discipline.

Buddhism in the
United States

The Buddhist community in the United States has matured more quickly than other American religions. Two visible signs of that maturity appeared in 1987 with the naming of the first Buddhist chaplain in the armed forces and the formation of the American Buddhist Congress. The congress will serve as a vehicle for building a more adequate understanding of Buddhists and Buddhism in American society and as a voice for the Buddhist community's opinions on matters of public policy.

(Melton, *Creeds*)

ON STUDY TO PRACTICE BUDDHISM

Of course, in Buddhist tradition, to study is considered very, very important. Without study, it is difficult to practice. You can practice without much study. The human mind is such that there are a lot of different parts or elements. In order to combat these different parts and in order to change your whole mental attitude, you need the various different methods, different practices. Therefore, study is very important.

Usually, among my Western friends, I give something like a warning or my suggestion that taking a new religion is not easy. Changing your religion is not a simple task. It is very complicated, or very delicate.

Universal Declaration on
Nonviolence (1991)

*. . . We declare that religion
must not permit itself to be
used by any state, group,
or organization for the purpose of supporting aggression for nationalistic gain.*
*. . . We have an obliga-
tion to promote a new vi-
sion of society, one in
which war has no place in
resolving disputes between
and among states, organi-
zations, and religions.*
*. . . Our declaration is
meant to promote . . . a
new global society, one in
which nonviolence is pre-
eminent as a value in all
human relations.*

Generally speaking, it is better to follow your tradition of your religion. Of course, you can adopt a certain different method from other traditions. Already some of my Christian brothers and sisters utilize some Buddhist method in their own daily practice. This is okay.

But I found some individuals, after exchanging their religion, sometimes develop a kind of mental confusion. I think two points should be kept in mind. One, even though you may have keen interest about a new religion, you should think again and again. Then, if you really feel that the new religion, or some dif- ferent tradition, really suits you and is more effective, then of course, it is the individual's right.

The second point, which I consider very, very important: Sometimes in order to justify your decision, there might be some kind of a tendency to be critical about the previous religion. That is very dangerous. Even though the new religion is more suitable, more effective, at the same time millions of people still care to benefit from the previous religion. This you must realize, you must acknowledge. This is very important, particularly at this moment when everyone is trying to have genuine harmony between different religions.

A MESSAGE FOR THE TIBETANS LIVING UNDER CHINESE RULE AND A MESSAGE FOR ALL PEOPLE

Usually I am telling those Tibetans who live in China proper that it is very important to keep their identity, their culture, although they remain in the Chinese towns and cities. Then I tell those Tibetans who live in our own country, although the situation is very, very difficult, we should not, under any cir- cumstances, give up. We should not give up the spirit of non- violence. It is very important.

Then, these days, I also say that, traditionally in our mind, the concept about the environment, ecological problem—we have not much idea about these problems because Tibet is a vast land and a small population and a dry, cold climate. So, the en- vironmental importance is something new to Tibetans. It is now very important to know these issues, and then protect with a sense of responsibility about the environment. This should be part of their life, from childhood—concern about water, the en-

vironment, the trees and animals. Clear awareness of the importance this must be a part of their life.

Compassion with fellow human beings, compassion with the
environment, and animals. That's it. That's it. I think that's the
only way. If we disregard the environment, other forms of life,
then without this, the human future, then it really is question-
able. After all, we are part of nature. If nature's balance is really
disturbed, then we'll disappear.

I think another basis of my hope is human nature is such
that when we really face a very serious crisis, then there are two
possibilities. One, that serious problem or crisis sometimes de-
moralizes us—depression. That is failure. That's very sad. Another possibility is, because of the seriousness, the human mind
says, "That's enough."

Then we try to find another alternative. Then we will find alternatives because of human intelligence. I think, now that we
are entering the twenty-first century, I think it is this century
that can give us many lessons.

So now, today, it seems among thinkers, among the people,
there is a real, genuine questioning. "Oh, our lifestyle or our
modern economic structure, these are really something we can't
sustain." I think these are the indications of a gradual response
to that crisis. This is a very hopeful sign.

*Know that the Truth is
sacred regardless of its
source, despite its seeming
vagueness or incredibility.*

—Tibetan Book of the Dead

BUDDHIST

MINDFULNESS

Dr. Chatsumarn Kabilsingh

Dr. Chatsumarn Kabilsingh, professor of religion and philosophy at Thammasat University in Bangkok, is the daughter of a monk and of the only living Thai woman who is an ordained Buddhist nun. Dr. Kabilsingh's mother established the first temple in Thailand for Buddhist women, where Dr. Kabilsingh grew up, as she says, a "temple girl" in a country that always thought of temple children as boys.

Dr. Kabilsingh's life work has been devoted to helping women out of poverty through Buddhist social activism. She frequently lectures throughout the world. Her topics include ecology and ethics, feminism, the role of Buddhist monks in forest conservation, consciousness after death, cross-cultural perspectives on nature, interfaith visions of reality, and international issues associated with achieving global peace.

Editor of the Newsletter on International Buddhist Women's Activities since 1984, Dr. Kabilsingh writes magazine columns and regularly lectures in Bangkok on Buddhism. But she is perhaps best known for her numerous books, which include: *Essence of Buddhism: Theravada-Mahayana* (1975), *Islam* (1977), *Christianity* (1979), *History of Buddhism in Thailand* (1981), *Buddhism in China* (1982), *A Comparative Study of Buddhist Nuns' Monastic Rules* (1984), *Women in Buddhism* (1985), *Philosophical Reflections on Life* (1986), *A Cry from the Forest,* and *Tree of Life* (both 1987).

In her most recent work, *Thai Women in Buddhism,* Dr. Kabilsingh examines the Bhikkhuni Sanga, the nuns' order. This order developed in India after the Buddha's death but subsequently waned for centuries as male-dominated Asian spirituality usurped the female's role. Today the female Sangha is once again flourishing and may offer many of the poorest girls in the country an opportunity to find a dignified lifestyle.

As an activist and conservationist, Kabilsingh's approach to ethics and interfaith dialogue is singular, as is her presence. She is the mother of three sons.

MINDFULNESS PRACTICE

You live in the present. Practicing Buddhism is to be mindful so every minute you are supposed to be mindful of what you are doing. So when you are feeding your baby, that is also a practice. So whatever you are doing, whether you are eating, you are studying—every minute is a practice for us.

To be mindful is to be aware of this present moment, to be in the here and now. Most of the time you tend to cling to the past, or otherwise you are projecting to the future so much so that you don't live the now, the present. I'm talking to you now. I should enjoy you rather than thinking about, "Oh, I'm supposed to. . . ." That is the practice.

If you get carried away with that kind of excuse you will never have time in your whole life to practice. You have to bring church into your home so that you can practice right now in this very moment. Then you can enjoy your life fully because wherever you are, you are in the present.

Sometimes you have to take one step away from what you are doing to meditate. But when you meditate enough, then that meditation should be for every moment. When you meditate, you know, you're supposed to be very calm and very watchful of what you are doing. You extend that meditation into your life.

SERVICE PRACTICE

Someone who would go ahead and choose the life of a monk or a nun is supposed to be more dedicated to their work. The message to be a monk or a nun is to be of help to others, to offer

Women in Buddhist Monastic Orders

Tradition says that the Buddha was reluctant to accept women into the Sangha, the monastic order, and that he allowed women to join only after his disciple Ananda's third appeal. The first female candidate for the Sangha was said to have been the Buddha's mother, Queen Mahapajapati, a wealthy woman who abandoned her domestic obligations, donned the yellow monastic robe, and shaved off her hair, but whom he refused at first. Her determination and sincerity played a vital role in bringing about the eventual admission of women to the Buddhist Sangha. The Buddha's reluctance has been used as an argument against the full acceptance of monastic orders for women in the Buddhist tradition.

Today, most Buddhist nuns are part of the Mahayana branch, mainly in Japan and Taiwan. Buddhist nuns are not generally accepted in Theravada Buddhist countries in Southeast Asia.

(Kabilsingh)

help to others. It doesn't mean that you are higher than the laypeople. Whether lay or ordained, we are the same. We are practicing, we are trying to find out who we are, and we are trying to practice living in this present moment.

So the monks and nuns are supposed to be the ones who have gone forth. They leave their home life in the background, go forth to study, to practice so that they can be of more service to others. Laypeople, because they have to work, may not have enough time to do for others as much as the monks and the nuns. To become monks and nuns in Buddhism really means to carry the message, "What can I do for you?"

ENLIGHTENMENT

Our spiritual goal is enlightenment. Enlightenment is for here and now. If you want to compare it to Christianity, you could compare it to the kingdom of God. Kingdom of God, each one of us, you do not know when it is coming. Only God will give you this kingdom of God. The same thing. Enlightenment could happen to you any minute. And it must be real for you now. Otherwise, Buddhism doesn't mean anything for me, if enlightenment is not for me, in this present life.

Many people, many Buddhists would kind of postpone the enlightenment. They are waiting for the coming of the next Buddha, so they will be enlightened in his time—but what about your life now?

The way of enlightenment, if you understand the teaching of Buddhism, is that this Prince Siddhartha went ahead into the forest, seeking to answer the question of how are we to get out of this suffering as human beings. That's the question that a Buddhist would try to get out of it. So to be enlightened is to be able to free yourself from this suffering of the fact that you are a human being.

Because of ignorance in this life, we cling on to this world. We cling on to ourselves, see that this is me, my, mine, cling to this existence, to this "Dr. Chatsumarn."

Whereas, there is actually no such thing as Dr. Chatsumarn. If you see each part of my body—these are my hands, where is

Vinaya, a collection of writings in the Buddhist Pali Canon, outlines the rules to be observed by the Sangha—the Buddhist monastic order. These rules are traditionally attributed to the Buddha; however, some of the Vinaya material appears to have been added several centuries after the death of the Buddha (ca. 480 B.C.E.). There is only slight variation in the Vinaya of different Buddhist traditions around the world.

Dr. Chatsumarn? This is a face. Then you go on analyzing it, you know, the nose, the lips, the cheeks, where am I? Where am I? Where are you? Who are you? When you start asking that question you realize that all this is—it's not there. This self is not there.

We accept that this self is here. But this self, in the eternal Self, is not real, because you do not have real ownership of it. I cannot say, "Well, I look very pretty today, I would like to remain pretty like this for the rest of my life." I have no control of myself. I have a headache, I cannot tell myself, "Stop headache." So in that sense we say that this self is not real because you do not have the real control of it.

By this message, try to remind yourself that you should not cling on to your self. It is impermanent. Everything is impermanent. Your self, your relationship with your husband, with your wife, with your children, that is also impermanent. So when you realize this, you don't suffer so much. You should learn to be detached so that when the time comes that you should be detached, then you really can.

If I understand the real nature of death and life, then I know life goes on to a certain extent and then it comes a time that there is death. Each one of us, when we were born, right away, we're being registered on the book of death. The only difference is that we do not know when we are going to die. If you know this nature of life and death, then, when the time comes, you accept death naturally. And if you can accept death naturally, then you do not suffer as much. But if you don't understand the true nature of life and death, then you cling on to it, and when actually death happens, you suffer so much. So the message of Buddhism is, "How are we to free ourselves from this clinging, this holding on to?"

In one level you do love your family. But in a higher level, let's say, in a transcendental level, you must realize that that relationship, also, is not real, is not permanent. So in Christianity, you would say that the real love would be the love of God. I think there is a passage when Jesus' mother and brother came to see him. He was questioning, "Who is my mother, who is my brother?" He is talking about two different levels of truth. In a higher level, only people who walk the path of God are his mother and his brother.

Buddhism in Thailand

Tradition says that Buddhism was brought to the Mon people, original inhabitants of Thailand, by missionaries sent from India by the Emperor Ashoka in the third century B.C.E. Buddhism is highly organized in modern Thailand and, as the state religion, is subject to a degree of state control. The king of Thailand must be a Buddhist, though his role as Defender of Religion compels him to protect all religions: Hinduism, Islam, Confucianism, Christianity. There is a Supreme Patriarch in Thai Buddhism, appointed by the king, and he is recognized as the leader of Thai Buddhists. More than 92 percent of the population adheres to Buddhism, specifically the Theravada tradition.

GOD IN BUDDHISM

We do not talk about God in Buddhism. We do not deny God, but our spiritual salvation does not depend on God, the Creator. Our spiritual salvation depends completely on us. This is the difference between Christianity, or any religion that has theism.

The image of the Buddha, it's a reminder for us that is our teacher. But the teacher cannot do everything for us if we do not practice what he teaches. In Christianity, you have holy communion. You accept Christ into you. You take in his body and his blood when you go to church every Sunday. What does it mean? It means that you must lead the life of Christ. But you if you do not take the life of Christ, you are no more Christian than any other people outside.

I draw a great strength and energy because I have faith in this spiritual power—if you like to call it God, if you like to call it enlightenment, whatever. And I could do wonders because I have this faith, I have this commitment.

THE COMMAND TO PROTEST: ON THE VIETNAMESE MONK WHO SELF-IMMOLATED TO PROTEST THE WAR

This was a Vietnamese monk practicing Mahayana Buddhism. In Thailand, we practice Theravada Buddhism. We couldn't understand that either. We thought, how could it be possible you kill yourself? That's the first precept: that you should not kill. Worse, to kill yourself.

But when you study Mahayana Buddhism you will understand they have fifty-eight Bodhisattva's precepts. One of the Bodhisattva's precepts says that you will not allow *adharma*—that is the power from the other side—to conquer you. You are supposed to protest.

According to this precept, you are commanded to protest. And that, I really appreciate what the Vietnamese monk did in the face of evil or in the face of oppression—the power of the other power that was trying to suppress Buddhism in Vietnam. He was not doing it for himself, he was doing it for Buddhism and for the world.

Buddhist Prayer

Now under the loving kindness and care of the Buddha, each believer of religion in the world transcends the differences in religion, race, and nationality, discards small differences, and unites in oneness to discuss sincerely how to annihilate strife from the earth, how to reconstruct a world without arms, and how to build welfare and peace of mankind, so that never-ending light and happiness can be obtained for the world of the future. May the Lord Buddha give His loving kindness and blessing to us for the realization of our prayers.

("Buddhist Prayers," World Conference on Religion and Peace)

Mahayana Buddhism

One of the two main branches of Buddhism, the other being Theravada. The Mahayana, or Northern School, is the larger branch of Buddhism and has assimilated many different beliefs of the cultures it has flourished in. Mahayana Buddhism traveled west from India in the first century B.C.E. and today flourishes in Tibet, China, Korea, Japan, Taiwan, and Vietnam. Several sects have grown out of Mahayana, including Pure Land, Ch'an/Zen, and Nichiren Buddhism.

When you have strong faith, you have commitment, conviction to something spiritual. That is a greater cause. It doesn't mean that this monk didn't love his life. He loved his life like us also. But he loved something more. So he was willing to sacrifice this part for the larger part, for the bigger part.

THE COMMAND TO PROTEST AND THE ENVIRONMENT

I happened to be a scholar and researcher for Wildlife Fund Thailand. What happened is that twenty years ago, we had 80 percent forest in our country. Twenty years after we have about 16 percent left. And at the very moment we are talking, they are cutting more trees. So that's going very rapidly.

The question is, "What happened—this is a Buddhist country? How is it that the forest is going so fast? Is there any connection between Buddhism and deforestation?"

So this project, what they are trying to do is to get the message across to the monks so that the monks could help to get out the message to the villagers trying to preserve the forest. There are some local monks who are very actively involved in trying to get the knowledge to the people, to the villagers' level. One particular monk, he actually received a global award in 1991 for helping the villagers to preserve the forest.

I think what we should try to help, the scholars as well as the monks, is to bring out Buddhist ethics on environmental issues so that it would be more known to the public that this is the message, the real message. Twenty years ago we didn't have any problem, therefore there was not much teaching about how we should conserve nature, how we should treat the environment. But now we have serious problem, and it's about time that we should do something. It doesn't mean that we should focus only from Buddhist resource. We try any means that we could get together.

In this project, we tried to make a blueprint. It could be in Christianity, you can adopt the same techniques. In Islam you can adopt the same technique, so that we could save this world.

The Bodhisattva Precepts are obligatory rules for a follower of Mahayana Buddhism, observed by monks and nuns as well as laymen. These precepts, 58 in all, are listed in the Brahmajala Sutra. The first ten are most essential—one must refrain from:

1. *killing*
2. *stealing*
3. *unchaste behavior*
4. *lying*
5. *using intoxicants*
6. *gossiping*
7. *boasting*
8. *envy*
9. *resentment and ill will*
10. *slander*

BUDDHIST BRAHMA KUMARIS JEWISH
JAIN NATIVE AMERICAN SUFI HINDU
CHRISTIAN ROMAN CATHOLIC MUSLIM
SIKH BAHA'I

PROTESTANT

ROMAN CATHOLIC PROTESTANT BUDDHIST
ZOROASTRIAN PROTESTANT CHRISTIAN

HINDU MUSLIM JAIN ROMAN CATHOLIC
TAOIST BAHA'I BUDDHIST SIKH SUFI
NATIVE AMERICAN BRAHMA KUMARIS
JEWISH PROTESTANT CHRISTIAN TAOIST
BUDDHIST HINDU ZOROASTRIAN JAIN
ROMAN CATHOLIC BAHA'I PROTESTANT
TAOIST HINDU SUFI NATIVE AMERICAN
MUSLIM BRAHMA KUMARIS BUDDHIST
SIKH SUFI JEWISH MUSLIM TAOIST
ZOROASTRIAN CHRISTIAN BAHA'I HINDU

PROTESTANT

PERSONAL TRANSFORMATION

Charles W. Colson

Charles Colson earned his B.A. at Brown University and finished his J.D. in 1959 at George Washington University. From 1959 to 1975, he practiced law, and he served as special counsel to President Richard Nixon from 1969 to 1973. Colson was key adviser to President Nixon and a major strategist of the 1972 campaign.

After a series of now legendary Nixon Administration imbroglios, and following much soul-searching, Colson surprised everyone by pleading guilty in federal court in 1974 to an obstruction of justice charge and was sentenced to one to three years in prison. In all, Colson spent seven months in jail for his Watergate-related activities. The Massachusetts Supreme Court decided to suspend Colson, rather than disbar him.

Today, Colson is chairman of the board of Prison Fellowship, a ministry he founded in 1976, that seeks to help people suffering at all points of the cycle of crime: prisoners, ex-prisoners, victims, and their families. Colson's Prison Fellowship program relies on a network of nearly 50,000 volunteers.

A frequent columnist in print and on radio, Colson has implemented some 18,000 matches between prisoners and pen pals on the outside. Through his Angel Tree program, families of incarcerated parents are befriended by churches through support groups. In addition, a Christmas gift-giving program for children of prisoners has been established. Colson founded the

Chicago Declaration
of 1973

*As evangelical Christians
committed to the Lord
Jesus Christ and the full authority of the Word of
God, we affirm that God
lays total claim upon the
lives of his people. We cannot, therefore, separate our
lives in Christ from the situation in which God has
placed us in the United
States and the world.*

*We confess that we have
not acknowledged the com-
plete claims of God on our
lives.*

*We acknowledge that
God requires love. But we
have not demonstrated the
love of God to those suffering social abuses.*

*We acknowledge that
God requires justice. But
we have not proclaimed or
demonstrated his justice to
an unjust American society.
. . . We deplore the historic
involvement of the church
in America with racism. . . .
We have failed to condemn
the exploitation of racism
at home and abroad by our
economic system. . . .*

Justice Fellowship program in 1993 to promote biblical reform
of the criminal justice system. The program has managed to organize volunteer task forces in twenty-five states to promote victims' rights, alternatives to prison for nonviolent offenders, and
in-prison industries. And Colson's Neighbors Who Care program is a church-based organization that meets victims' practical and spiritual needs. Colson is also chairman of the board of
Prison Fellowship International, a network of national prison
ministries chartered in fifty-four countries.

Colson compellingly describes his conversion to a deep
Christianity in 1973 in his book *Born Again*, which sold three
million copies. His other books include *Life Sentence, Loving
God, Who Speaks for God?, Kingdoms in Conflict, The God of
Stones and Spires, Why America Doesn't Work,* and *The Body.*

In 1986, Colson joined Jimmy and Rosalynn Carter in
Chicago to help in the construction of four houses in a poor
neighborhood under the auspices of Habitat for Humanity. Colson was quoted as saying, "The last time I worked for the president, I got one to three years. Now I'm just getting hard labor."

That sense of humor and honesty about who and what he
stands for has endeared him to tens of thousands of people.
John Buchanan, of People for the American Way, wrote of Colson in the December 17, 1990, edition of *The National Law
Journal,* "We disagree on many issues. But he is doing splendid
work. It is straight; it is good; it is real. It's a wonderful recla-
mation of lives gone wrong, and from where I live, that is the
essence of Christianity."

In 1993, Colson received the Templeton Prize for Progress in
Religion. Although Charles Colson was not an official partici-
pant in the Parliament of the World's Religions, we interviewed
him when he came to Chicago to receive his award during the
congress.

FROM A LIFE IN ASHES TO A LIFE IN JESUS CHRIST

I've got an eclectic background, to say the least. Chuck Colson,
ex-White House aid, ex-Marine captain, ex-lawyer, ex-convict,
now fulltime in a ministry to prisons with the gospel of Jesus

Christ. I guess it's one of the most remarkable transformations a person could go through.

Twenty years ago my life was broken. I was a lawyer who had lost my right to practice law in a number of states. I was run out of the White House and ended up in a prison cell. The president for whom I had served for three-and-a-half years was run out of office. I sort of looked around and saw no hope.

It was a life in shambles except that I had, a year before, given my life to Jesus Christ. And the remarkable story of Chuck Colson is how God reached into that prison cell, took a person who was broken and had lost everything, and used him as he has used me over this period of time to build what is the largest prison movement in the world and maybe the largest ever, certainly since the Salvation Army. Fifty-thousand volunteers in the United States, fifty thousand volunteers around the world.

My life, I'd hope, would give hope to everyone. That's what the power of Christ does in a person's life. You see where the real power is in the world. It wasn't at 1600 Pennsylvania Avenue. The real power is the power of God to transform the human heart through Jesus Christ. And that's what he uses to change the world.

Unfortunately, in the media age, we stereotype phrases and we turn them into clichés. When I came out of prison I entitled my first book *Born Again*, and everybody said, "Oh, don't use that. It's a tired cliché." And it became even more of a cliché. It became secularized. Everybody—basketball teams, football teams, antique cars, everybody—was "born again."

Jesus used that term with Nicodemus, a Jew who was seeking to know the truth, and he said, "You must be born again, born again of the spirit of God." It is a spiritual awakening to the truth of Christ. And we say, we ask Christ into our lives. We invite him to be the Lord of our lives. He is the Lord of the Universe, but we ask him and invite him to come into our lives. And we surrender our lives to him. That's the essence of what being a Christian is all about.

Sometimes I think we evangelicals, and I am an evangelical, make it all sound too simple, and we make it sound sort of like a formula. It is not. Jesus specifically said, we don't know how

We must attack the materialism of our culture and the maldistribution of the nation's wealth and services. . . .

We proclaim no new gospel, but the gospel of our Lord Jesus Christ, who, through the power of the Holy Spirit, frees people from sin so that they might praise God through works of righteousness. . . .

Then the king will say to those on his right, "Come, you who are blessed by my Father; take your inheritance, the kingdom prepared for you since the creation of the world. For I was hungry and you gave me something to eat, I was thirsty and you gave me something to drink, I was a stranger and you invited me in, I needed clothes and you clothed me, I was sick and you looked after me, I was in prison and you came to visit me."

(Matthew 25:34–36, NIV)

the Lord, how God, works in our lives. It's like the wind; we don't where it comes from or how it blows. But I believe that God touches people in their hearts, and I believe you know it. I happen to believe that there are no such things as atheists. I believe that there are only people who are suppressing the truth— that the truth of God is every single one of us. Most of us spend most of our lives rebelling from it because we don't want to face it because we think it may change our lives, and it will.

People will find a relationship with Christ when they honestly come to terms with God, when they really get to that point where they are willing to say, "I'm going to stop running. I'm going to turn. I want to know if it's true. Could it be possible that God sent his son to die on a cross that my sins might be forgiven?"

When you come in faith to that point, then suddenly you have a spiritual awakening. People can put it in formulas and phraseology and different language. It's that moment of reality, it's that moment of facing the truth of God.

WHY A PRISON MINISTRY?

When I got out of prison in 1975 and walked out of those prison gates and saw them slam behind me and realized I was free, I didn't look back because I never wanted to go into a prison again. Rotten holes! Stinking places. And depressing. You can see why they breed crime, which is what they do. But the first year I was home from prison I couldn't forget the men I'd left behind. In the middle of the night, I'd wake and think about them. I'd go back and visit. And then I realized that God was really calling me to go to the "least of these" in the world, the most unlovable people, the forgotten exiles of life, who are put away in penal colonies—to take the love of Christ to them.

In the summer of 1976, after my wife said she was willing, we committed ourselves to work in the prisons as God's call upon my life. I will keep working in the prisons. I work there because I believe that's what he's called me to do, and it's the place I would choose to work.

I think, in all of the twenty years that I have been a Christian, the man who most exuded the fear of God, who most exemplified the fear of God (which is the mark of a Christian, the mark of a post-Christian man is that he's lost his fear of God— the reverence, the worshipful sense of the presence of God in our midst) was a man on death row. None of the great theologians I have met or great religious and spiritual leaders most exemplified that for me; it was a man on death row eleven days before he died.

I spent an hour with him on an Easter Sunday, and this man talked about what Jesus meant to him in a personal way. He talked about the fact that he knew he was going to die and he was sharing Christ with people around him. I went to encourage him, and I spent one hour with him and came away just spiritually renewed.

I've seen this all over the world. I've been on death row in Zambia, in one of the most depressing physical places that I've ever been in my life. These men were allowed out to meet with me. When they came, we had prayer together. When I pray I kind of get down on my knees, gently; I suppose at my age you have to do it gently. But these men just dropped to their knees— and you felt the power of God in that room. They were leading others to Christ on the very day of their execution. I've been in prisons in thirty-one countries and have seen this.

In Brazil, a prison run by our ministry is run by Christian principles. They have a buddy system, and they have volunteer families that come in and work with them. They have chapel programs every day. They sing the Lord's Prayer before they eat their meals, plus psalms and proverbs from all over the world. That's one of the most uplifting atmospheres I've ever been in.

The recidivism rate, the repeat offense rate for crime, all over the world is 75 percent. The people that come out of that prison, São José dos Campos in Brazil, have a 4 percent recidivism rate. So I know that God in a person's heart transforms them and gives them a new life and makes the difference.

IS GOD CHRISTIAN?

I'm a Christian, so I believe what Jesus says is true. He says, "I am the way, the truth, and the life. No man comes to the Father but through me." Now that's an exclusive claim and, in that

Evangelical Christians in
the United States

*In the 1990s it is estimated
there are 40 million conservative evangelical Chris-
tians in the United States.
They have rejected tradi-
tional "mainline" Protes-
tant leadership, specifically
the National Council of
Churches.*

*Some of the largest
evangelical denominations
are:*

- *Southern Baptist
  Convention*
- *Holiness churches*
- *Pentecostal-Charismatic
  churches: Assemblies
  of God, United Pente-
  costal Church, Church
  of God (Cleveland,
  Tennessee), Church of
  God in Christ*

sense, it can be a stumbling block to people. But the truth is a
stumbling block often. I have preached Christ in Muslim gather-
ings in India. When I spoke and preached about the resurrection
of Jesus Christ from the dead, the president of the All Islamic
Congress in India there came up to me afterward and said, "I've
never heard that before. I'm really interested." And he sat and
began to talk with other Christians.

I'm a Christian—and I can fully respect other people's religious views. And I can dialogue with them. Certainly we should
have the most civil kind of a relationship. But I believe that
Jesus Christ is the truth, and I cannot be faithful to what is the
core belief of my life if I do not challenge other people with that
truth. So I do—lovingly, gently—at every opportunity I have.
Sure, I see wonderful people. I mean, I know people who are in
cults who are some of the best-living, most decent people I
know. But I know where their eternal salvation lies, and so my
job is to try to lead them to that. Righteous living doesn't get
you into heaven.

I've preached it through Buddhist and Hindu cultures.
They've never heard about someone dying on a cross for their
sins. I happen to believe that it is the truth. I can't impose it on
anyone else. I don't want it to be a stumbling block. I want
people to see the love of Christ incarnate in my life more than
anything else in the world. I want them drawn to sweet spirit,
the sweet fragrance of God's holy spirit. I can't hit them over
the head with a Bible and make them believe. Sometimes our
tactics turn people off. But not the truth of what we are pro-
claiming.

The doctrine can often get in the way of love. I'll notice
sometimes the volunteers will grab someone, push them up
against the wall, put a tract under his nose and say, "You've got
to believe this." Those volunteers we get rid of, because you've
got to earn the right to be heard wherever you are, whether it is
in a prison or whether it is walking the streets of Chicago, or
whether it's in a Parliament of the World's Religions, or anywhere else. People have got to see something authentic in your
life that they are drawn to, and then they are willing to listen to
what that is that they are drawn to—and it's the truth of God
revealed in Jesus Christ. But they have got to see Christ's
love first.

CHRISTIANITY AND LOVE

Jesus was asked the greatest commandment of all. He said it's to love the Lord your God with all your heart, mind, and soul and your neighbor as yourself. The Christians whom I know, the ones I work with, do precisely that. I work with fifty thousand volunteers in America. They are the true recipients of the Templeton Prize. They are out going on to the AIDS wards embracing people dying of AIDS.

We're the ones who are out caring for the families here in the inner city. Two hundred seventy thousand children in America last year received gifts at Christmastime through our Project Angel Tree. They have a mommy or daddy in prison. Remember one out of fifty children has a mother or father in prison. We're the ones that are out there bringing them their gifts, giving them an illustrated Bible, a gospel comic book, a gift that we say—and I love it—"This is from your daddy." And you see that little child's face light up and say, "My daddy hasn't forgotten me."

We're the ones bringing hope and compassion to the people in the inner cities. The people I know who are Christians do love their neighbor as themselves.

Oh, yeah, it's a very tough commandment. That is correct. The gospel isn't easy. C. S. Lewis said, "If you want pleasure, I don't recommend Christianity." You can get pleasure out of a bottle of Port wine. But if you want the truth, then you look at Christ and it's hard and it's demanding.

You value yourself as created in the image of God, yes. And you have to have a very strong sense of self-worth in the best way that God so loved me that he sent his only son to die on the cross for my sins. If I'm worth that in God's eyes, then I have to show that same kind of love that God showed for me to other people.

I was in prison. I learned that I had lost my license to practice law in Virginia. My dad had died. And the most crushing moment of my life was when I received a phone call that my son had been arrested in college for possessing an ounce of marijuana and was in jail.

One of those things that drives me on is the realization that God has used my life in a unique way, and I have an obligation to share that truth with other people. I run into them every day.

Keep on loving each other as brothers. Do not forget to entertain strangers, for by doing so some people have entertained angels without knowing it. Remember those in prison as if you were their fellow prisoners, and those who are mistreated as if you yourselves were suffering.

(Hebrews 13:1–3, NIV)

The world is a mess. Life is not easy. There is lots of pain and suffering. And we're not supposed to have an easy ride of it, but God uses the toughest times in our lives to build our character.

Adversity will turn out to be the greatest blessing. The greatest thing that ever happened in my life is as a result of the worst thing that ever happened to me. But that's the way God works. So take heart, people who may feel you are at a low point in your lives. Maybe this is the way God gets their attention and they discover that on the other side are blessings they had never hoped for otherwise.

CHRISTIANITY AND THE ENVIRONMENT

I'm always amused when I look at all the environmental movements going on in the world because the greatest environmentalist is the Christian because we are called to exercise dominion over what God has given us. We are called to be stewards of the earth and of all of creation.

I think Christians have been in the forefront of most of the great social reforms of the nineteenth century. I mean, you go back to the nineteenth century before government took all of these things over and who was it who cared for the poor? Who ran the poorhouses? Who cleaned up the insane asylums? Who stopped the child labor abuses? It was the Christians. It was the Wesley awakening in England, spread to America. I mean the great evangelical heritage was a concern for justice and righteousness and people and dignity and for the preservation of what God has given us.

Christians have been in the vanguard because we see ourselves as having a duty to God to care about these things, not a duty to some "Mother Nature," not a duty to some planetary matter, but a duty to a holy God, who created this universe, that we are to care for it and to protect it to preserve it and to have dominion over it and to cultivate and to till that universe—to work for the good to be in part of God's creation process, in that sense.

And to make it reflect the glory of God in every single way— to let God's justice be seen, his righteousness be seen in every area of life—which is the environment, of course, but it's every single area. It's human rights, it's human dignity, it's the life of the unborn. It is the concern for the prisoner. It is the caring for the poor.

We are to live every day in fulfillment of God's mandate and commission to make disciples, to teach people what he has taught us, to bring righteousness to bear on the earth and care about the creation, and most of all to care about those whom he has created—every single human being is to be treated as the child of the King. Christianity is the only religion that believes that.

PROTESTANT

ENCOUNTERS WITH GOD

DIANA L. ECK

Raised in Bozeman, Montana, Diana L. Eck is one of the world's leading scholars of Indian religion. A graduate of Smith College and the School of Oriental and African Studies at the University of London, since 1984 she has been a professor of comparative religion and Indian studies at Harvard University and a member of the Faculty of Divinity at the Harvard Divinity School.

Her academic specialties include Gandhi; Hindu myth and ritual; women and religion; pilgrimage; sacred space; Buddhist, Hindu, and Sikh traditions in America; and world religious dialogue. She has approached the Bhagavad Gita through the perspective of Christianity and has lectured widely on Hindu-Christian dialogue. She is especially noted for her outstanding contributions to the perspective of pluralism in world religions.

Dr. Eck's beautifully crafted books include: *Banaras, City of Light* (1982), *Darsan, Seeing the Divine Image in India* (1985), *Speaking of Faith: Global Perspectives on Women, Religion, and Social Change* (ed. with Devaki Jain, 1987), *Devotion Divine: Bhakti Traditions from the Regions of India* (1991), and *Encountering God: A Spiritual Journey from Bozeman to Banaras* (1993). In addition, Dr. Eck's essays have appeared in numerous journals throughout the world.

She has been the recipient of two Fulbright scholarships, a Lilly Endowment, a Melcher Award, a Guggenheim Foundation scholarship, a Social Science Research Council fellowship award, a Phi Beta Kappa award for teaching, and an American Express Grant for Ethics and is a Luce Fellow in Theology for 1995.

Eck is a tireless member of dozens of academies, commissions, international religious councils, and assemblies. She was the moderator and chair of the Working Group on Dialogue with People of Living Faiths from 1984 through 1991 and continues to play a major role worldwide in the interfaith dialogue movement.

THE PLURALISM PROJECT

I'd been teaching world religions and comparative religions at Harvard for some time, and gradually the whole context of teaching began to shift. I realized that the students in my classroom were different than they had been ten or fifteen years ago. There were far more Muslim and Buddhist students, South Asian Americans who had grown up in Cincinnati and were Sikhs, or Jains, or Hindus, who had been to Hindu summer camps and were now freshmen at Harvard.

The whole issue of talking about and teaching about world religions wasn't in some other part of the world but in our own university community and in our own urban setting. So I started by having a research seminar on world religions in Boston. As a group, my students and I visited the mosques and the Hindu temples and Sikh *gurdwāras* and whatnot in Boston.

We discovered there were really quite a few of them, something like twenty mosques in that part of New England, in the Islamic Council of New England. There was a great big Hindu temple that had been built from the ground up according to Hindu ritual temple specifications and consecrated with waters from the Ganges and from the Mississippi and Colorado rivers. There were other Hindu temples, Buddhist temples—Cambodians in the northern suburbs of the city, Chinese and Japanese, and lots of Euro-American Buddhists as well.

This exploration was one of the most exciting semesters I've ever had with my students, and it became clear that it would be interesting to do this kind of examination of the cities and towns of the United States. Just to figure out who's here. We don't ask a religious question on our national census. We could.

America's Religious Landscape

As of the 1990s, American religion can be divided into ten recognizable groups or denominations, each claiming a substantial number of adherents.

Tradition/ Denomination	Approx. Membership (in millions)
Christian	
Roman Catholic	56
Eastern Orthodox	3.5
Liberal Protestant	52
Conservative Evangelical	40
Holiness	3
Pentecostal-Charismatic	6.5
Non-Christian	
Jewish	6
Muslim	5
Buddhist	3
Hindu	3

Religious Diversity in the
World (approx. for 1989)

Tradition	Membership
Christian (33%)*	1.7 billion
Muslim (18%)	924 million
Hindu (13%)	870 million
Buddhist (6%)	312 million
Sikh (0.3%)	18 million
Jewish (0.3%)	17 million
Jain (.15%)	7–10 million
Confucian (0.1%)	6 million
Baha'i (0.1%)	5 million

*Percentage of world population

I think we probably ought to. We don't know who we are. For three years now, I have had students spanning out over the country in the summertime, doing what you might call hometown research on the religious landscape of Minneapolis, Oklahoma City, Denver, and Houston, documenting how many mosques there are, how many Jain temples, Hindu temples, Buddhist meditation centers and temples, *gurdwārās,* Zoroastrians, and so on. It is really astounding. The tremendous diversification of American cities is a reality. All of our cities are really multireligious cities now.

If you drove down the street in Houston, for example, many of the Hindu temples or Buddhist temples wouldn't look like much from the outside. Many of them are converted from other purposes. It might be a suburban home that has become a Vietnamese temple. It might be a building that looks a lot like an industrial park or a mosque in a shopping center or something like that. This is a new reality for us.

A DISTINCTION BETWEEN PLURALISM AND DIVERSITY

Pluralism really requires a kind of encounter with one another and requires a certain amount of mutual education and exchange and living together in the common give and take of life. It's creating that kind of pluralist fabric that is really a challenge for us in North America. It's not everybody do his, her, and their own thing in their own sphere, but the fact that we're challenged to a common life together as well. The old ways of what you might call exclusivism will not do for us anymore.

If you were to ask most people how Christians think about people of other faiths, they would say, "Well, it says in the Bible, 'I am the way, the truth, and the life, and there is no other way but through me.'" I am a religious person. I am also Christian and, in a theological sense, I deal with that by saying that's a misinterpretation of what it says in the Gospel of John. Jesus is responding to a question that Thomas asked out of his fear the last night of Jesus' life. Thomas is asking, "Where are you going?"

It's a pastoral response that Jesus gives. "I am the way." It's not a dogmatic response. People use that quotation from the Bible, from the Holy Scripture, as if you could use it to answer the question, "Master, are the Buddhists really going to reach the far shore on the raft of *dharma*?" or "Master, what will happen in six hundred years when the prophet Mohammed comes?" And it's not an answer to any question that we might want to ask. It's not the answer to that question, so we can't use it as the answer to that question. I think to do so violates our own, or at least my own, understanding of scripture as a Christian. It certainly is not the sort of scripture that can be used to beat our neighbors over the heads. I think that is a real abuse of Christian scriptures.

DIFFERING REACTIONS TO OTHER RELIGIONS

I think that it is important for us to hear the language of difference. We're not heading toward one world religion, and no one religion can somehow embrace all of the mystery and the multiplicity. It's important for us to be able to be in encounter and dialogue with both our differences and similarity—for our understanding, but also for our mutual discovery of what is true as religious people.

When I titled my book *Encountering God,* what I meant was not just that I have encountered the way in which Hindus understand God or the way in which Muslims understand God and have understood something about *their* perception. But, in and through the Hindu tradition, I've learned more about the one I refer to as God. My faith has become deeper and richer as a Christian because of the contribution of Hindus.

I wrote a little bit about that in my book that I subtitled *A Spiritual Journey from Bozeman to Banaras.* I grew up in Bozeman, Montana, in the United Methodist Church—very involved in the church as a child, as a person in the Methodist youth fellowship, committed to the social vision of justice in the church, very much influenced and shaped in my own personal life and faith by the experience of church fellowship. As a college student, when I went to India, for the first time I met people who were not Christians.

I didn't quite know what to think of them. I had no real knowledge of the Hindu religious tradition. I certainly grew up with a lot of language about using terms like *heathen* to describe non-Christians. But the people that I met certainly weren't any-

The function of comparative religion is to discern this essential Truth, this Divine Mystery beyond speech and thought-forms of each religious tradition, from the most primitive tribal traditions to the most advanced world religions. In each tradition the one divine Reality, the one eternal Truth, is present, but it is hidden under symbols, symbols of word and gesture, of ritual and dance and song, of poetry and music, art and architecture, of custom and convention, of law and morality, of philosophy and theology.

(Griffiths)

Let us speak in harmony;
Let our minds apprehend
*   alike.*
Common be our prayer;
Common be the end of our
*   assembly;*
Common be our resolu-
*   tion;*
Common be our delibera-
*   tions.*
Alike be our feelings;
Unified be our hearts;
Common be our intentions;
Perfect be our unity.

—Rig Veda, Hindu scripture

thing of that sort. These were people of faith. They were people who prayed. They were people who meditated. They were people whose religious life mattered a great deal to them, and whose religious life also inspired them to work, as I had, in issues of social justice, to work on behalf of the neighbor. They were some of the most wonderful people I ever met. And though their ways of worship and life were quite different from mine, they were not people you'd want to describe with any term except as people of faith whose faith was another faith. So that was a real challenge for me. It was really that challenge that drove me into the comparative study of religion, to find out those answers for myself, to come to some understanding of the other.

I can give the example of visiting a Hindu temple and finding in the moment when the curtain is pulled back and the people who have gathered for worship express their astonishment at the flowers that have been placed so elaborately upon the image of Krishna. Finding myself caught up in that astonishment myself and touched both by this *darshan,* or vision of God's presence, and also by the community of faith I was experiencing this with, I learned really more and more richly about what it means to speak of incarnation, from Hindus who understand incarnation in such a different way than I do.

It enhanced my religion. I feel this has happened over and over. Our dialogue is not simply about understanding one another, but developing a deeper understanding of ourselves. True dialogue is mutually transformative, and that doesn't mean that we cease to be who we are—that I abandon my Christian community and become something else. Or that you abandon a Hindu or Buddhist community and become something else. Through our encounter with one another, we have a deeper understanding of ourselves and of the mystery of the divine or of transcendence, or however we speak of this.

HINDUISM AND UNDERSTANDING GOD

The Hindu tradition has seen the divine in many ways, truly multiple ways, and has also imaged the divine in multiple ways. Part of my astonishment, part of the astonishment of many who might go traveling in India, for example, was with the images of the gods with so many arms. What are they, exactly? And I gradually learned in dialogue with Hindu friends and teachers that this word *idol* that we use as if people were worshiping a god—something that is not God—was certainly not at all the way in which Hindus understood the images of the divine. Yes, they were images. Yes, they were made of granite or of metal or something like that. They also were consecrated and the presence of God invited to be present for the time of worship.

Hindus would also say that, yes, there are many gods. There are three hundred and thirty million to be precise. There is almost the sense that the divine is so abundant in the world that our human challenge is to perceive the divine. And it's not limited to one place or form or time. So there are many gods, many ways in which, as Hindus would put it, God is present and manifest. It also is true that Hindus see God in particular forms. I mean, there are images that are made and consecrated of the gods and that's very hard for some of us who come from non-imaging traditions to apprehend. But it's not as if somehow the vision stops at this image. The image really is more a lens through which, or a window through which, one sees the divine. In fact, when Hindus go to temple, they don't speak of going to worship, but of going to see, of going for *darshan*.

They say, "I'm going for *darshan*." Or if you've been to the temple, I would say, "Have you had *darshan*?" That means, "Have you seen?" So there is the sense of the visual nature of our apprehension of the divine. We are people of the book and of the ear. It's "Hear, O Israel," or the sense of the *logos* as revealed. There is in the Hindu tradition a sense of the abundance of the divine. And our main human problem is opening our eyes, to be able to see the divine in the many, many places where God shows Godself, you might say. So polytheism isn't about the numbers of gods there are. It's about the abundance of the divine in the world.

As the web issues from the spider, as little sparks proceed from fire, so from the one soul proceed all breathing animals, all worlds, all the gods, and all beings.

—Brihad-Aranyaka Upanishad, Hindu scripture

A NEW VIEW OF THE WORLD

When the World Parliament of Religions first met in Chicago in 1893, someone said something at the opening session that I felt was really interesting: "We must try to listen for the understanding of our own faith, in the faith of the other." That's really an astonishing thing to try to do—to really attempt to hear one another, not simply so that we can make note of the differences and how one another is wrong.

But, one hundred years ago, when people gathered in Chicago for the World Parliament of Religions, one of the delegates from Japan came and took note of the fact that as he came through the West Coast there were all the signs that said, "No Japanese allowed to enter here."

He was very shocked at this as a Buddhist and said, "If this is your Christian ethic, we're perfectly satisfied to remain heathens."

We have a history, beginning in 1882, of Asian exclusion, of a racist immigration policy that gradually dilated to include not only Chinese and Japanese but other "Asiatics" as they were called, including people from India. It's important to note that people from India were all referred to as "Hindoos."

In fact, most of the immigrants in the early part of this century from India were Sikhs. They received, as many others did on the West Coast, a good bit of harassment. This particular case, involving a man who married an American woman and become a naturalized citizen, went all the way to the Supreme Court. He was stripped of his citizenship on the grounds that Asiatics, "Hindoos," could not be counted as, you know, sort of white, Anglo-Saxon. It was based on a racial issue, and Hindu was a racial designation.

Scholars at that time said that really people from India are part of the Indo-European family group, both racially and linguistically. The languages of India are related to the languages of Europe, Sanskrit to Latin. The Supreme Court decision said: Well, maybe the perception of scholars is that we have this common history, the brown Indian and blond Scandinavian. But this is not the perception of the common man. A number of people were stripped of citizenship on that grounds.

It wasn't really until 1965, with the new immigration act that abandoned the old system of national origins quotas, that there really was an opening of the possibility of immigration from Asia. That really is what accounts for this new religious landscape that we began with.

Pluralism is not simply a kind of, "Let's all hold hands and pretend that we agree." Because we don't—on many things. Our encounter is not only about mutual transformation enhancement, but also about gaining a clearer understanding of where we differ. That's a precious thing to have—an understanding of our differences of perspective. Pluralism really means that culture of encounter, not simply a culture in which we all turn on our own orbits somewhere.

Living love, yes. That's a good way of talking about it. I think that it is a real challenge for most of us because the issue of how one thinks about people of another faith is not just an academic issue that people in religion departments or theological schools might contemplate. It's a question in virtually every city. People in every parish if they are Christian, or in every synagogue if they are Jewish, or people who are quite secular and don't think of themselves as part of any religious tradition have to really encounter the question of their own identity in the context of people whose faith is different. And that's a challenge for us.

Multilayered Spirituality in America

In A Generation of Seekers, *Wade Clark Roof has found a considerable syncretism of religious belief and practice of young Americans today:*

"Members of this [baby boomer] generation have few inhibitions about multiple associations with vastly different groups, such as remaining a Presbyterian while at the same time exploring Zen Buddhist teachings. . . . Even more common is the phenomenon of picking and choosing a belief from a variety of sources, which results in 'multi-layered spirituality' found within organized religion: Vegetarian Unitarians, Lambs for Christ, Quakerpalians, Creation-Spirituality Catholics, macrobiotic kosher observant Jews. . . . There is a clear relationship between strength in belief in God and the exploration of new beliefs and teachings."

PROTESTANT

A RESPONSE TO FUNDAMENTALISM
MARTIN EMIL MARTY

Religious educator, editor, and writer, Martin Marty is an ordained Lutheran minister and has been the Fairfax M. Cone Distinguished Service Professor at the Divinity School of the University of Chicago since 1978. Since 1969, Dr. Marty has edited the journal *Context*. Senior editor of *Christian Century* magazine and past president of the Park Ridge Center in Illinois, an institute for the study of health, faith, and ethics, Dr. Marty has been the director of the Fundamentalist Project for the American Academy of Arts and Sciences since 1988. Some of the key findings and ideas of that particular endeavor surfaced during the course of the following interview.

Dr. Marty's unassuming nature and modesty conceal the fact that he is, in fact, one of the most prolific theological scholar/writers of the twentieth century. It is not possible to list all of his major works here, but some of them are of especial importance. Those include: *A Short History of Christianity* (1959), *The Infidel* (1961), *Second Chance for American Protestants* (1963), *The Search for a Usable Future* (1969), *Righteous Empire*, for which he won the 1971 National Book Award, *Religious Awakening and Revolution* (1978), *The Public Church* (1981), *Pilgrims in Their Own Land* (1984), *Protestantism in the United States* (1985), *Religion and Republic* (1987), *Second Opinion* (1990), and, as co-author with R. Scott Appleby, *The Glory and the Power* (1992).

Dr. Marty took his Ph.D. in American Religious and Intellectual History from the University of Chicago in 1956, having first studied at the Concordia Seminary and the Lutheran School of Theology at Chicago. He has been the recipient of a remarkable number of honorary doctorates from nearly fifty colleges, seminaries, and universities throughout the United States, including the University of Southern California, the University of Notre Dame, Hebrew Union College, Colorado College, Aquinas College, and the Virginia Theological Seminary. He is the past president of the American Society of Church History, of the American Catholic History Association, and the American Academy of Religion.

Dr. Marty's encyclopedic knowledge of Christianity, as well as other religions, is matched by his extraordinary charm, humor, and insights into contemporary life. In many respects, he is the dean of modern religious commentary. His editorials appear in major newspapers around the country. For example, when Pope John Paul II found himself embattled at the United Nations Cairo Conference in September 1994, Marty's full-page analysis of the Vatican versus most of the rest of the world was featured in the *Los Angeles Times*.

In person, he is jovial, decisive, and generous.

THE STUDY ON FUNDAMENTALISM

We're spending six years producing six volumes on fundamentalisms around the world. The first one simply looked at fourteen different fundamentalisms, from United States' Protestant to *Dackwa* in Malaysia to Egyptian Muslim Brotherhood. Then we spent two volumes on the world that fundamentalisms make, the worldview, the intimate part of life. All fundamentalisms care a lot about gender, sexuality, family. We're doing a volume on accounting for them, trying to explain why we think they exist now in the late twentieth century, when nobody foresaw that they would. We're doing one that formally compares them, and finally one on what are the public policy implications, statecraft, media, reporting, human relations.

We want to be sure to be very broad. We don't want to confine people. There is a line from William James, in his *Varieties of Religious Experience,* where he says, "If you could interview a crab, the last thing it would want to be is classified a crustacean."

The first Protestants were Lutherans, organized into churches in the sixteenth century by German princes who responded to the writings of Martin Luther (1483–1546) and rallied to his cause. Luther's emphasis on scriptural authority and on preaching the gospel and sacraments as a means of grace have remained central to Lutheranism. There are an estimated 8.3 million Lutherans in the United States grouped across three separate church organizations:

Evangelical Lutheran Church in America 5.3 million in 10,700 churches

Missouri Synod 2.6 million in 5,800 churches

Wisconsin Evangelical Lutheran Synod 400,000 in 1,200 churches

Liberal Protestantism

In the late nineteenth and early twentieth century, American Protestantism split into four major denominational groupings: Liberal Protestants, Evangelical Conservatives (whose most conservative element is Fundamentalism), the Holiness churches, and the Pentecostals (or Charismatics).

It would say, "I'm not a crustacean, I'm a crab. I'm not even a crab, I'm me." We start there. We really want to hear the voice of the fundamentalist. Most of the people we've talked with feel that we are dealing with them fairly.

Why in the twentieth century did we need a new word? You will not find the word *fundamentalism* before the twentieth century in any language I know of. It was invented, used first in the July issue of a 1920 Baptist magazine, *The Watchman Examiner*, in the middle of a Baptist church fight when the editor said, "Everybody wants to be called conservative nowadays. Moderates are conservatives, but they are not willing to do battle for the Lord. Those who want to do battle for the Lord—we'll call ourselves 'fundamentalists.'" The word was in the air, but he pushed it that way. And soon organizations were "fundamentalist."

They were passive for a long time because I think they thought, like the Amish, they could be off the road, let the world go by. But certain things happened. First of all the development of mass media. The signals come right into your home, and you can't keep your child from them. Or in the United States, the school prayer decisions of 1962 and 1963 that said the public school, which a lot of the Protestants ran as if it were their own, can't have devotions, can't have Bible reading, can't have prayer. This looked to them as if the world was sneaking in on us. And then the *Roe vs. Wade* abortion decision. Every culture had some things like that happen.

FROM SELF-PRESERVATION TO AGGRESSION

Most fundamentalists want to be in the middle of the world. They want to be in the thick of things. They can't run away. They might have home schooling; they still haven't kept radio or TV away or presidents away. In every culture this happens. Iran is an ideal case. In Iran, a lot of young Iranians studied in Europe, the United States, came back with masters degrees, doctors degrees, were in good with the Shah, had the power, changed the skirt lengths, put on makeup, played modern cinema, and most people weren't in on it. And the parents see their own young lured by this and say, "We're not going to get the goodies of modernity, we're only going to have the precious things overrun." Soon the veil comes back on, the skirts get long, the makeup is off, the MTV is out.

That's a typical pattern. You are challenged, you react. And once you start reacting, the first reaction is usually resentment: We're mad at the great infidel, the great Satan, the anti-Christ; we're mad at the liberal, the humanist.

Then they start getting power and it goes to their heads, just like anybody else. They think, we could run the show, and we could do a better job. We could produce an economy, we could create morality. And the politics of resentment became, very clearly in the United States in the early 1980s, a politics of a world of power.

In some religions, this was rather efficient and easily done. Islam was easiest because most, at least Arabic Islamic states, never really separated religion and regime, so they could really take it back over.

FUNDAMENTALISM, THE STATE, AND THE LOSS OF DEMOCRACY

Let's remember that in most places where fundamentalists prosper there never was democracy. And that's a very different thing. Typically, Algeria today is a secular military, nominally Islamic regime that has had a lot of repression. And somebody could come along and tell the young men, "Your years of generativity and sexuality pass you by because you can't have sex without marriage, you can't have marriage without housing, you can't have housing without a job, you'll never get a job, there go the years. This is not what Allah intended for you. Join the movement."

And by April of '91 when there were going to be elections, 58 percent of the people of Algeria, had they been free to vote, would have voted for such a party. They're not replacing democracy; there's a regime maybe more repressive than what was there.

Sudan is run by Islamic fundamentalists. It was repressive, it is repressive. So we really have to ask about the very few republics and democracies that are challenged by fundamentalism. Yes, their impulse is to say, we've got too much freedom, we've

Membership and Number of Churches in the National Council of Churches, 1989

Churches
- *United Methodist Church*
  9.1 million members
  37,000 churches
- *Evangelical Lutheran Church in America*
  5.3 million members
  10,700 churches
- *Presbyterian Church (USA)*
  3 million members
  11,500 churches
- *Protestant Episcopal Church*
  2.5 million members
  7,000 churches
- *African Methodist Episcopal Church*
  2.2 million members
  6,200 churches
- *United Church of Christ*
  1.6 million members
  6,400 churches
- *American Baptist Churches in the U.S.A.*
  1.5 million members
  5,800 churches
- *African Methodist Episcopal Zion Church*
  1.2 million members
  6,000 churches

Conventions
- *National Baptist Convention of the U.S.A.*
  5.5 million members
  26,000 churches
- *National Baptist Church Convention in America*
  2.6 million members
  11,000 churches
- *Progressive National Baptist Convention*
  1 million members
  1,000 churches

got too much pluralism, there are too many kinds of voices running around and if we ran the show we would get it back to the good old days when one set of people ran it.

Many of them may be of relatively tolerant temperament. They don't all want to kill you, they don't all want to repress you, but they definitely want to be the ones who will make the signals, to determine who writes the textbooks, what the books in the library will be, what the policies at the hospital will be. And so these would be the retreats from the notion of a fully open society. There's no doubt about it.

THE RELIGIOUS VISION OF TRUTH: SELECTIVE AND ABSOLUTE

All fundamentalists have a certain psychological cast. That is, they are people who by nature don't like uncertainty, they don't like the "maybe you have a point" approach. They don't like paradox, and so on. But a lot of people don't like that and don't turn fundamentalist.

So we have to ask what are these other features. We do want to stress that there is a religious vision. It's the particular kind of religious vision that wants to reduce the element of mystery, of drama, of doubt. In the Hebrew scriptures, for example, Jacob wrestled with the angel, and you don't really know who this angel is, you don't know the outcome. Job talks to the voice and never wins. Habakkuk asks why and doesn't get an answer. The Psalms are just full of these agonizing questions.

Now this is all in the book of the fundamentalists. They believe every word of it. But they repeat those texts that say that the truth is a rock to stand on. God gives you a sure word. God couldn't go against God's own word, and so on. So there's a very strong impulse to say religion is about a set of truths, and I can know them, and there can be no doubt about them.

What interests me and the people I work with is that fundamentalists are not simply traditional or conservative, in that they don't treat the whole tradition equally. If you could run the beliefs of a billion Christians through computers, certainly the vast majority would have at least two fundamentals—the doctrine of the Trinity and some view of the Eucharist, the mass. You would never come up with fundamentalism.

THE ETHICS OF CONVERSION

I think that the debate over the ethics of conversion, to a fundamentalist versus almost everybody else, results from the fact that almost everybody else says we operate with different modes of reality.

I think that the nonfundamentalist believes that God, in God's own time, has a way of dealing with people. I'd like to convert you to every cause I'm in. But I don't do it when the rules of the game are dialogue. I think that that's where the ethics of conversion issues have come about.

Now what has happened, of course, is most of us have our defenses up. If I'm in what's announced as dialogue and I know that the fundamentalist is ready to pounce, I am very careful. But I do believe that fundamentalists of various sorts have seen that to achieve certain goals they do have to be careful. The best illustration of that is some fundamentalist groups that want to be active in Israel, on some ground or other, almost have to sign an agreement that they are not going to proselytize.

I give you another illustration. Billy Graham is not a fundamentalist, but Billy Graham is normally an agent of conversion. That's what he's in the world for. Yet in 1992, I believe it was, he had a crusade in New York, which is a very Jewish city. He has many friends in Judaism, and, in advance, he told the rabbis, "Look, I'm not targeting Jews for conversion." And that drives a lot of fundamentalists crazy.

He drives a lot of Jews crazy, but he also gets awards from Israel for wonderful films he puts out about Israel. What I'm trying to say is that he is showing us there that he will deal with the government of Israel, he will deal with Jews, without trying to convert them, whereas another kind of fundamentalist will say of every encounter, "I've got to wait till your weak moment comes, and I've got to pounce on you."

COMMUNITY AMONG LIBERALS AND FUNDAMENTALISTS

The Christian Fundamentals

In 1909 a group of conservative American Protestants, later recognized as the first fundamentalists, organized a national movement to protect what they felt to be the orthodox truths of the Christian faith against modernism and liberalism. Their list of five fundamental doctrines was first published in a 12-volume series of booklets entitled The Fundamentals: A Testimony of the Truth *(1910–1912). The five doctrines were:*

- *The virgin birth of Christ*
- *The physical resurrection of Jesus Christ*
- *The inerrancy of Scriptures in every respect*
- *The substitutional theory of atonement*
- *The physical Second Coming of Jesus Christ*

More than 2.5 million copies of the series were printed and distributed with money furnished by two wealthy laymen.

Think of all the company that Jerry Falwell kept in his prime. He held a view of the state of Israel that Israel welcomed, because you have to have an Israel for Jesus' return. No Jew wants it for that reason, but they gave him an award and he gave Menachem Begin an award, because they were helping. His best allies on antiabortion were the Catholics. He hated everything the Catholic bishops stood for in social terms, the economy, but they were allies. And in a strange way some people began to know each other and form community.

A republic is made up of so many kinds of people that you can keep the integrity of your separate faith, but you soften some of the edges by finding out that other people who will never agree with you are fully human beings who care as much as you do about something else. So I think that's a beginning, on social grounds, on communion grounds. They—fundamentalists—are fellow humans and they do care about a lot of the same things others care about.

I'll pick a group in the 1990s, Focus on the Family. It has one edge that frightens me. I'm not a fundamentalist, and I don't like what it does about sex education at schools. I don't think it represents, to my view, the truth of the situation. I have real trouble with it.

It has another side. These people put real energy into trying to have families. They put energy into adoption. Where there is a single parent family, they try to surround the mother or the father with other company. There are a lot of the ideals there that are positive, that I could go along with.

I do not go along with censorship, with formal repression, but I have to say that some of the things that some of the groups are for in opposition to violence and misuse of the human body in sexual portrayal could be a positive goal. And I could find ways to work with them to do that.

A new combination of liberals, like People for the American Way, and fundamentalists found each other both saying that the textbooks unnecessarily, officially screen out the story of the role of the spiritual and religious in human life. The liberals were saying we can't use the public schools to teach this or that religion as the truth about life, which the fundamentalists want.

But we both can say let's restore it.

There were hilarious textbooks that would not allow Martin Luther King to be identified as a black Baptist minister. And that's his whole soul. One text defined Pilgrims as people who travel a lot. You miss the heart of it. You can't make sense of Lincoln's speeches, you can't make sense of the Civil Rights movement, without it. And so we're bringing it back in.

I don't believe we dare despair of keeping dialogue going on those levels. But I'm not a naive optimist who thinks we're going to start by finding a sole communion between fundamentalists and nonfundamentalists on the deepest things of their religious teaching.

PERSONAL FAITH

My own faith, along the way, is a very open version of Lutheran Christianity. I relish it because it is so full of contradiction and paradox and ambiguity. Martin Luther came down on two sides of most things, but not on the notion of grace, not on the notion of the fact that the divine God reaches into our world with that. And I apprehend it.

But he also believed that God works through people who aren't Christian. He is said to have said—I've never found where, but it fits—"Better be ruled by a smart Turk than a dumb Christian." He really did believe that people out there could be agents of God's good work and good will even if they weren't converted. On the one hand, I try to be a faithful member of that communion. On another level, I have to move with real freedom among the other religions and the nonreligious people in the world, who can also serve God's purposes.

PROTESTANT

SCIENCE AND RELIGION

John Marks Templeton

The simple beginnings of the life of John Marks Templeton, who was born in the small Tennessee town of Winchester in 1912, held little indication of the enormous financial empire he would one day oversee. A graduate of Yale University, a Phi Beta Kappa member, and a Rhodes Scholar, he began work on Wall Street in 1937, and opened his own fund management company three years later. From 1937 to 1941, he was president and director of Templeton, Dobbrow & Vance, Inc. in New York. Later he was chairman of the Templeton Camroth Corporation, then vice president of the First Trust Bank Ltd. in the Bahamas.

In 1954, Templeton began the Templeton Growth Fund, an investment corporation that has become legendary. By 1992, Templeton's companies were controlling more than eighty mutual funds around the globe, including his Growth, Global, and World funds, managing over $20 billion in assets, far more money than the annual GNP of many countries combined. In a most unusual gesture of recognition of the investor's wideranging accomplishments, Queen Elizabeth II knighted him Sir John in 1987.

Templeton, a Presbyterian elder, has long maintained that spirituality, not economics, has been the single most important aspect of his life. A combination of studious business practices with an unfailing devotion to seeking a higher truth have become the hallmark of Templeton's life. He feels that both disciplines have limitless potential, but that only spirituality can bring real advancement to an individual and to the world. Templeton's actions give credence to his tenets.

One accomplishment indicative of his beliefs was the establishment, in 1972, of the Templeton Prize for Progress in Religion. Convinced that the Nobel awards overlooked achievements in spirituality, Templeton created the prize to honor what he considered to be more important than all categories of the Nobel prizes combined. The Templeton Prize, currently worth more than one million dollars, is the world's largest award. Under a formula designed by Templeton, the monetary amount is annually adjusted to ensure that no other annual award exceeds it. In his stated objectives of the award, Templeton says that "progress is needed in religion as in all other dimensions of human experience and endeavor. There has been a long departure, at least in Western culture, from the last synthesis when religious knowledge and scientific knowledge were organically related. It is urgent that progress in religion be accelerated as progress in other disciplines takes place. A wider universe demands deeper awareness of the dimension of the spirit and of spiritual resources available for man, of the infinity of God, and of the divine knowledge and understanding still to be claimed."

The first recipient of the Templeton Prize was Mother Teresa of Calcutta. Others have included: Chiara Lubich, founder of the Focolare Movement in Italy; Professor Thomas Torrance, Moderator of the Church of Scotland; the Rev. Dr. Billy Graham; the writer Alexander Solzhenitsyn; the Rt. Hon. Lord Jakobovits, Chief Rabbi of Great Britian; Dr. Inamullah Khan, Secretary-General of the World Muslim Congress in Pakistan; Sir Sarvepalli Radhakrishnan, former President of India and Oxford Professor of Eastern Religions and Ethics; and the Rev. Nikkyo Niwano, founder of Rissho Kosei-Kai, Japan.

Templeton has eloquently argued that we should be spending at least "$100 million each day" in a scientific search for the meaning of God. On a smaller scale, the importance of spirituality in Templeton's life is evidenced in how the annual meetings of his mutual funds are always opened with a prayer. Templeton says the prayers are not designed to make stocks improve but rather to calm and clear the minds of stockholders.

Presbyterians in the United States

Presbyterians belong to the group of Liberal Protestant denominations in the United States aligned with the National Council of Churches, a group that numbers perhaps 52 million. In 1989, there were approximately 3 million members of the Presbyterian Church (USA) worshiping at 11,500 churches across the country.

John Templeton is a prolific author, recipient of numerous awards and honorary degrees, and financial analyst, with frequent appearances on such television programs as "Wall Street Week in Review" on PBS. His recommendations are listened to with zealous sobriety by laypersons and professional money managers worldwide.

A New Beginning

To a large extent, the future lies before us like a vast wilderness of unexplored reality. The God who created and sustained the evolving universe through eons of progress and development has not placed our generation at the tag end of the creative process. God has placed us at a new beginning. We are here for the future.

—Sir John Templeton

THE TEMPLETON PRIZE

We wanted to say to the world that progress in religion is more important than progress in chemistry, medicine, literature. We felt that Alfred Nobel had made wonderful benefits by giving prizes for tremendously new improvements.

When we began the prize twenty-one years ago, one of the first people we invited to the board of nine judges to make these choices was the head of the World Council of Churches. He and I were talking and we agreed that surely the Creator created every human being, not just some of us. Therefore we're all brothers and sisters, therefore we ought to love each other and go another step beyond that and learn from each other. So a prize for progress in religion should be for every human being, every child of God, and for those people who had done something totally new and original.

Progress in religion can come in many forms. Of the twenty-three different prize winners, no two are alike. The first winner was Mother Teresa of Calcutta. The judges selected her because they felt she had provided the whole world with a new understanding of the meaning of love, where she left her convent, went out on the streets with only two dresses and a few rupees and picked up the most pitiful dying people and took care of them. From that has developed this enormous world organization. I regard her as a living saint.

WHY WE NEED RELIGION

Our antagonisms come from human ego or self-centeredness. You don't find people fighting each other over their doctrine. You find them fighting each other over the territory, over the authority. Throughout history when the high priest and the dictator were the same persons, they fought over territory, over authority, not over religion. Religion has always been a tendency toward peace.

There are people working toward uniting the different faiths and denominations. But I don't think that's God's purpose. As I study God's creations, he didn't create one kind of insect, he created more than a million kinds. As you go down through geologic history, the variety has not gotten less but greater. And I think the same is true in religion or the study of spiritual matters.

It is part, too, of God's purpose to have his children study from every different aspect and then to love each other, talk to each other, learn from each other. I rejoice that there is a wonderful rich variety of religions now. Surely we'll not only love each other, but also learn from each other. And that is a far greater blessing than if we just had a uniform concept without any progress.

If you had one concept, one dogma, and nothing else, we would not have the incentive to learn more. If we have dozens or hundreds of different viewpoints, different religions, different faiths, different denominations, then as we exchange our ideas with each other on a loving and friendly basis, we have eyes opened to new aspects of God we might not otherwise have understood.

It's the benefit of freedom. Any society, any group of people that have freedom will disagree with each other and in their disagreement they develop new thoughts and progress they wouldn't develop if they didn't have that disagreement.

We can admire what is done by everybody. There is no form of worship of God that I don't admire. I admire the ancient scripture, I am an enthusiastic Christian, and I believe that the gospel of Christ is marvelous revelation. But at the same time, I can learn by reading the Jewish scriptures, or the Hindu scriptures, or the Buddhist scriptures. They are all approaching the question of God and God's purposes and more about spirituality in different ways. It adds a rich variety to my knowledge and yours if we have all these people trying to share their most beautiful insights, their most beautiful triumphs.

Syncretism

The four International Interfaith Organizations all reject "syncretism," which implies an artificial mixing of religious beliefs and practices; they also reject "indifferentism," which suggests that it does not matter what you believe. None of these four organizations are trying to create one world religion. . . . The interfaith organizations assume that most of their members will be loyal and committed members of their own faith communities. Respect for the integrity of other people's faith commitment and religious practices is essential.

—Marcus Braybrooke
(SourceBook)

GOD-MADE, NOT SELF-MADE

I'm not a self-made man. No human being could make a person. Your body is so miraculous with hundreds of billions of atoms cooperating to produce you. And not just to produce your body, but to produce your spirit, your personality, your soul, to produce *you*. Oh no, no human being could possibly be self-made.

I feel very humble that God has entrusted me with so much in my lifetime. And I am always seeking to find out how I should use these resources and abilities that God has given me to work in accordance with his purposes.

I have the opinion that it is God's good pleasure to give you prosperity and good health and happiness. All of those things come to you because of God's gifts, his abundance, his blessings.

Now they come to you if you are in tune with his principles or his purposes. For example, in business. If a person starts out in business to make money for himself, he's not likely to do it. But if he starts out in business to provide for the public a lower cost, higher quality, or productions not yet dreamed of, he's likely to be a great success. Business is only one example.

The secret of success is to try to give it away. If your life is focused on getting, you're going to be miserable. If your life is focused on giving, you are going to be an automatic success.

ALL ARE EQUAL IN GOD'S EYES

It's part of God's ongoing creative process to have every human being different and to have a wide variety of religions and a wide variety of denominations and churches. But to every human being he gives some talents. Not the same talents. He didn't give me the musical talents he gave you. And not the same quantity of talents, either. But the parable of the talents in the Bible teaches us that whatever talents God did give us, it's our duty to use them to the utmost.

The lord of the manor went away and gave to one servant five talents, another two, and another one. The first two servants multiplied the talents and gave them back to the lord. The one with one talent was fearful and buried his talent and gave the lord back only what he had been given. So the lord said to

---

Unity in Religious Diversity

Similar to the chain of being, with its unending variations and suprises, is the mosaic of human opinion about God. The sheer variety of opinions concerning the nature of God should give us pause. We should admit humbly that other theologies contain valuable insights into God that our own may lack. In many ways, [humans] attempting to describe God encounter the same difficulties as the proverbial blindmen describing an elephant. No one sees the entire picture, yet each feels and understands a part necessary for the full description.

—Sir John Templeton

the other two, "Enter into the joy of the kingdom." And the other man he banished from the kingdom.

It's a dramatic, clear lesson that you should discover what your talents are and then use them to the utmost, to do the most good in accordance with God's purposes.

If you start out to gain happiness for yourself, you'll never achieve it. But if you start out to give happiness to other people, you can't help the happiness coming back to you.

SCIENCE AND SPIRITUALITY

Science has discovered coal, and then petroleum, and then nuclear energy, and now renewable types of energy. But it goes far beyond that. Science is discovering the creations of the creator. For fifteen billion years, our universe had been in the process of creation. And for the first time, just in the last seventy years, scientists have been able to see what did happen a billion or fifteen billion years ago. We never knew, until seventy years ago, that there was any galaxy outside our own little Milky Way. Now we know there are a hundred billion other galaxies—surely all created by the same creator.

So the majesty of God, the infinity, the eternity of God is becoming more and more apparent because we are seeking. And that is what we should be doing in religion. My efforts now, for the rest of my life, are focused on spirituality. How can people grow spiritually the way we have grown scientifically and materially?

I'll give you one illustration. One of my foundations is publishing a book called *A Bibliography of Research by Natural Scientists on Spiritual Subjects*. We have collected over a hundred and fifty articles from learned, peer review journals of the highest scientific standard where scientists have been studying spiritual matters. For example, none of us doubt there is such a thing as love, and yet what little has been done scientifically to study love. It is beginning, though. Or prayer, or worship, or all these other things that are of a spiritual nature can be studied. And if they were studied it would be a *marvelous* thing.

Let's put it this way. The amount that is being spent worldwide for scientific research today is about a billion dollars a day.

Science and Religion

Humanity's attempts to progress toward a more humane future are blocked by two mutually exclusive world views. One segment of our population pursues facts at the expense of values, while another section is preoccupied with values at the expense of facts. These two worlds, the world of science and the world of religion, are separated by a deep, harmful and unnecessary chasm which has lasted too long. . . . If the founders of the world's religions were with us now, they would implore us to benefit from new facts, new knowledge, and new insights as well as wisdom and teachings of the religions.

—Erika Erdmann (SourceBook)

Suppose we spent one-tenth that much on spiritual research. That would be a hundred million dollars a day spent on spiritual research, and that is more than what has been spent on spiritual research in the history of the earth. And I hope that eventually, not too far away, we'll be doing it.

The clearest way to express that is the old saying that you learn God's purposes from two books: one is the book of revelation—ancient scripture—and the other is the book of nature. As you study nature, you are studying the creations of God and from the creations of God you learn more about God, himself, aspects of God and purposes of God.

We are publishing a book called *Evidence of Purpose*. There are twelve chapters, each one by a famous scientist writing about his own field, physics, genetics, and other sciences. Each one is saying that in recent times, within the last forty or fifty years, the discoveries have been so extraordinary they could not possibly have happened by chance. And if it didn't happen by chance then there has to be a creator, there has to be a purpose in the universe. Some of us like to call that purpose under the name God. It doesn't matter what name you use for it, but the scientists are coming around to the viewpoint that the universe was not created by accident and you were not created by accident.

I have established prizes for progress in religion and some of those have gone to people who are doing this type of research. Let's take Sir Alister Hardy. He was one of the prizewinners. After fifty years he became world famous and was knighted by the Queen for his work in botany because he was the world expert on the varieties of plankton in the ocean and in the air. Then he stopped all of that and said he was going to do the same thing with the varieties of spiritual experience. So he spent the last thirty years of his life collecting, classifying, and studying the varieties of religious experience and wrote a whole long list of books with wonderful titles like *The Biology of God*.

We're now thinking of having a survey to find out among the professors of hard sciences, such as chemistry, medicine, and so forth, how many of them pray. And we think it's going to be a very high proportion. To be a scientist doesn't mean you close your mind to the underlying realities. Scientists are only studying those things that are tangible, visible things. But that's not the total reality, the underlying reality. The thing that sustains and improves the outward appearances is a spiritual matter. So scientists, more and more, are coming to believe that the real underlying facts are religious and that science is just the study of the manifestations.

Everything that we touch, or see, or hear is temporary compared to the underlying reality that has created the universe and has created your body, but more important, has created your mind and your soul. So all of these things are going on and that is the basic underlying reality and most everything else is simply a temporary appearance.

THE PROBLEM OF EVIL

Why do bad things happen to good people? Shelves of books have been written about that for centuries, but nobody knows the full answer. I'm prepared to believe if I had created the world, I would have created a world with no problems. But fortunately I was not asked to create the world. The one that did create the world was far, far wiser than I. And he has created our world *with* problems. I'm prepared to take a humble approach that he is right, although I don't know why.

Take a little example. You may have young children, going to school. You have a choice of sending them to a school where there are no examinations or a school where there are examinations. I choose the one that has examinations. So maybe God has put us on the earth, where, in a sense, we are going through a school, and if we don't have any tests or any hardships we may not grow spiritually as rapidly as we would otherwise. That's only one possible human explanation of a much greater mystery.

The problem of evil has always been with us. But I must say that I think the quantity of evil is decreasing. Now you may not get that impression because the progress in media has been so marvelous that we now hear about the evil that we never would have heard about otherwise. We hear about these pitiful problems and evil going on in so many places, we just would not have known about it.

Try to study it from a mathematical standpoint, I think you'll find there are less people being killed by violence today than in any previous ten-year period in world history, a smaller proportion. The number of people that were killed in the time of the Romans, or the times of the Greeks, or the times of China, in relation to the population, there was far more violence then than there is now.

THE NATURE OF GOD

Some people have called it the "ground of being." Others have called it "the original clock maker" who put the clockwork into process, which is not just running on its own. I prefer to think of it as the only reality.

If you push me on it, I would have to say Creative Reality is the closest thing that I could come to, to avoiding the word *God*. That's not an adequate thing though, because God goes far beyond "creative reality," because God lives within each of us. Among the hundreds of billions of molecules and atoms in your body, you have a soul, you have a spirit. You are motivated and all of those spiritual qualities represent an indwelling God that has numbered every hair of your head. So God is not merely transcendent in a big sense, God is also intensely imminent in every one of his creations.

We are here on earth probably for some purpose. Whatever those purposes are, we didn't put ourselves here. And whatever those purposes are while we are here, we should try to discover them, live our lives in accordance with those purposes and try to improve and reveal those purposes to other people. And I think there would be a great benefit to do that.

In fact, we need to work on discovering the laws of life. All the great religions have brought up basic principles of life and they have been very useful. Like in Christianity or in Judaism, the Ten Commandments have been very useful. There are laws of life, and if you learn them and live by them you will not only be more productive, you will be healthier and happier. I think that the more we study the underlying reality the more likely we are to be useful. And from the usefulness come back to us health and happiness.

The God who made the world and everything in it . . . he made all nations to inhabit the whole earth . . . that they would search for God and perhaps grope for him and find him—though indeed he is not far from each one of us. For "In him we live and move and have our being"; as even some of our own poets have said, "For we too are his offspring."

(Acts 17:24–28, NRSV)

AT HEART, THE WILLINGNESS TO SHARE

To love, to give. It seems to be one of those basic principles we are talking about, that we should love every human being without exception and without limit. Try to think of everyone you know or everyone in history. Do you genuinely love everyone?

There is nothing in the Bible that said you have to agree with anybody, it only says you have to love them. And you can love people without agreeing, as you probably do with your children quite often. So it's our duty to love people and to give love. Some people worry about getting love. If you try to get love, you're not likely to get it. People won't want to associate with you. But if you are always radiating love and trying to give love, people will give it back to you. You can't stop them from doing it.

I'm just a beginner. I'm a sinner. I'm a student. I'm only starting to learn. I'm only trying with the rest of my life and the resources God has given me to encourage thousands of people to do serious research on the things we're talking about.

BDDHIST BRAHMA KUMARIS JEWISH
LIN NATIVE AMERICAN SUFI HINDU
RISTIAN ROMAN CATHOLIC MUSLIM

ROMAN CATHOLIC

NDU MUSLIM JAIN ROMAN CATHOLIC
OIST BAHA'I BUDDHIST SIKH SUFI
TIVE AMERICAN BRAHMA KUMARIS

WISH PROTESTANT CHRISTIAN TAOIST
DDHIST HINDU ZOROASTRIAN JAIN
MAN CATHOLIC BAHA'I PROTESTANT

OIST HINDU SUFI NATIVE AMERICAN
ISLIM BRAHMA KUMARIS BUDDHIST
KH SUFI JEWISH MUSLIM TAOIST
ROASTRIAN CHRISTIAN BAHA'I HINDU

ROMAN CATHOLIC

MAKING A DIFFERENCE

THEODORE MARTIN HESBURGH

The Reverend Theodore M. Hesburgh was born in Syracuse, New York, in 1917, joined the Order of the Congregation of the Holy Cross in 1934, and was ordained a Roman Catholic priest in 1943. After being the head of the religions department at Notre Dame and executive vice president, he became president of the university in 1952, a post he held for thirty-five years, the longest tenure at that time among active presidents of American institutions of higher learning.

Between 1954 and 1990, he was awarded an astonishing 129 honorary degrees—the most ever awarded to one person. In addition, he has held fifteen residential appointments over the years, involving him in virtually all major social issues—civil rights, peaceful uses of atomic energy, campus unrest, treatment of Vietnam offenders, Third World development, and immigration reform, to name only a few.

Father Hesburgh is the recipient of numerous awards, including the Presidential Medal of Freedom in 1964, the American Liberties medallion of the American Jewish Congress, the Merit award of the National Catholic Educational Association, the U.S. Navy's Distinguished Public Service award, and the French Ordre des Arts et des Lettres.

As chairman of the International Federation of Catholic Universities from 1963 to 1970, he led a movement to redefine the nature and mission of the contemporary Catholic university. He is the first priest to be an overseer at Harvard University, and in

Catholics in the United
States

In 1993, Catholic member-
ship in the United States
was estimated at more than
56 million, or 22 percent of
the total population. There
are roughly 23,000
Catholic churches across
the country.

Top Five Countries
with the Largest Catholic
Populations (1991)

Brazil	*135 million*
Mexico	*83 million*
U.S.A.	*56 million*
Italy	*55 million*
Philippines	*52 million*

(1994 Catholic Almanac,
Huntington, IN

1994 he was elected president of the Board of Overseers. He
was also the first priest to serve as director of the Chase
Manhattan Bank. He has served as a trustee or director or chair-
man of numerous foundations and institutes, including the
Rockefeller Foundation, the United Negro College Fund, the
Overseas Development Council, and the Academic Council of
the Ecumenical Institute for Advanced Theological Studies in
Jerusalem.

Former director of the Woodrow Wilson National Fellowship Corporation, a member of the Carnegie Commission on the
Future of Higher Education, Father Hesburgh was Chairman of
the U.S. Commission on Civil Rights from 1969 to 1972. From
1977 to 1979, he was chairman with rank of ambassador of the
United States delegation of the UN Conference on Science and
Technology for Development.

Father Hesburgh is the author of such well-known books as
Theology of Catholic Action (1945), *God and the World of
Man* (1950), *Thoughts for Our Times* (1962), *The Hesburgh
Papers: Higher Values in Higher Education* (1979), and *God,
Country, Notre Dame* (1990).

In his preface to Father Hesburgh's *The Humane Imperative: A Challenge for the Year 2000* (Yale University Press,
1974), Kingman Brewster, Jr., wrote, "Father Hesburgh's contribution to the continuing and unfinished effort to make the
Declaration of Independence and the Bill of Rights a living reality for all Americans is so widely appreciated that it needs no
embellishment. . . . There is no gloom in his dedication, since it
is sustained by a confidence that the Holy Spirit is at work in us
all, in the world, and in the cosmos. At a time of lowered expec-
tations, it is good that there are voices of hope, seasoned by experience, still capable of believing that we can fashion a better
world."

CHALLENGES FOR THE YEAR 2000

If I could be dramatic I would say the first challenge is to survive
because we've been facing, the last forty years, a nuclear threat.
Fortunately we're cutting back on the warheads now, but
they're still around. We're just taking them off the delivery systems, and we don't have a clue how to get rid of them all.

Then we have an ecological threat which won't blow us out of the water as quickly as the nuclear. This may take a hundred years, but it will just as surely. If we make our air unbreathable and our water undrinkable and our land untillable, the planet becomes uninhabitable, like all other planets we know.

I've always been an optimist, and I think we're going to make it. But we don't make it just by drifting. We don't make it by no change, business as usual. You make it by understanding, first of all, what the dimensions of the problem are today. What we can do about them and then bringing all the forces to bear to do that, and we've got to do it together.

I think there's always been greed in the world, and there always will be. There's always been power seeking, and there always will be. But I think the world is full of a lot of very good people who don't want to die tomorrow morning, or don't want their kids to die in a nuclear disaster. There are people who love this earth and don't want to see it go into a cinder.

There are a lot of good people out there, and somehow one has to educate them. One has to rally them around—set ways of getting at the problem in a realistic way. And, you know, one has to live and hope.

These problems are big; they're huge; they are global. But they are not unmanageable if we put our minds to it. I think we have to approach the world with a certain amount of confidence and optimism knowing that there are lot of good people out there that we can count on if we get them to accept a few basics.

Statistics on Catholics by Continent/Worldwide

Area	
Americas (63%)*	461 million
Europe (40%)	285 million
Africa (14%)	89 million
Asia (2.7%)	86 million
Oceania (26%)	7 million
Worldwide (18%)	928 million

(*Statistical Yearbook of the Church,* Vatican City, 1990)

Indicates percentage of population.

A NEGATIVE OPTION MORALITY

I think what you and I know is that a lot of people don't want to get involved. They may be good in a personal way. They don't shoot people. They don't cheat people. They don't underpay their help.

But if you say, as the Lord said he is going to ask us in judgment, "When did you feed me when I was hungry, and when did you give me something to drink when I was thirsty, and when did you visit me when I was in prison, and when did you take me in when I was an alien? Whenever you didn't do that you didn't do it to me." That becomes a pretty hard test for being good or not being good, at least in the judgment of the gospel.

What I try to get to our students is, you can make a difference, anybody can make a difference. I've known a zillion people in my life who have made a difference. I'll just take one. We wouldn't be talking about environment now if it weren't for a lady named Rachel Carson. She wrote a book. Some woman writes a book on some crazy subject—environment, ecology—and today the world is conscious of ecological problems.

People are careful about keeping this earth a little bit close to its current beauty and making it even better. As a kid, I was sitting in a car, eating a candy bar, get finished and throw it out the window, everybody did it. You don't do it any more.

So I think that's one thing. You can make a difference. But then you have to decide where and how and when, and are you really going to do it? And that, that requires a bit of a change.

PERSONAL CHOICES FOR CHANGE

Everybody has to come to are they going to make a difference or are they just going to drift through life, maybe not landing up in jail, but maybe not landing up in heaven either? You have to, I think, consciously say, "I can make a difference."

I want to train young people to carry on for the future. I want to see a younger generation who has these same feelings they can do something about human dignity and human rights, they can do something about world hunger. In the Rockefeller Foundation, we multiplied the world's food supply about six times through the Green Revolution. It can be done. It took some time. It took probably forty years. It took a lot of research. It took a lot of hard work in the field. It took a lot of education in the Third World.

The pesticides and artificial fertilizers were done by commercial farming, mainly to get more production, to sell more food for more money. We did very simple things. We taught them how to keep rats, who eat, I guess, about 25 percent of the grain in India, out of the field. If you can get rats out of the field at night, you've made a big jump in your production level.

You make a target, you work it out, and you do something. For example, the world's been eating rice for about eight thousand years. No one's ever decided this rice is the best in the

Rachel Carson (1907–1964), marine biologist and writer, set in motion the American environmental movement with the publication in 1962 of Silent Spring, *a book uncovering the widespread and irresponsible use of long-lasting poisons—pesticides and herbicides. She attacked the cozy relationship between the scientific community, the large chemical companies, and the government regulatory agencies. Up until that point, government agencies relied on the chemical companies they were supposed to regulate to set allowable tolerances for dangerous pesticides. Beyond opposing the indiscriminate use of poisons as a danger to all life, Carson made clear the basic irresponsibility of an industrialized, technological society toward the natural world.* Silent Spring *inspired the movement that banned outright dangerous pesticides, like DDT, and brought many others under stringent control.*

(Biography)

world for this particular climate, this soil, and this rainfall. We did it. Of course, we've got computers now. We looked at forty thousand varieties, came up with the very best for this country, for that country, for another country, and lo and behold we're raising six times more rice than we used to. We did the same thing for corn.

TO BE RELIGIOUS IS TO SERVE HUMANITY

I think anything you do to serve humanity in his and her needs, anything you do to uphold the dignity of the human person, anything that you do to work for peace, which only comes from justice—and the world's so full of injustice, full of war (there are about forty wars going on right now, large and small)—is to be religious.

Because the world comes from the creative hand of God, the Christian recognizes that the goods of creation exist to serve the needs of all. No one has the right to arrogate to oneself an excessive amount of those goods at the expense of the legitimate needs of others nor does anyone have the right to be destructive or wasteful of those goods, in disregard or contempt of the generations to follow.

(McBrien, *Catholicism*)

God himself told us about his kingdom. It's a kingdom of justice and peace. So I think you can praise God by kneeling down in a dark room and praying, but you can also praise him by going up and upholding the rights of some women who are being run roughshod over, or some men who are being persecuted because they happen to be Muslim or something. You can do anything for justice and peace and you are serving the kingdom of God, and serving God; you are serving religion.

That doesn't mean I don't offer Mass every day. It doesn't mean I don't do my breviary, which the monks do in the monastery. I do that every day. It doesn't mean that I don't meditate now and then. It doesn't mean that I don't have to make a retreat every year and see how I'm doing, which generally isn't all that great. But in any event, I do the things I should do. I preach and I do pastoral work.

For the ordinary person, religion has a lot to do with it. When I went to Notre Dame originally in 1934, we had one fellow who was doing something good for other people. He was taking the food left over in the dining hall to the hobos down where they gathered in the outskirts of town.

Today, 75 percent of our students are doing something in the way of service. They take care of 250 kids with Down's Syndrome. About 850 of them tutor kids who otherwise might drop out. They are Big Brothers and Big Sisters; they work for the

The Parable of the Good
Samaritan

*A man was going from
Jerusalem to Jericho, and
fell into the hands of robbers, who stripped him,
beat him, and went away,
leaving him half dead. Now
by chance a priest was
going down that road; and
when he saw him he passed
on the other side. So likewise a Levite, when he
came to the place and saw
him, passed by on the other
side. But a Samaritan while
traveling came near him;
and when he saw him he
was moved with pity. He
went to him and bandaged
his wounds, having poured
oil and wine on them. Then
he put him on his own animal, brought him to an
inn, and took care of him.
The next day he took out
two denarii, gave them to
the innkeeper, and said,
'Take care of him; and
when I come back, I will
repay whatever more you
spend.' "Which of these
three, do you think, was a
neighbor to the man who
fell into the hands of the
robbers?" He said, "The
one who showed him
mercy." Jesus said to him,
"Go and do likewise."*

(Luke 10:30–37, NRSV)

homeless; they work for the people just coming out of jail with
no place to go. Now, are they more religious than when only
one fellow was doing something? I think so.

Religion is not just something private between you and God,
although it can start there. It's how that private relationship between you and God gives you an opportunity to serve him.
"What you did for my least brethren, you did for me."

Having compassion isn't worth anything if you are not
moved by it to do something. I always tell the youngsters, compassion is where you start. You see something bad, and you feel
sorry for it. Commitment is when you do something about it.
That makes the change. Compassion doesn't change anything
except maybe make you feel badly.

DEALING WITH VIOLENCE

The whole fabric of human society, its laws and its ethics, is
based on the dignity of every human being. In other words,
you're a world in yourself. You have dignity, I've got to respect you.

I have to respect you whether you are a man or a woman, or
white or black, or Jewish or Christian, or whatever. These all
have nothing to do with it. What has to do with it is that you
are someone, a world in yourself, a microcosm, who has the
image and likeness of God in your very being because you have
a mind to know and a will to do. You're free. We are the only
free creatures in the whole world.

Now if everybody respected that dignity of the human
being, whether it is a child or an unborn child or a person that
is ninety years old dottering around, you wouldn't have kids
thirteen years old going around shooting up other kids twelve
years old.

It's that respect for the dignity of the human being, if we
could ever get that through to all peoples and all religions and
all races, that no matter who the other is, if he or she is a human
being, by golly, you respect them, you give them their rights,
you practice justice toward them. You love them. And together
you work for peace, not for conflict or violence.

PEACE THROUGH JUSTICE

There's an old saying, "Peace is the work of justice." And if you want to work for peace, work for justice, because every single war, it's injustice that causes it to happen.

For example, if you're living in Bosnia-Herzegovina and you happen to be Muslim, you've got the Orthodox climbing all over you to the east, and you've got the Croats climbing all over to the north. Now if you happen to be Croatian, then you've got the other two. Or if you happen to be Orthodox, you have the other two.

I want to say, in the name of God, *quit!* You are destroying the human beings who are made in God's likeness or his children whom you are bound to respect and to honor and to help. Instead of that you're blowing them up, you're raping them, you are treating them like garbage? And they are all doing it, it isn't just one or the other, they're all wrong, all three are wrong.

I was talking to Cy Vance. He's the one who began, with Lord Owen, trying to negotiate the thing, and he wore himself out for a year and a half. He called me up one day when he was back in the States, and he said, "You know, Ted, something terrible about that war. I finally got the religious leaders together and they spoke hatefully to each other. And I said to them 'Gentlemen, I was brought up to believe that religion was about love, not about hate. You people act as though you're strange dogs in a cage growling at each other.' Well, they said, 'We've been doing it for hundreds of years.'"

So quit. It's been a bad thing for hundreds of years—stop doing it.

Lord,
Make me an instrument of thy peace.
Where there is hatred, let me sow love.
Where there is injury, Pardon.
Where there is doubt, Faith.
Where there is despair, Hope
Where there is darkness, Light.
Where there is sadness, Joy.
O Divine Master,
Grant that I may not so much seek
To be consoled, as to console;
Not so much to be understood, as to understand;
Not so much to be loved, as to love.
For it is in giving that we receive.
It is in pardoning that we are pardoned.
It is in dying that we awaken to eternal life.

—St. Francis of Assisi
(1182–1226)

ORIGINAL SIN

I happen to believe in original sin, which is not all that popular today. You don't hear much about it, that in the beginning, in a sense, humanity sinned in the person of Adam. He was given a beautiful setup, and God said, "Just don't do one thing. You're free to do anything you want but just don't do this one." This is the way Adam would say to God, "You're supreme and I'm a creature." And so what does he do? The one thing he isn't supposed to do. This is all, of course, put in a story that even simple people can understand. But the point behind the metaphor is very real. God says don't do this.

God had to take a chance. The moment he made us free, he had to allow for evil, because if we are free we can do good or we can do evil. We do evil, and there are all kinds of ways that evil spreads after we do it.

It's about choice. It's about choosing that which you know God would have you choose—which is called conscience, an inner voice saying, "God wants you to do this." People tend so easily, as Adam and Eve did, to choose evil.

As St. Paul said, "I do the evil things I don't want to do and don't do the good things I want to do." I mean, we all know in our conscience that we are not saints. We all know that we often go against what we know in our conscience to be the will of God. But the moment God puts freedom in the world, he's got to allow for the possibility of evil in the world.

FORGIVENESS AND LOVE

I am optimistic about people. I don't think a lot of people go to hell, although a lot of people are heading that way. I think God's grace is greater than evil. I think God made men to be good, not to be evil. And he made them to serve him and to create a beautiful world and not to make a crummy world and to be constantly fighting.

There is always forgiveness. That's the other beautiful thing. Everyone can be forgiven anything, because, as creatures, we can't possibly do more evil than God can forgive. God has infinite forgiveness, no matter what evil we do.

I remember a wonderful little ditty from a medieval poem, "Between the Stirrup and the Ground." It's about this guy who's been doing evil all his life. He's a bad knight and he's galloping over the countryside and his horse hits a furrow and throws him. He knows that he's going to land awfully hard and probably going to be killed, and it says, "Between the stirrup and the ground, mercy sought and mercy found." I don't think you can presume on God's mercy, but, by golly, it's always there.

One great thing about being a priest is that if anybody tells you anything they have done wrong, no matter how monumental, you've got to forgive them if they are sorry. It isn't you forgiving them, you have to give them God's forgiveness. You start judging, and pretty soon you find out you're guilty of the things you are judging.

When I see people who are worried and stewing and they think everything is going to hell in a basket and I say, "Hey look, don't worry, God's providence and care is up and working before the dawn." If you really believe that, and you've got reason to believe it, no point in stewing and being upset and thinking your life isn't going to amount to anything, that you can't make a difference. I say the same thing for myself.

Love. When you shake it all down, that's where you wind up. I've talked a lot about justice and peace but it springs from love—love of God, love of your fellow human beings, love of this world and all the beauty it's got.

ROMAN CATHOLIC

A GLOBAL ETHIC
Dr. Hans Küng

The Golden Rule in Various Religious Traditions

Judaism
What is hateful to you, do not to your fellowmen. That is the entire Law; all the rest is commentary. (Talmud, Shabbat, 31a)

Christianity
In everything do to others as you would have them do to you; for this is the law of the prophets. (Matthew 7:12, NRSV)

Islam
Do unto all men as you would they should do unto you, and reject for others what you would reject for yourself. (Mishkat-el-Masabih)

Buddhism
Hurt not others with that which pains yourself. (Udana V.18)

Born in 1928 in Switzerland, educated throughout Europe, Hans Küng took his Doctorate of Theology from the Institut Catholique, Sorbonne, at the University of Paris in 1957. Ordained as a Roman Catholic priest in 1954, he is on the faculty of Catholic Theology at the Institute of Ecumenical Research of the University of Tübingen in Germany.

Dr. Küng lectures throughout the world. His more than twenty books have been translated into numerous languages and published in more than one hundred editions. Those books include: *Justification: The Doctrine of Karl Barth and a Catholic Reflection* (1957), *The Council and Reunion* (1961), *Truthfulness—The Future of the Church* (1968), *Infallible?* (1970), *Does God Exist? An Answer for Today* (1978), *On Being a Christian* (1974), *Eternal Life?* (1982), *Christianity and Chinese Religion* (1988, with J. Ching), *Mozart —Traces of Transcendence* (1991), *Theology for the Third Millennium—An Ecumenical View* (1987), *Global Responsibility* (1991), and *Judaism* (1991).

A staunch church reformer who has long attempted to reconcile Catholic and Protestant theology, Küng was rebuked by the Vatican in 1973 when the Holy See's Sacred Congregation for the Doctrine of the Faith issued an official declaration entitled "Mysterium Ecclesiae," which ordered "the world's Catholics to reject Küng's theories," according to the magazine *Newsweek* at the time.

Küng is today thought of as one of Christianity's greatest intellects. Adept at nine languages, he was the principal author of the Global Declaration of the Parliament of the World's Religions at Chicago in 1993, signed by representatives of virtually every religion on the planet.

THE NEED FOR A GLOBAL ETHIC

We need a new basic attitude of humanity. Take only one very simple rule: "Don't do to others what you do not want done to you." Five hundred years before Christ, that was stated. That was already pronounced by Confucius. Rabbi Hillel said it before Christ. And we have even a positive formulation in the Sermon on the Mount, where Jesus said, "Do to others what you would want they do to you."

I know, of course, that everybody needs success. But it is a very different situation if you make success your god. If a businessman is just working for success, then he has, of course, no limits. If a politician is only working for success, well, he is even able to lie, to kill, to do everything that is really against humanity. So we think you have to come back to the basics. In the declaration of the Parliament of the World's Religions is the most basic thing, not at all self-evident—that the human being should behave in a truly human way, in a truly humane way. Often we behave like beasts.

To have a common ethical foundation does not mean that we have to agree on everything, so to speak. It's the question of behaviors and not the question of beliefs. We could discuss forever and ever what is the relationship of the Torah, you know, for Jews, and of Christ for Christians, and how this goes together. I am involved in all sorts of dialogues where we are discussing these problems. But my personal experience is that even people who didn't agree on questions of faith, dogma, and so on, can agree on certain attitudes and behaviors. And so my formula is, we do not need one religion.

We do not need one religion but we need one global ethic. I think it is inadmissible that you have different rules in Japan and in America and in Europe. We cannot permit that ethics are divided. As a matter of fact, you will find from Japan to Russia

Confucianism
Do not impose on others what you yourself do not desire. (Analects XII.2)

Hinduism
Never do to others what would pain thyself. (Panchatantra III.104)

Jainism
One who neglects or disregards the existence of earth, air, fire, water, and vegetation disregards his or her own existence, which is entwined with them. (Mahavira, 6th century B.C.E.)

Bahā'ī
Desire not for anyone the things that ye would not desire for yourselves. (Gleanings from the Writings of Bahā' Ullāh LXVI)

Sikhism
Treat others as thou wouldst be treated thyself. (Adi Granth)

Zoroastrianism
Do not unto others all that which is not well for oneself. (Shayast-na-shayast 13.29)

Taoism
Regard your neighbor's gain as your own gain and your neighbor's loss as your own loss. (T'ai Shang Kan Ying P'ien)

to Europe you will have common convictions and also, I would say, common problems.

I remember a conversation when the whole revolution went on in Russia, from a physicist, a famous Nobel Prize winner in physics. I said, "What is your view of the situation?" He said, "Well, our ultimate problem is a problem of morals. Our people do not know anymore for what to work, for what to live. So they are muddling through and they need again to know the purpose of their lives and what are really certain standards." Here I think such a declaration could really help.

VICTIMS OF OUR OWN SUCCESS

The record of humanity is ambivalent. That is the reason why I speak about to be truly human, or to be humane—that is the positive side of humanity. We have a great deal of achievements, and we have a great deal of failures. Our century has seen tremendous successes in science and technology, but on the other hand, we seem to be very behind in our moral attitudes with regard to all these successes. We are not any more able to control our success. We are the victim of our own success.

I think of all those people who see that they are destroying nature, the environment. Well, we are the victim of the success to control and to be the lords of nature. You see, what is in my mind and I think in many minds in the Parliament, we had already a change of conscience with regard to the environment and nature.

I think nobody, if he or she is honest, will not agree that thirty years ago we didn't think the same way about nature as we do today. Second, nobody thought thirty years ago about peace and warfare as we do now, that we should abolish the wars. Third, nobody thinks about the relationship between men and women the same way today as thirty years ago. We have a real change of consciousness.

What I want to provoke with my book on global responsibility toward a global ethic is precisely to provoke the same change of consciousness with regard to ethics.

I am well known by many to be very critical about religion, about my own church sometimes, the Catholic Church. I think I have to be. But I also see that religion can function in a very positive way. You would not have had a peaceful development and a peaceful revolution in 1989 in Eastern Europe, without religiously committed people. The same is true for Africa. You had a lot of very religiously motivated people who tried to change the situation by peaceful means. The same with the Philippines, in Haiti, and I could go on.

This Declaration for a Global Ethic is precisely self-critical with regard to religion too. We have especially to change our self. But at the same time, religions could really promote in a tremendous way the peace of the world. And I am very much convinced there will be no peace among the nations without peace among the religions.

Can there be peace? It's a good question. But if I see, for instance, the history of Catholicism and Protestantism in Europe, well, since the sixteenth century and the time of Luther and Calvin, we had many wars. The history of France and Germany was a terrible history of enmity, hereditary enmity, they said, at the origins of World Wars I and II. Today, you could not anymore imagine that there would be a war between France and Germany. Why? Because after World War II we had religiously committed people who suffered a great deal under the Nazis.

You see, if it is finally possible to have peace between Germany and France, then it must also be possible to have peace between Arabs and Jews. It must be possible also to have peace in Northern Ireland. We need peace in India between the Muslims and Hindus. We need peace between Singhalese and Indian people in Sri Lanka. We need to give to the younger generation again a horizon of meaning. They must know for what they are living.

Hans Küng was invited by Pope John XXIII to be a peritus (Lat., "expert") at the Second Vatican Council, 1963–1965. Later, Vatican authorities conducted a series of investigations into his publications, beginning with The Church *(1967), which the Sacred Congregation for the Doctrine of the Faith forbade to be translated or even discussed. Proceedings following the publication of Küng's* Infallible? An Inquiry *culminated with a formal declaration on December 18, 1979, against his teaching, with the judgment that he could no longer be considered a Catholic theologian.*

(McBrien, *Encyclopedia*)

CENSURE IN THE CHURCH

First it depends upon what you call the church. Here you have a great center for public opinion research. My friend Andrew Greeley will tell you that, for controversial issues in the Catholic church, the greatest part of the Catholic population have the same view as I do. On contraception, for instance, on the evaluation of how to treat divorced people, on how to treat women

*Charles E. Curran, one of
the most prominent
Catholic moral theologians
and from 1965 professor of
theology at The Catholic
University of America, was
removed from his teaching
post in 1986 because of his
dissent against the Vatican
encyclical* Humanae Vitae,
*which prohibited birth con-
trol by artificial means.
Since 1991 he has been
Elizabeth Scurlock University Professor of Human
Values at Southern
Methodist University.*

(Melton, *Leaders*)

in the church, how to have better relationships and eucharistic services together, and so on. I don't think that is a question of the church; the church is a community.

There are a few people, maybe not so much in Chicago, but in Rome, who think still we should go back to the Middle Ages. And they, of course, misunderstand. But you know, I do not want to polemicize here. I see that our church is nevertheless quietly moving all over the world in the same direction.

I am really a man who is always defending religions in public, but of course, you cannot defend everything in religion. We have in all religions things that are just terrible. If the religions themselves are not really humane, then I think it is really not very helpful for them to preach this truth to the world. And so, I really believe religion has got not to be regressive.

Regressive means, in the sense of psychoanalysis, to go back to your childhood. Sometimes in religion people are treated like children, and a lot of people, they pray like children, even if they are fifty years old. Good religion, humane religion, true religion has to make people mature.

Sometimes in religious communities and in churches, you are not allowed to say the truth. We had a very sad cases in the Catholic University of America. My good friend Charles Curran has just been eliminated because he has taken a stand on the question of birth control. That is, of course, repression. And we have to abolish that. That is a problem for Orthodox Jews, for Orthodox Muslims, for fundamentalist Protestants at their seminaries. You have everywhere the danger of repression.

CRITICIZE RELIGION, BUT DON'T ABANDON IT

Religion, fortunately, is not concentrated on what I would call the human machinery of religion. People who have power in Thailand, in the Buddhist establishment, or who have power in the Vatican, or who have power in a Protestant organization, these are human things. Religion is ultimately directed and sustained by a different reality.

There must be something I cannot prove, but I have reasons to trust that what we see, what we can touch, what we can calculate, what we can manipulate, that is not all. That there is another dimension, that there is a deep meaning in our lives we have to discover, that we are coming from somewhere and going to somewhere, that even death is not the end of everything. So that is, of course, religion. We call this God in our Jewish/Christian/Muslim tradition. Others call it a different way. But there is an ultimate reality that the human being is not alone in this tremendous universe. That is the heart of religion. And to give up that would be very, very unreasonable, I believe. And ultimately, also, not very human, not very humane. If you look at this long history of five hundred thousand years, from the beginning people believed in something. They made their symbols, they had their images, they had their prayers, they had their customs giving them things to live for a new life, and so on.

Is this all wrong? Are all these mosques and churches and synagogues built around a nothing? I don't think that is the truth. It is, of course, important to know that because this ultimate reality we call God is precisely something absolutely different, you cannot prove this as you can prove in mathematics or in physics that it is. If it would be that, it would not be God. And so, it's a challenge, it's an indication for what I call a reasonable trust that there is an ultimate reality which sustains us, which is ahead of us, and which ultimately will save us

The aim [of ecumenism] can only be a critical or self-critical differentiation which measures any religion critically by its own origin and by a humane ethic, without claiming it for itself. We do not arrive at peace through syncretism but through reform of ourselves; we arrive at renewal through harmony, and at self-criticism through toleration. So what is being fought for here is a theology of peace which finds the way to peace not by bracketing off the questions of truth but by incorporating it and responding to it, and which above all discloses and helps to work out those conflicts and points of unrest in the world of which the religions themselves are the cause.

(Küng)

ROMAN CATHOLIC

LIFE AFTER DEATH

Robert Muller

Robert Muller holds degrees in law and economics from the universities of Strasbourg and Heidelberg, as well as from Columbia University. A native of Belgium, raised in Alsace-Lorraine, he fought in the French Resistance and was imprisoned by the Nazis.

After thirty-eight years of service at the United Nations, culminating in the position of Assistant-Secretary-General and special adviser to Secretary-General Javier Perez de Cuellar, Robert Muller is now Chancellor Emeritus of the University for Peace in Costa Rica. Muller has been hailed as "the philosopher of the United Nations," and its "Prophet of Hope." He was one of the main architects of the UN institutional system, leading the Economic and Social Council. He coordinated the efforts of thirty-two UN specialized agencies and was the trusted collaborator of Secretary-General U Thant. He is the author of numerous books, including *New Genesis, The Birth of a Global Civilization, My Testament to the UN, A Planet of Hope, The Desire to Be Human,* and *Dialogues of Hope.* Muller was awarded the 1989 UNESCO Peace Education Prize for his World Core Curriculum for Education, which has been adopted by schools around the globe.

From his unique vantage point of top-level global statesmanship, Muller saw the strong connection between spirituality and politics, and it is that relationship that has given him a truly unique voice in world affairs. Few have had the wisdom or audacity to insist on an ecumenical spirituality as a crucial corollary to more practical spheres. Raised a Catholic and deeply influenced by Buddhism, Muller created the Pacem in Terris Society in the Secretariat of the United Nations to allow staff to hold discussions on spirituality and to broaden their work in that domain.

His dream has always been to form a strong alliance between all the major religions of the world and the United Nations. It was U Thant who used to say that until humanity rightly perceived its place in the universe, none of our problems would be solved. Muller has seized upon the message of major religious leaders—Christ, Buddha, Mohammed—and promulgated through his assiduous labors a spiritual joy, brilliant corridors of light, rather than focusing upon darkness. And it is this uplifting side of the man that has so endeared him as a spiritual mentor to many throughout the world.

Even during the darkest days of the Cold War, as the United Nations found itself perpetually deadlocked over countless issues, Muller's optimism prevailed. He managed—amid seas of safer atheism—to implement a practice of beginning and ending sessions of the UN General Assembly with a minute of silent prayer and meditation.

Norman Cousins has written of Muller, "Having lived at the center of events in a period of unique human evolution, he has attempted to share with others the formulas that let him remain happy and hopeful in the face of somber and complex problems. His formulas derive from a perspective essential to happiness. ... He has asked himself, 'What is the objective and meaning of life?' His answer: 'To be happy, to feel fully the miracle of life, and to be endlessly grateful for it.' "

In 1993, Muller was awarded the Albert Schweitzer Prize for the Humanities.

The United Nations

An international organization established immediately after World War II, the United Nations replaced the League of Nations. The need for an international organization to replace the League of Nations was first stated officially on October 30, 1943. The founding conference was held in San Francisco in 1945 to draft the governing treaty, the United Nations Charter. The General Assembly and Security Council first met in London in 1946. The UN took residence in its current home along the East River in New York City in 1952.

(Columbia)

A PERSONAL STORY OF HOPE AND PEACE

I would say that it is the United Nations that has made me hopeful, because when I entered the UN in 1948, I had just come out of the Second World War. I saw incredible horrors. I was imprisoned by Gestapo at the age of seventeen. I was in the French

*Until one is committed,
there is hesitancy, the
    chance to draw back,
always ineffectiveness.*

*Concerning acts of initia-
    tive (and creation)
there is one elementary
    truth
the ignorance of which kills
    countless ideas
and splendid plans:*

*That the moment one defi-
    nitely commits oneself
then Providence moves too.*

*. . . Whatever you can do,
or dream you can, begin it.
Boldness has genius, power
    and magic in it.*

Begin it now.

                        —Goethe

underground later on. I saw people killed. I saw Germans and French acting toward each other like animals. I really could not understand it.

As a matter of fact, when I was a little boy, I thought that life was divine. I used the adjective divine because it was the biggest word I could find. I was happy to be alive. I was happy to look at nature, to look at the moon and to look at the stars. Really my basic inclination was to be grateful for life as a little boy. And people said, look, what a strange little boy who goes around saying that life is divine.

And then later on I saw that there was a border which you were not supposed to go on the other side of because there were Germans. We were evacuated twice from our home town. Just within two hours, get out of the town, become a refugee. Then came the whole ordeal of the war. And all this was absolutely contrary to my love for life and my ideal for life.

I decided that I would try to prevent this for my children, that I am not going to accept these horrors and I am going to do something against it.

When I came back, my father asked me, "What are you going to do with your life?"

I said, "Oh, it's very simple, I'm going to work for peace."

He said, "You're crazy, there is no peace profession. We are poor hat makers. You will never make it."

I said, "Well, I don't know whether I'm going to make it, but I'm going to devote my entire life to peace because I do not want to see what I have seen at the age of seventeen or eighteen."

And I have. Two years later I was in the United Nations. I went to university, wrote an essay sponsored by the United Nations Association, and was sent to New York.

SEEING PROGRESS THROUGH EVOLUTION

There is evolution, and in this evolution humanity is learning. As a young man at the UN I gave us twenty years before we had a world war. We haven't had one in fifty years.

We were told that decolonization would take one hundred to one hundred fifty years. We did it in forty years. We are going to have a completely different millennium because what I see today as progress, I would have never believed as a young man.

Who would have thought that the Cold War would end? I was predicting that the Cold War would end before the year 2000. Now that it has ended, you begin to demilitarize. Practically in every country the military is out.

LIVING WITHOUT ENEMIES

We're going to work together. The money you spare on stupid armament expenditures you put into social security. We have enormous new problems coming up. For example the aging of the world population. By the year 2025 we will have a population of old people. We will be doubled more or less by the year 2100. And no government thinks of it. But you have to live with the problem and to correct it.

We, ourselves, by saving the children, have created the population explosion. Then we warned the world, "Something is wrong with population. Take it easy. Reduce your number of children." And you have the Pope and all the Latin American countries making an enormous building block, and continuing. You have the right-to-life people against the whole idea.

Nevertheless, in 1970 the world population was forecast in the UN to be 7.3 billion in the year 2000. We are down to 6.5. In other words, thanks to the world population conferences, thanks to the warnings the UN gave, we have saved the birth of 1.2 billion people. And we continue.

So the estimate is now that there will be 8.5 billion in the year 2025 and at the present rate the world population will stabilize at 11 billion. But I make you a prediction. It is going to stabilize at much lower than this because the UN is going to hit the population policies, and governments will have to recognize that they have to do it.

THE CONNECTION BETWEEN RELIGION AND POLITICS

I've come to the conclusion that all politicians in the United Nations should be like U Thant was, like Dag Hammarskjöld was,

Decide to Forgive

For resentment is negative
Resentment is poisonous
Resentment diminishes
*   and devours the self.*

Be the first to forgive
To smile and take the first
*   step*
And you will see happiness
*   bloom*
On the face of your human
*   brother and sister.*

Be always the first
Do not wait for others to
*   forgive*
For by forgiving
You become the master of
*   fate*
The fashioner of life
A doer of miracles.

To forgive is the highest
most beautiful form of
*   love.*

In return you will receive
untold peace and happi-
*   ness.*

—Robert Muller

a mystic. You have to consider your political function as a sacred function. It is the most sacred function of all because you can do good or bad. You can prevent war or you can have peace. You can do good for the poor people because you have a very powerful position. I believe that politics, politicians should again become spiritual people.

But I think spirituality is above religion. I would like people to behave in a spiritual way. For example, in the United Nations we start the General Assembly of the UN with a moment of silence for prayer or meditation. I would like all governments to do it. We have in the United Nations a meditation room. And the Americans copied us, and the Council of Europe copied us, and the Australian Parliament. Why should the guy sitting in the skyscrapers selling all kinds of stuff not start the day with a prayer and ask, "Well, am I selling the right thing?"

Can you imagine? As a matter of fact, I remember when the first world environment conference took place, the Ford Foundation hired a consultant to see what was the end result of the conference.

I met him in the UN corridors, and he said, "Robert, you will be very interested in my finding. I've come to the conclusion that the environmental question is a spiritual question."

I said, "What?"

He said, "Yes. I give you a very simple conclusion: If a businessman makes business without thinking about future generations, he will not give a damn about the environment. But if a businessman thinks of his children, of grandchildren and the future grandchildren, he will watch out what he does. He will do the right thing and from that moment he will have taken a spiritual decision." How interesting! How interesting.

So this is why the United Nations and this Parliament of the World's Religions is beginning to move toward the new global morality and spirituality. And this is something which is progressing too.

I can see a global spirituality binding all the religions, as long as they believe in spirituality and the soul and the spiritual dimension which is the highest dimension of our life. We go from physical, to mental, to sentimental and the highest is the spiritual—when we see ourselves as units of the universe or as children of God. And then the religions, they can have turbans, or they can have trousers, or they can kneel or they can sit or they can pray—that's irrelevant. And even there they could find out what is the best.

Some of them pray, the others meditate, the others. . . . It would be fascinating. Some religions, for example, like the Zoroastrians, the Jains, the Franciscans among the Christians, they have had an environmental view for a long time. The Jains were environmentalists for the last 2400 years.

We have much to learn. Some scientists also have this view by saying be frugal and simple in order not to tax God's creation. How beautiful that is. In other words, do not reduce your consumption because you going to save money. No, because you have to be respectful for the earth. So the religions have quite a lot to offer and with a great variety.

PERSONAL AND GLOBAL DECISIONS

I think that you can decide in the morning when you wake up, to be happy, or to be miserable. I was in prison from the Gestapo, with thirty people standing one next to the other, nobody even lying down—and I said, well I'm going to decide to be happy even here. And I composed a novel in my life, where I saw the blue skies, because I said to myself, "You Germans are not going to get me down."

You have always, as a human being, the possibility to take one side or to take the other side. You can say, "Oh, I feel lousy today." If you say, "I feel lousy today" that is the beginning of sickness. But when I wake up, I say, "My God, how wonderful, I feel so young and happy and healthy today," and then all your cells are encouraged. Those little cells, they need encouragement; your heart needs encouragement; your brain needs encouragement.

I never think that something is impossible. In the UN I am the expert of impossibilities, which is great fun.

I met a lady here and she said, "Well, I was in Hawaii and I found your poem, 'Decide to Forgive.' And when I read this poem, it changed my life because I decided to forgive the people who killed my husband. And from the moment I forgave, ever since I have tried to do good in the world."

I believe that the religions have many of the answers which the political world is seeking . . . they have been here many more years than the United Nations. We should consult them. Dag Hammarskjöld and U Thant were absolutely right when they considered that world affairs needed to be inspired, guided, elevated, and ruled by a global spirituality, and that political leaders needed similarly to be guided by a personal spirituality.

—Robert Muller

THE POWER OF FORGIVENESS

That was wonderful. You see, just decide to forgive. As a matter of fact, in Kansas City now, there are people who have created a center for the study of forgiveness, to study the power you have to forgive. I would propose to them that they should give a yearly prize for forgiveness. The first person to whom I would give this prize is to Mrs. Chamoro, the Prime Minister of Nicaragua, who had the courage also to forgive the people who killed her husband. What a wonderful example this would be to the world.

How wonderful it would be that governments would come to the General Assembly and say, I ask you for forgiveness. Or others to say, I forgive you. It would be beautiful. Forgiveness has really something in it. In other words, you put it aside, and you go on a positive way, on a different way.

There is something which is magic in forgiveness, the power to heal.

POWER AFTER DEATH

I have all ready my dialogue with God, to ask him, "How are you going to use me after death? Are you going to use me to needle those heads of state and to make peace?"

Let me tell you a very recent event. It was the sad departure of my wife. She was a wonderful woman from Chile. She was a delegate to the UN. She gave up her career to beautifully raise four children. And she had Alzheimer's disease for the last four years. I found a magnificent nursing home for her in Costa Rica and two months ago, she died. Today, as a matter of fact, would be her birthday.

When she died, I cried tremendously. I was prepared by her Alzheimer's disease, but it was terrible. I had never suffered a loss like this. And looking at her, she was beautiful again after all the sufferings, I said, "What would she say to me? Would she say to me 'Be unhappy, cry'? No! She would say, 'Go on with your work. Work more than ever for peace.'"

Whenever I wanted to leave the UN, she said, "Under no circumstance. You must stay. The UN is your place." And then, when I got this message from her, I said, "This is it. I will do what she expects me to do, what she would request me to do." And I said to her, "I'm going to work more for peace than I've ever done before in all my life. I will never postpone any initiative, any action, and I am going to count them every day. I am going to write them down every day. And I am going to report them to you in writing and orally."

Every day when I go to the University for Peace, I stop at her tomb, and I have a conversation with her. I say, Margarita, this is what I did today, and yesterday. I have a whole pile. After one month, on the second of August, I counted how many peace initiatives and actions I had taken—one hundred and eleven—which I have never done before. I never postpone it. If the idea comes to me to write a letter to the Pope or to a president, or to a minister, or to someone who can do something for peace, it goes out. Why? Because I have to report it to Margarita.

PERSONAL MOTIVATION

Of course, over life you become very experienced. Also there must be some strange forces in the universe that help you when you are open. For example, I have now made another discovery with the death of my wife. It is that, since I have decided to do this, since I am open, I now have the impression that she is helping me in ways. I wake up in the middle of the night, some idea comes, and I write it down and go back to sleep.

Now, from where does the idea come? Is it from my own mind or is it in connection with something else?

I give you something which makes me almost shudder; it's almost spooky. Since I want to have a woman become Secretary General before the year 2000, I put the book of her heart in her coffin, because she was my first lady of the world.

From here in Chicago, I will go to Costa Rica, invited by the wife of the president of Costa Rica, the first lady of Costa Rica, to meet on the sixth of September with twenty-one first ladies of all of Latin America and Central America. Now where does this come from? Why would they invite me to this?

Of course, the first item I put on the agenda will be, "You have to make sure that, at long last, after fifty years, we should have a woman as Secretary General of the United Nations." I have a whole program already of what I want to discuss with them. Now it is quite possible that this was figured out by Margarita in outer space.

Today I have a new beautiful union with my wife. I am still alive, she is up there, we work together. And I am thinking now, I'm planning now, how we are going to work together when I am dead. I am not going to remain dead. I will organize this.

I am sure that when I die, if there is a God up there, he will receive me and say, "My dear Robert, you were very lucky that you planned to be of use to me, because I could not make you a spirit in the universe if you had not asked for it."

If you had not asked for it—this is the key. In other words, everything is in yourself. You have to decide, you have to ask, you have to open yourself. If you close yourself, something cannot penetrate. This is why I am open in every direction, the whole day long, seizing every occasion. And as Goethe said in a fabulous poem, once you are committed, once you are pure, once you are honest, providence moves in, and then all kinds of surprising things happen.

Providence moves in. And it helps you meet people, coincidences which you could have never thought of. Even the material help will come to you because, in total commitment, as he says, there is boldness and there is magic. And this is what I find out more at the age of seventy, that I always had the instinct of it.

But now I have almost the impression that I have the proof by what I see happened with my wife. And her death for me is not a degradation for me. Her death has elevated me. Can you imagine! And this could be a lesson. I think we should teach people how to die and to believe in afterlife.

We ought to have a help when we pass from life to death. This is a very important moment. But why not tell the people that even in the face of death you can make it something positive? This is why I know that when I am dying we're going to have another union up there.

But you can hear from me only if you are open. I am sure that this whole planet is surrounded by spirits, by saints, by our ancestors, and that they see what is happening and they almost beg you, "Why don't you ask me to help you? Because I can help you only if you ask; if you are closed I cannot penetrate."

This is why the religions are so important. I'm Catholic. And it was very strange, as a matter of fact, that my French education almost eradicated my religion, my divinity, which I believed in when I was young.

It was in the United Nations at the age of forty-seven that I was working with U Thant, a Buddhist and Secretary-General, who taught me that spirituality is a way of life from the moment you wake up until you go to bed. He was the most spiritual person I ever met in my life. And then I remembered my Catholic faith; that's exactly what the Christ has said.

I didn't become a Buddhist. There was no need, because my own faith said the same thing. So I became again a practicing Catholic because this is what Jesus said. But it was a Buddhist who reconverted me to Catholicism. And I am very happy because, without the spiritual dimension of the whole universe and the purity and the goodness and to see yourself in the stream of time as having a responsibility, the possibility to help to a better world, when you do this you are serene, you are happy, and you always know what to do. You always distinguish what is good and what is bad. But it was strange that it was a Buddhist who made me again a good spiritual person.

U Thant (1909–1974), a Burmese diplomat, was Secretary General of the United Nations from 1962 to 1972. He served as chairman of the Burmese delegation to the UN from 1947 and was appointed Burma's permanent representative to the UN in 1953. He succeeded Dag Hammarskjöld as Secretary General in 1962. In the early years of his tenure, he was deeply involved in the settlement of major international disputes, including the removal of Soviet missles from Cuba in 1962 and the achievement of a cease-fire in the 1965 India-Pakistan War.

(Columbia)

ROMAN CATHOLIC

THE HEART OF MEDITATION
BROTHER WAYNE TEASDALE

Brother Wayne Teasdale was educated at St. Anselm College, at the McAuley Institute of St. Joseph College, and at Fordham University. He did additional work at Yale, Trinity College (Hartford, Connecticut), and several monastic institutes and seminaries. While a member of Hundred Acres Monastery, a lay monastic community in New Hampshire founded by Father Paul Fitzgerald, a Trappist monk, Teasdale spent long periods in India. He was eventually initiated into Sannyasa as a Christian by Dom Bede Griffiths, an English Benedictine monk, and spiritual teacher/superior of Shantivanam Ashram in the southern Indian state of Tamil Nadu. It is as a Christian sannyasi that Brother Wayne is a monk.

In 1988, Father Thomas Keating, a great Christian spiritual master and one of Teasdale's teachers, invited him to accept election to the North American Board for East-West Dialogue, now called Monastic Interreligious Dialogue, a Roman Catholic organization representing Benedictine and Cistercian monastics of North America, and mandated by the Holy See to sustain such dialogue. Prior to that time, Brother Wayne befriended the Dalai Lama, and with him developed the Universal Declaration on Nonviolence. Brother Wayne and the Dalai Lama continue to work together on a number of projects of mutual concern.

Brother Wayne is a board member of the Parliament of the World's Religions. He has worked for several years to establish solidarity among all spiritual traditions. He regards nonviolence as an absolute organizing principle of universal civilization and a trust for which humanity is responsible to all other species.

In Brother Wayne's lectures and writing, one is made cogently aware of the inherent powers of the mystical quest. He says, "The spiritual journey is the greatest single resource we have to change the world and bring about the birth of a new civilization that possesses, and is animated by, heart."

He suggests that only such heart will be sufficient to sensitize humanity, and human behavior, to the earth itself. According to Brother Wayne, three trends characterize this sensitizing: community between and among religions, interspiritual wisdom, and the earth as a matrix of interfaith dialogue and collaboration. He believes that the religions have an enormous responsibility to facilitate this huge transformation of culture and cultivate it while disseminating the techniques and message of global responsibility.

Brother Wayne Teasdale personifies that multicultural affirmation. Soft-spoken, as at home in Rome or the United States or India, he is an outstanding example of a roving spiritual ambassador whose gentle message gathers inspiration from both East and West. When Father Bede initiated Brother Wayne, he gave this Roman Catholic from Connecticut the name of Swami Paramatmananda, meaning the Bliss of the Supreme Spirit, Self, the Atman. In Christian terms, Brother Wayne says, the translation would be something like "Joy of the Holy Spirit."

Roberto DeNobili (1577–1656) was an Italian Jesuit missionary to southern India. To further his conversion work, DeNobili adapted his missionary activity to native customs, adopting a saffron dress, wooden clogs, and a vegetarian diet of a sannyasi (Hindu holy man). In 1618, the Portuguese Grand Inquisitor tried to censure DeNobili for these adaptations, but after investigation, the Pope formally approved DeNobili's methods in the apostolic constitution Romanae Sedis Antistes in 1623. DeNobili was the first European to get firsthand knowledge of Sanskrit, the Vedas, and Vedanta (the philosophical system inspired by the Upanishads).

A SANNYASI

I'm a Catholic sannyasi. In Sanskrit it means renunciate, monk, and I'm a Catholic monk but in the Indian tradition. There have been Catholic sannyasis since Roberto DeNobeli, an Italian Jesuit, took sannyasi in the seventeenth century. That is, Christian monks who have [accommodated] their monastic life to the conditions of India. So this is a way a monk dresses in India, and I was initiated into that tradition.

I have found that if you are deeply rooted in the spiritual level, the mystical life of your tradition, and you have a spiritual practice—meditation, prayer, liturgy, periods of contemplation—you deeply appropriate your own tradition. You integrate

*Bede Griffiths (1906–
1993), an English monk,
went to India in 1955 to
assist in the foundation of
Kurisumala Ashram, a
monastery of the Syrian rite
in Kerala, in the southwest.
In 1968 he went to live in
Saccidananda Ashram, a
Christian community fol-
lowing the customs of a
Hindu ashram and adapt-
ing itself to Hindu ways of
life and thought.*

it. It becomes part of you. Then you can venture out into Hinduism, into Buddhism, into Jainism, into Sikhism, Taoism, or
the various indigenous traditions on a deep, deep level. You find
that you can relate those other traditions to the depth of your
own tradition. And what it does is, it enriches your whole understanding of your tradition.

The ultimate experience of the Christian tradition is what we
call transforming union with God. This is beyond faith, beyond
liturgy, beyond the structures of the church, where the soul is
united with God in an experience of union which is the aim of
the beatific vision, for instance. In Buddhism, Tibetan tradition,
Soto Zen in the notion of *satori,* in *fena* in Sufi tradition, in the
Kabbala in the Jewish tradition, and in various other experiences of the mystical, deepest level of unity, there is that kind of
consciousness, that kind of experience.

So, when you relate that to your own tradition, you see that
there is a similar level of mystical insight there. You see, it's like
the palm of the hand, and the five great religions are like fingers
on the hand. Father Bede would make this point. And on the
surface they are distinct, like the fingers. But then they all come
together in unity on the deepest level of reality. And that's spirituality, as opposed to religion.

Spirituality is the mystical path that is the essence of religion,
which has generated all the traditions. And religion itself is a
crystallization or an institutionalization, a hardening, an attempt to grasp the experience and to fix it. But spirituality is living, it's dynamic, you know, it's every day. It's now. We are
engaged in a spiritual experience right now.

A COMMUNITY OF RELIGIONS

I think we have to emphasize for the future this idea of the community of religions. Not a syncretism. We don't want to build a
super-religion. That's not the point. But there is such value in
the rich diversity that exists.

As the Dalai Lama has often said, we have a universal responsibility for the earth. I think that one of the ways to begin
to become conscious of it is by building this sense of community

among the religions. And that will replace the competitive relationship, the hostility, the suspicion, and the fear that leads to a kind of fundamentalist mentality in the various traditions. This mentality of fundamentalism exists in every religious tradition and every social group. At the base of it is a psychological type of mentality that is really fear and insecurity. Fundamentalism gives an intellectual—if that's not an oxymoron—security. They can exclude everyone else and they have all the answers and they have the truth.

Fanaticism is what we have to get beyond. Truth can't be owned. But fundamentalism, as a mind-set, is conducive to divisiveness, and hostility, and war, conflict among traditions.

I think we forget, in the Christian tradition, what Jesus said—not to judge and to forgive. Now there are many holy and wonderful fundamentalist people, but when it becomes fanatical, then it becomes exclusivistic, then it has the potential for violence. And, at the basis, it is a judgmental attitude which puts down every other group as wrong.

In each religion it is necessary to go back beyond its formulations, whether in scripture or tradition, to the original inspiration. All scriptures and traditions are historically conditioned; they belong to a particular age and culture and are expressed in a particular language and mode of thought. But behind this historic form of expression lies the original Mystery, the revealed Truth.

(Griffiths)

WHAT RELIGION IS ABOUT

I think in the long run it isn't about being right. The Pharisees wanted to be right and they were right up to a point.

It is about *being.* Being kind, being patient, being loving, not judging, drawing out the best in the other, seeing the presence of Christ or the divine in the other, not pigeonholing, being totally open.

Something really struck me a few years ago when a reporter for *Time* magazine asked the Dalai Lama, who was badgering him, to give him the secret of what he believed. His Holiness looked at him and smiled and started to laugh. He simply said, "My religion is kindness, my religion is kindness."

As a Christian I have to say my religion is love, my religion is compassion, my religion is kindness too. That is the essence. Kindness, love, compassion, patience, gentleness, nonviolence, inclusivity, including more, not being an elitist circle. This is the fruit of spirituality in action. So it doesn't matter what you believe. It is important but it doesn't matter in the long run. It

The Seville Statement
on Violence

*Five propositions written in
1986 by an international
team of specialists for the
United Nations-sponsored
International Year of
Peace. Based on scientific
evidence, the statement was
endorsed by scientific and
professional organizations
around the world.*
   *"It is scientifically incor-
rect to say that:*

1. *we have inherited a tendency to make war from
   our animal ancestors . . .*
2. *war or any other violent
   behavior is genetically
   programmed into our
   human nature . . .*
3. *in the course of human
   evolution there has been
   a selection for aggressive behavior more than
   for other kinds of be-
   havior . . .*
4. *humans have a violent
   brain . . .*
5. *war is caused by instinct
   or any other single motivation. . . ."*

matters what you are. And that is seen in how you treat people,
how you can be to them, and how you can look beyond simply
your own needs.

I would like to hear the fundamentalist talk more about love
and less about being right or who is right. Only God can judge
who is right and who is wrong. He knows the heart, and goes by
the heart, not by the appearances or the words. What they do in
their actions? Whatever you do to the least of my brethren—and
that is universal in every tradition.

In other words, in every tradition how you treat other people
is indicative of the degree of spiritual enlightenment you have. It
is the measure. A person can claim to have that consciousness of
knowing the ultimate mysteries of the universe, knowing God
directly, being united with God, but if that person is unloving or
unkind in his or her behavior, then I would be a little on the
skeptical side. I don't think you get there unless you pay the
price of transformation.

LEARNING TO MAKE PEACE

I think what we have to do is simply begin to conceive that a
new civilization is possible—a new global civilization that has a
basis in compassion, in kindness, in love, in a sustainable relationship with the earth. That is to say where economic development and consumer life of the people does not result in a deficit
to the planet but is in harmony with the natural rhythms of the
planet and can build up the forests and purify the water and
the air.

I hope that the Parliament of the World's Religions can articulate a vision, a direction for the planet, and we can begin to
move in that direction.

I think nonviolence is the way to teach peace and to spread
peace in the world. It means for instance to be patient with
everyone, to be present to them, to be kind, to be humble, to listen. If anyone asks you for something to help them, that you respond to them, that you have a sense of humor. You *always*
keep perspective. You see, it is hard for us to keep perspective.
In every situation we are in, we think what is going on in that
moment is so important, and we can get irritable and aggressive.

It would be in how you drive the car. Do you drive it with a sensitivity to the other drivers or are you cutting them off? Nonviolence is an attitude, and if you have it to its ultimate degree it is *ahimsa*. Ultimately *ahimsa* is love.

Ahimsa is the Jain term for nonviolence, but it's a very comprehensive term. An attitude of nonviolence means one is patient in day-to-day life, one listens to others on a deep level and responds to people's needs. Reality speaks to us often through the needs of others and the whole situation that we are in each moment.

I think the key to changing the world, making the world over and turning it into a nonviolent peaceful world, of course, will require every individual to awaken spiritually and to develop. Spirituality, automatically, if one really is transformed, will lead to that type of nonviolent, nonharming attitude.

I personally am opposed to abortion and for many, many reasons. The spiritual consequences are never talked about. I think though that in the future we must find a way to balance the rights of the mother with the rights of the unborn. There must be a way, a technology or something that would allow both realities to be protected.

What I'd like to see is a consistency about life. No death penalty, no war, a more enlightened view toward rehabilitation of criminals and things of that nature—to be consistent about the value of life.

And if you are pro-life, it also means the fifty million children in India who are on the street. You want to see them have a better life. Or the Brazilian children who are being shot, being eliminated by the government because they regard them as social parasites. We have to be consistent about our protection of life.

In terms of society, there are some things we can do. I know this may be an unpopular view with Hollywood, but I think there is a direct relationship between the violence in our society and the portrayal of violence in movies and in television. I think that Hollywood and all those people have got to be called to task, to accountability and responsibility. They are educating society to violent behavior. It's as simple as that. If you're constantly bombarding people with violent images, on a subconscious level you are teaching them violent technologies.

Sannyasin

There are four asramas ("stages") in a Hindu's life:

1. Brahmacharya, *the period of adolescence as a celibate religious student*
2. Grihasthya, *a married householder and member of the community*
3. Vanaprasthya, *literary "forest-dweller" or hermit, a householder who has discharged his duties and retired to live a solitary life of meditation*
4. Sannyasa, *one who totally renounces the world except for the minimum of clothing and a begging bowl. A sannyasa is a mendicant holy man, searching for the final liberation from all worldly attachments.*

I think the religions need to embrace together, formally, a new relationship among themselves and articulate a relationship among nations of nonviolent peaceful resolution of conflicts. We say this is the pillar of the new civilization. And we begin to think beyond the need for violence or the need for military. We can slowly change. It's going to take a long time.

It is not possible to be a spiritual leader, a religious leader, a spiritual person, if you are encouraging violent acts of any kind. There is no justification for it. It's an oxymoron to call someone a spiritual leader who is violent. I think the religions have to say that this behavior is intolerable. It is no longer acceptable. We have to set these standards. And one way is that the religions must declare their independence of governments who make war or who practice terrorism. I think if we set that standard, it will eventually have an impact, as the Magna Carta did, as the Bill of Rights has, as the Universal Declaration on the Rights of Man. All these documents have had a historical impact on the development of, say, the rights of citizens, and their relationship to their government. So I think the religions can play a very strong role in bringing that change and also articulating a whole new vision of what a new global civilization that has a *heart*, that is coming from a deeper place, is.

BECOMING SENSITIVE TO THE RIGHTS OF OTHER SPECIES

We have to come to a point to realize that to harm other life, other than to sustain your own life, is profoundly evil. I am extremely opposed to hunting and even to fishing. All life manifests the Divine. We should just take what we need and not harm the rest of creation but live in harmony with it. As Thomas Berry remarks in his book *The Dream of the Earth*, this is the earth community, the whole living being, and we're part of that. But as a species we are a failure in terms of our stewardship of this planet and our relationship to other species. We have harmed them. We have dominated them. A million species have become extinct because of us. So I think we have got to begin to become sensitive to the rights of the entire earth community, particularly the other species.

In each religion it is necessary to go back beyond its formulations, whether in scripture or tradition, to the original inspiration. All scriptures and traditions are historically conditioned; they belong to a particular age and culture and are expressed in a particular language and mode of thought. But behind this historic form of expression lies the original Mystery, the revealed Truth.

(Griffiths)

THOSE WHO NEED US ARE OUR TEACHERS

They are projecting that within ten years, half of India's population could disappear because of AIDS. And now there is a tremendous amount of AIDS in Thailand and in China. And now there are more virulent viruses, if you can imagine. It could be that the population explosion could be severely reversed by attrition from these new diseases. And I view that as partially the earth itself protecting itself from the human species.

We have so far been a failure. We have not been responsible to our place in creation that the earth itself is beginning to make adjustments. And so our duty in the face of those incredible viruses, plagues, and diseases is to be a heart of compassion. It's an opportunity for us to respond to those we know who may have this disease, or some other disease, or any illness, to respond to the vulnerability from another. Suffering is an education in compassion. Everyone we meet who needs us, in some way, they're teaching us. They're leading us.

They're the teachers. I once saw that so beautifully in Dharamsala, meeting a leper on the road, whose fingers were all gone and he was begging there. But in his eyes was the most intense serenity that I ever saw. I realized that he was a holy man. It gave me a deep sense of the mystery of life, the mystery of encounter. Like Martin Buber says, all life is meaning. All of life is in the meaning of people, in the encounter, the existential encounter of people, the exchange of spirit that goes on.

It's like Mother Teresa said, all she sees is Christ in all those people. It's all Christ. It is overwhelming, so you respond with each person that you're able to respond to in the situation, as you're able.

That's enough, I think in the long run, if everybody does it. It's like Dorothy Day, of the Catholic Worker movement, used to say, that if every American family took in a homeless person there would be no homeless. I don't think most people could do it because homeless people are often very difficult to live with. It's tough, and often there may be psychological problems. It is difficult. Only as we get to know the homeless and see the good that's in them—there's some violent ones—but I don't think there is anyone that can't be led beyond it in time.

I'm hopeful because I really think the Spirit is with us. I really do, and I've seen so many examples of holiness and love all around the world that I know there is hope.

UNITY WITH THE DIVINE

I think we need to realize that the exercise of meditation, or any spiritual discipline, is a way in which you make space psychologically for a relationship with ultimate reality, with the divine to unfold in your life. And if you do that it is going to change you, it's going to transform you. You cannot sit still if you begin to meditate.

There are thousands of ways, and each person is unique. Their needs and their history are different. So, therefore, they have to find the rhythm that will work for them. And I think, in time, that will be revealed to them through trial and error, or through a teacher, or something they just stumble on. You just come to it.

I think ultimately, for me, the essence of meditation is to become aware of how intense silence is. In the silence is a dynamic presence. And that's God, and we become attuned to that. In Tantra Yoga they say that God is a very subtle vibration, frequency. With meditation you're slowly tuning yourself to that level of vibration of the Divine. So there are more and more subtle states of consciousness. Tibetans have really explored this.

It is very interesting that we have to develop and open what the mystics call our spiritual senses. We have inner senses that are closed because we are so extroverted as a people and a culture. So we must awaken those. And those gifts, they call them the gifts of the Holy Spirit in the Christian tradition, they're implicit in the faith of any Christian but they're not aware of it. They stay on this very external level of faith.

But it's God. It's grace. And it depends on how ready you are and how attuned you are to it. If our inner senses, our spiritual senses, awaken then we become alert to another level of consciousness. God is so subtle that it takes time and a process to adjust, to be able to experience those other levels of consciousness. But I find that in the quiet it's possible to become aware of God—very deeply.

The Christian is not to become a Hindu or a Buddhist, nor a Hindu or a Buddhist to become a Christian. But each must assimilate the spirit of the others and yet preserve his individuality and grow according to his own law of growth. . . .

—Swami Vivekananda
(1863–1902)

That's what we're meant for; that's what we're made for. That's our source of being, as far as I can see. And that's love. That's pure love. And then to not just experience it as external, but as you are taken up in it like a great song that the Divine is singing. You are resilient, and you are being breathed into existence.

I experience the silence, ultimately, as a dynamic breathing. The whole universe is breathing. It's the Divine breathing. Energy is ultimately vibrations of this cosmic type of breathing, and meditation is, for me, becoming more and more attuned to the quiet so that I can be united, or realize that unity, with God. So I can live out peace. And that's the source. Then, of course, for me, as a Catholic, it's in harmony with the Eucharist. But I think when you get into mystical life, you're getting into the promise that's implicit in the Eucharist—as a state of intimacy with the Divine.

"Do not judge, and you will not be judged; do not condemn, and you will not be condemned. Forgive, and you will be forgiven; give, and it will be given to you."

(Luke 6:37–38 NRSV)

IDDHIST BRAHMA KUMARIS JEWISH
IN NATIVE AMERICAN SUFI HINDU
RISTIAN ROMAN CATHOLIC MUSLIM
KH BAHA'I JEWISH ZOROASTRIAN
MAN CATHOLIC TAOIST BUDDHIST
ROASTRIAN PROTESTANT CHRISTIAN

HINDU

NDU MUSLIM JAIN ROMAN CATHOLIC
OIST BAHA'I BUDDHIST SIKH SUFI
TIVE AMERICAN BRAHMA KUMARIS
WISH PROTESTANT CHRISTIAN TAOIST
DDHIST HINDU ZOROASTRIAN JAIN
MAN CATHOLIC BAHA'I PROTESTANT
OIST HINDU SUFI NATIVE AMERICAN
SLIM BRAHMA KUMARIS BUDDHIST
KH SUFI JEWISH MUSLIM TAOIST
ROASTRIAN CHRISTIAN BAHA'I HINDU

HINDU

LOVE

His Holiness Sri Swami Chidananda Saraswati

Swami Chidananda was born Sridhar Rao, in Mangalore, Southern India, in 1916, the first son of an Orthodox Hindu Brahmin family. Raised on stories and songs from the scriptures, he found a great early influence in the thrilling narration of tales from the puranas by Ananthayya, an old retainer in his grandparents' household in Mangalore. He read, as well, tales and teachings of modern Indian saints, such as Sri Ramakrishna, Swami Vivekananda, Ramana Maharshi, and Swami Ramdas. Educated principally in Christian schools, he developed a love for Jesus Christ and all the virtue of his teachings. Swami Chidananda attained his undergraduate degree from Loyola College in Madras in 1938.

His first acquaintance with the sage who was to become his teacher, Swami Sivananda Maharaj, was through the monthly *My Magazine*. He joined the Himalayan Ashram of Swami Sivananda, founder of the Divine Life Society, in 1943. The guru's life was one devoted to the service of others in the underlying belief of the unity of all mankind.

Swami Chidananda took up his guru's work of healing the sick as he served in the Sivananda Charitable Dispensary of the Ashram. There, regarding his service as worship, he gained a reputation for having healing hands. He inspired something of a legend when he saved the lives of both an itinerant saddhu leper and a gravely wounded dog.

Swami Chidananda believes that God's spirit infuses every atom of matter—animal, vegetable, and mineral. All living creatures,

An ashram is a place dedicated to spiritual practices, usually in a natural setting away from cities, where spiritual seekers live together and follow a specific discipline, having the common goal to reach God-consciousness.

(Crim)

Hindu Sainthood

A Hindu saint is usually a swami ("monk") who is recognized as continuing the ancient spiritual tradition begun by the great Rishis ("seers"), those who had direct experience of the divine and communicated this mystical knowledge to their immediate disciples and subsequent generations. The Rishis are the legendary spiritual founders of Hinduism.

all particles of this earth are God. He says, "To do violence to God—it is not worship, it is not religion, it is the opposite." Not surprisingly, his favorite Christian saint is St. Francis of Assisi. On December 3, 1943, in this spirit of the active practice of nonviolence, his teacher, Swami Sivananda, initiated the continuous chanting of a peace prayer. Begun in the midst of World War II, the chant continues without interruption to this day.

In addition to the dispensary, Swami Chidananda worked in all departments of the Ashram. He was General Secretary of the Divine Life Society until he was elected its president. He participated in Swami Sivananda's historic All-India tour in 1950.

Since 1959, when Swami Sivananda sent Swami Chidananda as his personal messenger to spread his teachings to the West, he has traveled extensively. Although entertained by dignitaries and received with honor, he has remained the modest ascetic whose most precious commission is the service of lovingkindness to the sick and needy, teaching through example the principle of "doing unto others" whether they might be a desperate leper, a neglected and hungry child, an aggrieved animal, or the earth itself. As God indwells all, says Swami Chidananda, "The protection of the environment is built into the various Hindu visions of this world and the universe."

Swami Chidananda is held as a living Hindu saint.

SELFLESS SERVICE

Some timeless mass of wisdom happens to be the source of our religion and that mass of wisdom is called Veda, from the root Sanskrit word *vid,* to know. We don't know the origins. These Vedas were all beyond human history. They did not exist in written form. They were only memorized: Teacher put in mind, passed to his student, teacher to student, generation after generation, passed down in this method.

When the great sage Vyafa realized ten thousand years ago that man will lose his power of memory, and therefore this living philosophy will be lost to humanity, he took upon himself the mission of putting down in writing whatever Vedic knowledge existed in four big poems, called the four Vedas. And it is a very difficult, classical Sanskrit language. So to bring the truth home to the common man in the street, he wrote eighteen big verses. They are called the layman's *Vedas,* giving all the subtle truths of vedic philosophy in ordinary conversation, dialogue, stories.

Vyafa has only two things actually to say, and that is—do good unto others, serve others selflessly, that is the noble life. And to hurt or harm others in the least bit, that is indeed ignoble and the consequences will be dire—karmic consequences will be dire. Unless your life is lived in a selfless, dedicated manner, full of love for others, cultivation of others, your prayers and deep meditation, your yoga, and other things will be fruitless. It will be going around and around in a circle. It will be a waste of time.

Life is based upon the spirit of selfless service—expecting nothing.

THE POWER TO FORGIVE: THE DIVINE PRINCIPLE

The power to forgive is inherent in all beings, because within every human individual there is a spark of divinity. That is the central spiritual discovery of all those who have entered into transcendental spiritual experiences.

The Upanishads, the ancient Vedic vision, discovered this, and proclaimed it in the verse *"Eko devaḥ sarvabhutesu gūḍhaḥ devodevah sarvabhutāntrātmā."* One divine principle is hidden in all human beings. It is all pervading, and, at the same time, it is also indwelling. This reality that resides in the heart of all beings is perfect. It is full of all divine perfections that inhere in God—infinite love, infinite forgiveness, infinite purity, infinite peace, infinite joy. All that is auspicious, blessed, and beautiful is inherent in every human individual, like a great towering tree with its spreading branches, height, fruits, foliage, and flower is inherent in a tiny little seed.

This message is the central content of the teachings of all the prophets, the messiahs, the messengers of God that have come and taught from time to time in different parts of the world. And the core of the teachings is in their living words. And this is what each religion tries to bring to its followers.

May there be peace on Earth, peace in the atmosphere and in the heavens. Peaceful be the waters and the plants. May the Divine bring us peace. May the holy prayers and invocations of peace-liturgies generate ultimate Peace and Happiness everywhere. With these meditations which resolve and dissolve harm, violence and conflicts, we render peaceful whatever on earth is terrible, sinful, cruel and violent. Let the earth become fully auspicious, let everything be beneficial to us.

(Atharva Veda, XIX–9)

THE NEGLECT OF RELIGION

Man is too much involved in the world, too much in pursuit of immediate pleasure, immediate present sensations, wanting to possess, wanting to enjoy. But he has no time for the cultivation of his inner being. Therefore anything that comes in the way of his rush, his mad crazy rush of the environment, there is a mental block, he puts it away.

It's a problem of self. Man has no time to pay attention and anything that is uncomfortable and inconvenient he does not want, even though it is ready for him out of which to enrich his life, he doesn't want it because it comes in the way of his getting immediate pleasure. So for the sake of immediate pleasure, he sacrifices his own lasting happiness and peace and that of others, also. Because it is on two dimensions—man's connection with God and man's connection with man. Love God with all the heart, love thy neighbor as thine own self.

So without selfless service, prayer and meditation is not possible. They have to become one because God is as much in you, He is as much in the Creation that He created, He permeates all creation, He indwells all creatures, even the ant and insect—everything.

Through meditation you contact this presence of God within. Through selfless service you contact, within yourself, the God who is in all.

WHAT IS PRAYER?

Prayer is a restoration. It is not necessarily asking or seeking anything. It is just, once again, abiding in God. Consciously attach yourself to God. Put off all other thought. Think, "I live, move, and have my being in God," not in some removed god somewhere far off, not some hidden god—the now, here, God. Think, "I abide in him. I am in Him, He is in me, we are never apart." And come to that state and abide. That is prayer.

Unasked questions are answered. Before you pick a problem which is vexing you, solution comes. And it goes on happening from early morning till late night. Every day. If you only feel that, this is what God is for you.

Hinduism in the World

- *In 1989 there were approximately 870 million Hindus worldwide.*
- *95 percent of all Hindus worldwide live in India.*
- *80 percent of India's population is Hindu.*
- *In 1989 there were approximately twenty organized Hindu churches in the United States, combining the Vedanta Society and the International Sivananda Yoga Vedanta Centers.*

WHEN WE MEET A STREET BEGGAR

Let each one put oneself into the other person's place. If you were that person, what would you want someone else to do for you, just walk past? Or just throw a dime and go? Or something else? Put yourself in the other person's place and then whatever you feel would have been your wish, do that. Then your question will be answered. Then they will do the right thing.

COMPROMISE AND PROSPER

In this world, when you have dependents and you have to support people, if the work is not 100 percent honest, maybe you are compelled to compromise to some extent. But if it is either criminal or immoral, the decision is there. You have to try to change and go to some other work. You cannot save your conscience. And if you do that, if you have the courage, leave. If it is immoral or if it is criminal, you should have the courage to do it—some work will be waiting for you. God will provide. This law is unerring. If it is something that's not quite decent, a little bit of compromise is inevitable in ordinary life.

You compromise and pray at the same time. That is, 20 percent maybe, but if it goes beyond a certain limit, no compromise.

Place your devotion wholeheartedly at the service of the ideal most natural to your being, but know with unwavering certainty that all spiritual ideals are expressions of the same Supreme Presence. Do not allow the slightest trace of malice to enter your mind toward any manifestation of God or toward any practitioner who attempts to live in harmony with that Divine Manifestation. Kali, Krishna, Buddha, Christ, Allah—these are all full expressions of the same indivisible Consciousness and Bliss. . . . Blessed is the soul who has known that all is one, that all jackals howl essentially alike.

—Ramakrishna (1836–1886)

MAKING MORAL CHOICES

Are we to exercise birth control or are we not? You see this is a much discussed topic over the past sixty, seventy years. These questions were put to Gandhi, also. He says, marriage is part and parcel of a normal human life.

In the first stage of life, as student, you have to control yourself, keep yourself in full possession of chastity. Give all your time, attention, energy in study, building of good health, character.

Then, in the second stage, you marry, have a partner, be a father and be a mother and have a family. Contribute some ideal children to the next generation. That is your contribution

Hindu Scriptures

*Written in Sanskrit, the an-
cient language of India,
Hindu scriptures are di-
vided into Shruti (revealed
scriptures) and Smriti (traditional scriptures). The
Shruti is made up of the
four Vedas ("knowledge"):*

***Rig Veda**—Royal songs
praising gods*

***Sama Veda**—Hymns with
instructions for chanting*

***Yajur Veda**—Hymns with
instructions for sacrifices*

***Atharva Veda**—Collections
of sayings*

to society. Bring them up well. Feed them. Make them healthy,
good children, and that is your contribution for the perpetuation of the species. That is why the very principle of sex was put
by the powers that be in all creation. If the power of sex, the
power of reproduction had not been put the world, man would
come to an extinction.

The very need for putting this sacred power, this holy power
of being able to reproduce, procreate is brought about by the
phenomena of death. When God created, God did not create the
physical immortality of man. Children are imperative, otherwise
within one generation humanity that has been created by God
will become extinct.

Therefore we must have children, but how many is too
many is something it depends for you to decide. Some say two
is enough, three is too many. But then, the way of limiting or
restricting should be through a mutually agreed upon self-control
and not any artificial means that may even remotely tend to
violence toward life. It should be something that prevents the
conception of children. It can only be done through a mutually
agreed upon act of self-control on the part of both partners.
And unless that harmony and mutual cooperation between
partners is there it is—ah—not possible. Therefore great emphasis is laid upon living your life in such a way that such a
self-control becomes possible. The ideal of self-control is not
impossible.

Fall in love with parenthood. When you are only thinking of
yourself as a husband, you are only thinking of yourself as a
wife, as man and woman, then the entire emphasis is upon trying to get maximum enjoyment of this relationship. After you
have been man and woman, you have one child, you have two
children, you have three children. Afterward say, "Look here.
They have been the joy of our life. Now let us make ourselves
the joy of their life. Now our relationship should be of mother
and father, parent looking after these children to see that we
make them a happy home—make them happy."

So if psychologically one can start seeing oneself not as two
individuals related by sex of man and woman, husband and
wife, they start now thinking of themselves as parents of these
children.

ENVIRONMENTAL CHOICES

Every religion has something to say about [God within man] in its own way. Islamic religion says, "The light of Allah is in man." The Quaker says, "That of God is in man." The Bible says, "God created Adam and breathed his spirit into him." Christianity says, "The kingdom of God is within, the kingdom of heaven is within." Hinduism says, "God is the indwelling reality in man," in the Bhagavadgita.

So about man, everything is clear. But what about the world, this universe? God is that spirit, that reality which vibrates in every atom of matter, which is present in every speck of space.

To kill a species, in a certain sense, is to do violence to God. It is not worship, it is not religion, it is opposite. Swami Ji [Sivananda] said, "He is that Being who sleeps and slumbers in the stone, in the mill. He breathes and respires in plants. He moves in insect, beast and animals, and He thinks, feels, and reasons in man."

So He is not only in man, He is also in the stone and the miller, but in different degrees of expression. But the presence is there. The entire universe is pervaded with the presence of God. The first evidence they gave to this experience was in the very first Upanishad, the very first word, the very first line. They said this entire universe is pervaded by the presence of divinity. Whatsoever is in this universe, it is pervaded by the presence of divinity; therefore the entire vision of life is everything, is sacred.

Everything is sacred. Therefore, the devout Hindu, when he wakes up from bed, before he stands up, he says, "O my God, thou who are created in the ocean waters, thou whose breast is mountains, forgive me because at this moment I'm about to step my feet upon you."

From this prayer, man gets up and starts walking upon earth. Sanctity of all nature, everything here around us is recognized. Tread even upon grass with reverence, with respect. Do not walk just inconsiderately and roughly, tread gently.

Everything in our environment, water, air, fire, sky, plants, all—everything's sacred. So the ancient Aruvedic physicians, before they went to cut an herb for their patient, they asked permission of the plant. "Forgive me cutting out this plant,

Each Veda is divided into four sections:

Samhitas—*Priestly commentaries*
Brahmanas—*Priestly writings*
Aranyaka—*"Forest stories," teachings for those living outside of society*
Upanishads—*Important teachings*

The Smriti, passed down through generations orally, is divided into three sections:

Laws of Manu—*A book of ethical guidelines*
Epics—*Including the Mahabharata, the great story of ancient India*
Bhagavad Gita—*A poem about Lord Krishna*

uprooting the plant." And therefore the protection of the environment is inbuilt into the various Hindu visions of this world and the universe.

In whatever way and path, humans worship Me, in that same path do I (meet) and fulfill their aspirations and grace them. It is always My Path that humans follow in all their different paths and journeys, on all sides.

(Bhagavad Gita IV:11)

TEACHING OTHERS

I do nothing unless they ask me a question. If they seek guidance, then I tell them, "Look here, whatever you are doing, please pause and think for a while. Where were you?"

I ask him his age usually. He says, "I am thirty-seven."

I ask him, "Where were you thirty-nine years ago?"

"Huh, hum? I, I don't know."

I say, "No, you know."

"What do you mean?"

"You know that you were not here. You did not have a body. You did not have a name. You did not have a human identity, you were not in this human world at all. This much at least you know." And I tell him, "Another eighty, ninety years afterward, where will you be?"

He's a little surprised. He never thought about this. Then he says, "I won't be here."

"Well, sir, that state in which you were, before you came into this state and became a human actor on the stage of the world in this drama called life, and that state which once again you are to attain the moment you quit this body house, is that more continuous and real or [is] this temporary state in which you are?"

"Oh, I never thought that way."

And look here, this is a temporary little journey. All the world is a stage, you come and play your part and afterward are done and go out. But you are only here for a little while.

So I begin to make them take a look at their entire life in a different way. That opens some dimension of thought for them. They start thinking, "Yes, yes, I never thought about it before."

FULL CIRCLE TO SELFLESS SERVICE

The service starts with our own family unit. Then you begin to feel that what I am feeling, what gives me joy, what gives me sorrow should be the same in all beings. Therefore, just as I will do these acts of kindness to make my children happy, why don't I get some Christmas presents and meet someone else who won't have very good odds of doing it? Identify some homes where you feel that they may not have the same ability.

If you have three children, get Christmas presents for five children, make your three children happy and make some poorer children happy in some other family.

Expanding circles. Charity begins at home, they say. Make it not stay within the four walls of the home. Make gradually your neighborhood your home. Then your community your home. Then make your city your home. Then begin to feel that the world is my home, humanity is my family, and I will try to do anything that I can for anyone, known or unknown, near or far.

I think this is the expansion of consciousness which is the essence of part of the evolution of the spirit of service. And I do this because I feel kinship with the entire global human family. But I also know—I have been told—within everyone dwells that Being who is our common parent, from whom we all have our being. Therefore every human being, every human individual, is a living temple of the living God within.

So I help my brother man, and, in that, I also am able to worship Him who is enshrined in this body temple in the heart shrine.

As Swami Chidananda recites Christian scripture to make his point, the interviewer joins in, "Whatsoever you do to the least of these, believe that thou has done unto me."

That is the spiritual heart of selfless service.

Let us be united;
Let us speak in harmony;
Let our minds apprehend alike.
Common be our prayer;
Common be the end of our assembly;
Common be our resolution;
Common be our deliberations.
Alike be our feelings;
Unified be our hearts;
Common be our intentions;
Perfect be our unity.

(Rig Veda in *Earth Prayers*)

JAIN

JAIN

PEACEMAKER

His Holiness Acharya Sushil Kumar Ji Maharaj (June 15, 1926–April 22, 1994)

It was late afternoon on a hot and humid New Delhi spring day. At his ashram, His Holiness Sushil Kumar sat on his bed in a lotus position, repeating mantras. He was found sometime later, lying comfortably against a pillow. He had passed away. Three nights later, his mortal remains were consigned to flames. A motorcade meandered through the narrow lanes of the walled city of Delhi. Around the world, millions of followers mourned. In truth, the Jains were not mourning, but paying homage. For in Jainism, there is no beginning and no end.

Sushil Kumar (known as Guruji by his devotees) was an enlightened master who embraced nonviolence even as a child when confronted firsthand with Hindu-Muslim fighting in India. Later, he established a universal brotherhood among the conflicting religious traditions of India. In 1986, when politicians were attempting to solve the crisis in the Punjab, it was Guruji who accomplished reconciliation between the opposing groups. He did the same between Muslims and Hindus in 1991. And when Pope John Paul's proposed visit to India was opposed by various factions, again Kumar inspired moderation and tolerance from all involved.

Esteemed by presidents and prime ministers throughout the world, Sushil Kumar was one of the first Jain monks to take his message outside India. He began an ashram in New Jersey and was deeply involved in countless projects of significance—global conferences, alliances of faith and spirituality. When he died, he was setting the groundwork for a university of nonviolence in Manhattan, a nongovernmental organization recognized by the United Nations.

Founder of the World Fellowship of Religions, of the Jain Studies Program at Columbia University, of the Mahavir Jain Mission, and of the World Jain Congress, he was director of the Temple of Understanding, a founding member of the Global Forum of Spiritual and Parliamentary Leaders on Human Survival, president of the Punjab Peace and Unity Committee, and a founding member of the Vishwa Hindu Parishad.

For much of his life, he wore a mask (*mulpatti*) consistent with his Jain tradition, to protect insects. He organized animal rights rallies, discussed world peace with Mikhail Gorbachev in Moscow and Kyoto, and with environmentalists at the Rio Summit. He met with Saddam Hussein in an attempt to help him find some way out of the Gulf Crisis. When terrorist bombings and riots killed more than 1,200 people in Bombay, Guruji walked from district to district preaching peace. And he convened a World Religions Conference with more than 1,200 representatives from twenty-seven countries. Five hundred thousand people attended.

For fifty years he lived as an ascetic, convinced that *ahimsa*—nonviolence—and universal love could prevail. He was, himself, a follower of Mahavira (599–527 B.C.), the twenty-fourth Tirthankara or sage of Jainism, an elder of Buddha. In fact, it is believed that Buddha studied under Mahavira for several years. Mahavira emphasized the interdependency of all beings and asserted that every organism has a soul that must be cherished and allowed to evolve in its own free manner.

Toward this goal, Sushil Kumar devoted his all-too-brief life. He had great wit, sparkling eyes, flowing hair, a boyish grin, and a charismatic manner that was selfless. One felt good in his presence. Many will miss him. The material in this chapter is taken from one of his last recorded interviews.

"Traditionally when we are talking, or giving answer—any ceremony—when we start we are chanting a little bit." Sushil Kumar began with these words and then chanted.

Ahimsa

*Know other creatures' love
    for life, for they are
    alike ye.
Kill them not; save their life
    from fear and enmity.
All creatures desire to live,
    not to die.
Hence to kill is to sin.
A godly man does not kill.
Therefore, kill not thy self,
    consciously or uncon-
    sciously,
living organisms which
    move or move not,
nor cause slaughter of
    them.
He who looketh on the
    creatures of the earth,
    big and small,
as his own self, comprehen-
    deth this immense
    world.
Among the careless, he
    who restraineth self is
    enlightened.*

—Lord Mahavira,
    (599–527 B.C.E.)
    Jaina Sutras

THE PAÑCA-NAMASKĀRA MANTRA

You know the whole world is based on creation, preservation, destruction. Nature is based on the three things: endowed with production of a new state; destruction of an old state; and something remains constant.

This is what lord Mahavira told: I saw this universe, the whole universe based on the three principles: something is taking on, giving birth; something is going to die and finished; and one thing is the middle. That is the eternal, imperishable. The *Namaskāra Mantra* (*litany: salutation to five holy beings*): namo arihantanam, namo siddhanam, namo ayariyanam, namo uvajjhayanam, namo loe sarva sahunam. [Editor's Note: literally, obeisance to the Arihantas—perfect souls—Godmen; obeisance to the Siddhas—liberated bodiless souls; obeisance to the masters—heads of congregations; obeisance to the teachers—ascetic teachers; obeisance to all the ascetic aspirants in the universe.]

EVERY LIVING BEING IS GOD

If a drop is not ocean, then how is it possible that we can understand the ocean is drop? Drop and ocean is not big difference. If you know one, you know all. You know all, you know one. One and all is the same thing. The ocean is a bigger drop.

Soul is God. Self is perfected soul. Your own self can become perfected soul. If you want to see and realize God, everywhere is God. Any living being has God but covered or uncovered. That is a difference.

When you have this kind of hunger to know, how we can see—who is asking this question? This is God.

What Lord Mahavira is suggesting is if you are killing any living being, then you are not killing any living being, you are killing yourself.

Without tree we can't survive. Without us, they can't. And this is the principle of this whole universe.

This way he told the way of nonviolence. Meaning to feel oneness with all living beings.

Jain Monasticism

The vows required of monks and nuns resemble those of India's ascetic movements in general: truthfulness, not taking anything not given, renunciations of possessions, celibacy, and noninjury—with the last vow of noninjury (ahimsa) becoming a hallmark of Jainism. The Jain ascetic is obliged to take extraordinary pains to avoid injuring any living being. As a teenager, Guruji entered the sacred order of Jain Munis, receiving from his guru two traditional symbols of nonviolence: the mukhpatti, a white mask worn over the face to keep the wearer from accidently uttering harsh words or swallowing an insect [and thus killing a living soul], and a pinchi, a broom for sweeping surfaces before sitting lest a living entity be harmed.

(Tobias, *Life Force*)

Jainism and Ecology

The ancient Jain scriptural aphorism Parasparopa-graho jivanam *(all life is bound together by mutual support and interdependence) is refreshingly contemporary in its premise and perspective. It defines the scope of modern ecology while extending further to a more spacious "home." It means that all aspects of nature belong together and are bound in a physical as well as a metaphysical relationship. Life is viewed as a gift of togetherness, accommodation and assistance in a universe teeming with interdependent constituents.*

—Singhvi

In India, two or three years ago, one person got an export license to export the legs of frogs. And he killed maybe two hundred thousand frogs or more. What happened? After one year, the whole population of village—finished. Why? Died. Killed by mosquitoes. Mosquitoes are biting. Then there was so much fever and all died.

When the whole population died, then scientists came. They found when the frogs were eating mosquitoes, the whole population was perfect. But people killed frogs, then the mosquitoes killed the populace.

JAINS AS OUR FIRST ECOLOGISTS

First and end. It's the same thing. One year ago I was in Rio de Janeiro. There was biggest, largest worldwide conference—maybe 159 countries had sent prime ministers and foreign ministers, or what they have. The president of Argentina was stating that we lost, already, 140 species.

And, when I was presiding in a secular summit, I asked, how many species there are?

He said, "I do not know, but you know?"

I said, "Yes. Eighty-four hundred thousand kind of species are existing."

And I gave all the accounts. Two senses, three senses, four senses, five senses—and what kind of animal, what kind of trees and vegetables, or the one million different kind of trees. And then the fungus, fourteen-hundred thousand kinds. [Editor's Note: Jainism recognizes that all organisms have from one to five senses depending upon their state of neurological–spiritual evolution.]

When I gave complete account, eighty-four hundred thousand, he said "This is beautiful. How do you know these things?"

I told him, "That is our religion." Morning and evening, that is our religion. Morning and evening we are doing and we are talking, "Oh, my living being, if I hurt, if I killed, if I smashed you, give me forgiveness. I like to grant forgiveness to all, but please, give me, grant me forgiveness. I have no space for animosity, but I have only in my mind, friendship. And a universal friendship I am going to start. I am your friend."

Mahavira's challenge: If you have no oneness with all living beings, if you are killing trees, living beings, we are killing ourselves.

MINIMIZE VIOLENCE

Mahavira is telling if you are cutting tree and making coal, and selling, you are bringing so much sin. Don't destroy the beauty of the ocean and mountains, don't destroy this ark. Don't destroy any living thing.

But it is not possible in this life that we can become totally nonviolent. The main principle is maximum nonviolence, minimum violence. You can minimize violence. That is your work.

If you are a householder or if you are monk there is a difference. You are a renunciate, you give up every kind of rights. We are ready to protect the rights of the others. We are not demanding any rights for ourselves. That is the system of nonviolence. We are not ready to form rights, we are ready to ask you our duties.

According to our system, we can't ask for rights. Don't fight and don't make any slogan for rights. Give up your rights. If you protect rights of others, automatically they will protect your rights.

PEACE IS NOT POSSIBLE THROUGH POLITICS

The United Nations is a beautiful, wonderful idea. But for fifty years they are doing the big efforts to bring peace, but by politics. It is not possible. Politicians, or politics, can't bring peace on this earth. You know why?

What is the system, one person comes representing India, or Germany, or any country? He is representing his own government, and they have election. By election one party got success. They selected one person to go. And he is not representing India, he's representing the party and he's representing the

A Jain (Universal) Prayer for Peace

*Lead me from Death to
    Life,
from Falsehood to Truth.
Lead me from Despair to
    Hope,
from Fear to Trust.
Lead me from Hate to
    Love,
from War to Peace.
Let Peace fill our Heart,
our World, Our Universe.*

—Satish Kumar

prime minister or he's the head of the party. How is it possible they can bring peace?

I was selected as a spokesman for a meeting at the UN in 1981, a meeting on peace. I said, "You like to bring peace by politics. And politicians can misuse the power any time. But we are bringing peace through nonviolence. When you bring peace through nonviolence, that time nobody can misuse." Nonviolence means you give up your rights.

A Jain Prayer

May my mind remain always steady and firm, unswerving and unshaken; may it become stronger every day. May I bear and endure with patience the deprivation of dear ones and occurrences of undesired evils.

May universal love pervade the world and may ignorance of attachment remain far away. May nobody speak unkind, bitter and harsh words!

May disease and pestilence never spread, may the people live in peace, may the highest religion of ahimsa (noninjury) pervade the whole world and may it bring about universal good! Amen.

The main thing is that, if you are fighting for your own rights, you are bringing one fighting in place of another. You are adding violence and war.

Be ready. The nonviolent, we have to prepare. Then we have to sacrifice our life to protect all the other life. That you can teach to the people. People can learn. This principle I use so many places. In Punjab, in Kashmir, everywhere.

First I went to the Sikh Golden Temple in Amratsar. Rajiv Gandhi was prime minister and on very good terms with me, and he requested I come.

Everybody was so fearful. So many people had fled Punjab. Nobody could walk without help of police. I went and first, my request was, you remove the police from the area, from Golden Temple. I do not want any police.

All terrorist leaders were there, all the heads of the Sikhs were there. Six days I was talking. So many hours. And they felt so much love. I was thinking, we are responsible for terrorism. We are monks, what is our duty? Religious leaders, religious teachers, what is their duty? They have to teach nonviolence, service for the other. They accepted.

No conditions. Everybody was ready. I was working, I was talking with them. They accepted my proposal. But unluckily the government was very doubtful.

WILL GANDHI'S WAY PREVAIL?

Basically, principally, he was Jain. His mother was Jain, his family spiritual teacher was a Jain monk. Mahatma Gandhi wrote that "I have so much influence of Tolstoy, Ruskin, but ultimately, I was so much impressed from Sri Raychandbhai

Mehta, a Jain householder. He was a jeweler, and he was a great person of wisdom. He really was interested in everything."

I went, a few months ago, to his birthplace, Porbandor (western India). I was four days there, and I was looking and studying how Mahatma Gandhi got the nonviolence principle, how he was thinking, why his mother was worried about sending him to London or a foreign country. But, ultimately, he became a complete follower of nonviolence. And he was thinking, I can leave my body, my life, but I can't leave the principle of nonviolence. Nonviolence is my life and hope. And I have so much hope for India.

JAINISM ABROAD

Every time, when you do the new things, revolutionary things, well, people will oppose. People have a habit to follow the traditional system. When you start a new path, new system, they will oppose, for good or bad. Why people were opposing to Lord Christ. He was a great man. I love him, and I like him, and I respect him. But why people were opposing him?

Mahatma Gandhi got so much opposition. I am very small in this respect. But I got the same small, proportionally, opposition from the people in India when I came to the United States.

I discuss with them, "Do you love me?"

"Yes."

"Do you love nonviolence system?"

"Yes."

"Then why you want to monopolize about the nonviolence principle in India? Why are you keeping it here?"

I did all work in India I could do. Lord Mahavira taught only that mankind is one. There's not any difference. Like a cow, there are so many colored cows you can find but there is no real difference in milk. Milk is the same.

We have some old scripture, the scripture describing that, before so many monks were going outside, Alexander the Great and some, maybe naked, monks, they went to Greece. And so many monks went to Egypt, one thousand years ago. They traveled in Moscow, in other countries, doing so much work. And

Jains in the United States

Since 1965, along with Hindus and Sikhs, Jains began to immigrate to the United States, though due to certain restrictions on travel (to avoid harming organisms, as with jet engines), not in numbers as great as members of other Indian religious groups. Among the immigrants were individuals associated with the International Mahavir Mission, founded in India in 1970 by Guruji Muni Sushil Kumar. The Mission was brought to Europe and North America by its members. Today there are more than 50,000 Jains in the United States.

(Melton, *Creeds*)

even Lord Mahavira, and all the acharyas, they were traveling by boat. They were crossing the rivers. What's the difference—you cross the ocean or rivers, the same thing?

ON HUMAN RIGHTS AND RIGHTS FOR ALL LIVING BEINGS

Vegetarianism is a basic way of life for a Jain, taking its origin from the concept of compassion toward living creatures (anukampa) and nonviolence (ahimsa). The practice of vegetarianism is regarded as a potent instrument for the practice of nonviolence and peaceful, cooperative coexistence.

(Tobias, Naked Man)

I was in Australia at a World Conference of Religions for Peace. After three or four days of the conference, many representatives realized that I had not taken much food. We were every day eating roasted chickpeas and a special kind of vegetarian root and milk or tea or something like that.

You know what happened? They completely changed the menu and eating time. After sunset Jain monks are not taking anything. I was sitting down, so they told me to go up, I could take the food.

I said, "No, this food is not good for me."

And they said, "Oh, there's no meat, completely vegetarian food. Muni Ji, you're right, we have to change our habits. When we are thinking about human rights, we were not thinking about animal rights."

Yes, that time they started to think.

Today people are very aware, and you look at the situation and see how people are crazy for vegetarianism. And they are thinking meat is not good for health, for our bodies. Unknown diseases are entering in human bodies. I read an article by a doctor in Denmark, who was a doctor in a butcher house. He was testing animals. What he said was in his whole life of testing animals, 33 percent of the animals had tuberculosis, and 33 percent had cancer and different kinds of unknown diseases.

And the same thing with the poultry farms. If you could see them. Oh, so bad, bad smell, bad treatment.

Basically our good friends are the trees and the vegetables. By vegetables you can become more healthy.

Today or tomorrow, people will think oneness with all. *Ahimsa* is coming. Nonviolence is coming. The name of health, the name of prosperity, the name of economics or ecology, but anyway you have to think without trees, without animals, we can't survive. We can't exist. Nature has power to maintain the balance. But what we are doing—we are destroying the balance of nature also and bringing disaster very soon. And we are afraid, what man is doing to this world.

THE FUTURE

If tomorrow will come, then it will come with nonviolence. Without nonviolence, there will be no future of this world. But nonviolence according to Jains, when we are talking about nonviolence, it is not only the no violence, no violation of nature, our body, our . . . no, no. Nonviolence means we love all. You feel oneness with all living beings. Love.

When somebody asked this question to Mahavira, "What is the definition of nonviolence?" he said, "*Parasparopagraho ji-vanam.*" All beings are interdependent. This is the first principle of *ahimsa*.

JAIN

NONVIOLENCE
Dr. L. M. Singhvi

A born Jain, Dr. L. M. Singhvi is an eminent jurist, leading constitutional expert, distinguished parliamentarian, well-known human rights exponent, doyen of the Indian Bar, and author, poet, linguist, and man of the world. Living presently in London, he is India's High Commissioner to England, one of the most important political posts in India. Dr. Singhvi has been a leading Senior Advocate of the Supreme Court of India as well as the president of the Supreme Court Bar Association. Educated in India, and with degrees as well from Harvard and Cornell, Dr. Singhvi has received honorary law degrees from numerous other universities in England and India. He received the Inter-Faith Gold Medallion from the International Council of Christians and Jews; was appointed as a president of the Council to the Parliament of the World's Religions; and in 1987 he was elected as Honorary Bencher and Master, The Middle Temple (U.K.), one of the highest honors in England for a judge and lawyer.

As a life member of the Commonwealth Parliamentary Association, and chairman of numerous legal reform services and commissions, such as the Institute of Sociology and Communication, and the Centre for the Study of Law and Society, Dr. Singhvi's energies and convictions are inspirational. He is, for example, the past chairman of the Indian National Federation of UNESCO, the founder-chairman of the Dishantar theatre movement, founder of the Prabha Institute of Fine Arts, Culture, and Handicrafts for the Handicapped, former chairman of the National School of Drama, and a trustee and/or chairman of other schools and prestigious award committees.

It is Dr. Singhvi's ethical humanism, in keeping with his Jain principles, that one might cite as most characteristic of this truly renaissance individual, and the basis of his being awarded the Jain Ratna in 1988. In fact, he is one of only three persons to have ever been given this highest of commendations among the Jains.

Dr. Singhvi chaired the Plenary session of the World Hindi Conference on Literature and Human Values, and was founder and president of the Temple of Understanding in India. His literary interests include his having chaired the Veda Pratishthan, which has published fourteen volumes (out of the projected twenty-four) of Vedas in English translation, and his having been the former president of the Authors Guild of India. His own poetry, in Hindi, has been published in India.

A citizen of the world and leading exponent of rationality and empathy, Dr. Singhvi's international efforts have been noteworthy. He is an elected member of the UN Sub-Commission on Human Rights and the Chairman of the UN Human Rights Working Group on Accession of Member States of the UN to International Covenants and other human rights instruments. For eight years he was the UN Special Rapporteur (ECOSOC) on the Impartiality and Independence of the Judiciary, Jurors, and Assessors. He has chaired working groups on the prevention of crime and chaired the Asian Seminar on Asian Approaches to Human Rights organized by the UN University and UNESCO. Dr. Singhvi received worldwide acclaim for his Report on the Independence of Justice and his Draft Universal Declaration on The Independence of Justice in the UN Human Rights Sub-Commission in 1987. As Chancellor of Gandhi Vidya Mandir, a rural post-graduate Institute with extension education and social self-help services for the disadvantaged, Dr. Singhvi has been able to help put his human rights insights to work in dozens of villages.

In 1991 he was elected president of the World Congress on Human Rights. Many of his legal and social justice views and insights were published in his recent book, *Freedom on Trial*. In addition, he has been a co-author and editor of many

Ahimsa

For [Jains], ahimsa is the most important credo, encompassing one's behavior as well as intentions. One is forever duty-bound to avoid causing harm; to minimize all forms of violence; to stringently renounce cruelty.

(Tobias, Life Force)

Lord Mahavira (599–527 B.C.E.) was born in north-eastern India, near the modern town of Basukunda in the State of Bihar, and lived at nearly the same time and in much the same area as Siddhartha Gautama, later known as the Buddha. Born into a warrior clan, Mahavira was convinced at age thirty of a need to seek enlightenment and release from worldly existence. He then abandoned his household life and went out into the forest alone. Mahavira's ascetic program lasted for twelve-and-a-half years, and was single-mindedly directed toward detachment from physical existence. At age forty-two he achieved enlightenment and began teaching others and eventually collected a distinctive group of followers.

(Tobias, *Life Force*)

monographs, literary essays, research papers, and about sixty diverse titles. Most recently, he authored the Jain "Declaration on Nature," which was presented to Prince Philip at Buckingham Palace on behalf of all the millions of Jains throughout the world.

Whether speaking of civil rights, ecology, ancient or modern literature, drama, or international jurisprudence, Dr. Singhvi is unflinching in his concern for maintaining human dignity and equality in the face of conflict. As a Jain, and as a human being, Singhvi's views on tolerance, legal fairness, and the respect for all people has given a compelling tenor of enlightened secularism to his diverse body of work.

THE BASIS OF JAINISM

Ahimsa is a very ample concept which applies to all aspects of life. First of all it is nonviolence in words, deeds, and thoughts.

You must not torment anyone. You must not oppress anyone. You may not even insult anyone for that is a form of violence. You must observe restraint. You must not waste the resources of the universe. That is, waste is a form of violence.

There is definitely a hierarchy of life. In fact, the Jains engaged in one of the most scientific and elaborate classifications of life forms, levels of consciousness, and it is very well described in the Jain code of conduct.

Jains declare that the greatest religion, the greatest creeds, the greatest commitment of man on earth is nonviolence. And of course, a more practical interpretation of this, the minimum of violence.

In the Jain perspective, which is a perspective of realism, you must not ignore the reality of life. You must bring to bear upon it your precepts, your perspectives, your politics. And that is why Jainism is important and relevant and valid today, even more than in days of lesser violence in the world in which it was developed.

It is a very ancient tradition. Jainism goes back to many thousands of years ago. Lord Mahavira was only the last of the twenty-four tirthankaras. Now that was in the sixth century.

RELATIVE NONVIOLENCE AND RESTRAINT

Nonviolence is a very vital contribution to civilization. And from the treasure chest of the Jain tradition and philosophy you find unfolded the story of civilization. The first tirthankara, for instance, established agriculture.

It is true that some violence is involved even in agriculture. When you are growing plants, plowing in the fields, some forms of life are taken, but this is relative nonviolence.

This is important because what is unique about the Jain tradition and the Vedic tradition and the Buddhist tradition is that they empathize with all forms of consciousness, all levels of life. It's not just human beings. You have a particular shape and form, you are bipeds. But that does not mean that quadrupeds do not have life. That does not mean that they do not have an awareness of pain and happiness.

Modern science now tells us that plants have life, but thousands of years ago Jains developed a concept of life in which they clearly identified that plants have life. Now there is a lesser level of life. There is a lesser dimension of life. But you have to practice relative nonviolence.

I think this is what demonstrates the pragmatism of Jainism. Monks are expected to practice a higher, a more severe form of austerity. On the other hand the mandates that must be observed by the householder are relatively less severe, less exact. That is to make sure that the householder is able to engage in pursuits that are necessary. Jains are to live normal lives. They have families, they have children. They create wealth. They produce books; they enjoy the arts. They have their own aesthetic structure. So it is not a denial of life, it is restraint.

One practice of restraint is vegetarianism. This is relative nonviolence. You are not eating the forms of life which have five senses. You are not eating the forms of life which have four senses. We're eating plants, we're eating vegetables. And vegetables, too, have life. This is in full consciousness of the fact that this is what we call "relative nonviolence." When you are eating vegetables, they too have a certain sense perception, but that is a lower stratum of life, and with that lower stratum of life you have to make these compromises. Even when you breathe, for

There is nothing so small and subtle as the atom nor any element so vast as space. Similarly, there is no quality of soul more subtle than nonviolence and no virtue of spirit greater than reverence for life.

One who neglects or disregards the existence of earth, air, fire, water and vegetation disregards his own existence which is entwined with them.

—Lord Mahavira

instance, you are putting an end to millions of lives in these very fine particles of life.

Even that is violence, but that is a violence which is a necessary part of one's living. That is why I say that one has to practice the maximum of restraint.

For instance, in dealing with politics, you must practice truth and honesty because dishonesty and falsehood is a form of violence. And this is how you apply the whole science and philosophy of nonviolence to situations of life and come to your conclusions with regard to what is the maximum restraint you can practice. This maximum restraint is what ennobles you and ennobles society. It shows your consideration for the world.

Take for instance the five principles that are the Jain code of conduct. The first is nonviolence in thought, word, and deed; the second, to seek and speak the truth; the third, to behave honestly and never take anything by force or theft; the fourth, to practice restraint and chastity in thought, word, and deed; and then, the fifth, to practice nonacquisitiveness, that is to say, you do not accumulate wealth beyond a reasonable limit. Now these are all principles which have to be practiced in a relative context. You can't possibly say, "Well, I'll acquire nothing."

The Jains, in fact, are a very wealthy community, and they do tend to acquire a great deal. How do they balance it? They balance it by making vary large donations with charitable purposes. They give their time to the society, to the community. These are the principles on which you build up a nonviolent form of life. You try to see that there is the maximum of restraint in your life. It doesn't mean that you deny yourself what life offers.

It means that one aspires to be more civilized than one would be if one did not have the awareness of the code of conduct of nonviolence. But it becomes easy for me, born as I was in the country of Mahatma Gandhi. Mahatma Gandhi put nonviolence in the perspective of life, in all its ramifications, in all its applications. Nonviolence is a sort of talisman that he gave to the world.

And he said, here is a principle which you must apply in the forum of your conscience, in that forum of conscience you must make a decision whether it serves the cause of truth and nonviolence. Because, as Mahatma Gandhi said, "Truth and nonviolence are only two sides of the same coin."

Gandhi and Jainism

In the twentieth century, the most vibrant and illustrious example of Jain influence was that of Mahatma Gandhi (1869–1948), acclaimed Father of the [Indian] Nation. The central Jain teaching of ahimsa (nonviolence) was the guiding principle of Gandhi's civil disobedience in the cause of freedom and social equality. His ecological philosophy found apt expression in his observation that the greatest work of humanity could not match the smallest wonder of nature.

—Singhvi

VIOLENCE IN THE WORLD

That is because, I think, mankind's greed often exceeds their needs. What they do not practice is restraint because restraint is not regarded as a principle of civilization. Not yet. I think consumerism is, for instance, a negation of the principle of restraint. That is to say, if we go on exploiting the resources of the earth, without any level of interest, without any sense of restraint, we will end up by causing an ecological disaster. This we are beginning to realize only now, when that disaster is hovering over our heads, when the greenhouse effect and ozone hole threaten the possible destruction of the whole world.

The point is, what is humankind doing to itself and to other forms of life by this excessive indulgence in the exploitation of resources? Take what you need! But greed, when it is bigger than your need, not only destroys yourself but it destroys others. And this is where, I think, the principle of Jainism, the principle of nonviolence, comes in.

But that brings me to the whole question of violence, in terms of dealing with each other—the violence between religions, economic violence, political violence, military violence. After all, physical violence is only an expression of the violence in the minds of men and women. And we are, in a sense, becoming insensitive to the essential human goodness in us by allowing violence to be enthroned as if violence, power, raw power, is by itself something good.

It is important for us therefore to realize what Jains have said, what many of the religions in many different parts of the world have said, that nonviolence is a principle of bringing the maximum good to yourself and to others. Because, when you resort to violence you not only destroy something else, you're destroying yourself.

Lord Mahavira said it beautifully on one occasion: "You are that which you intend to hit, injure, insult, torment, persecute, torture, enslave, or kill." You are that.

It's important to realize it. Once you realize the unity of all life, the reciprocity of all life, the interdependence of all life, you have realized Jainism.

If you were to understand that the victim and the one who victimizes are one, the one who victimizes will consider this a

Nonattachment

Jain religion focuses primary attention on nonattachment (aparigraha) toward material things of life through self-restraint, fasting, abstinence from overindulgence, voluntary curtailment of one's needs and elimination of the aggressive urge. The rituals and practices prescribed for monks (mahavrata) are more rigorous than those (anuvrata) prescribed for ordinary followers. Apargraha and ahimsa taken together imply supreme respect for ecology and the conservation of the environment through avoidance of injudicious exploitation or wanton destruction of nature.

—Dr. N. P. Jain (SourceBook)

self-inflicted offense, a self-inflicted violence. That does not happen because moral perception, the psychological perception, is missing. Once that dimension is given, I think we will be more civilized human beings.

But the world itself is becoming more and more violent, although there is no reason for it to be so. For all these centuries of civilization should we find ourselves in a situation where violence is the norm and nonviolence only an idealistic exception? It should, in fact, be the other way around. Violence is a crime against humanity. It is a crime against humanity within yourself and humanity elsewhere. And this is where I think it is important for us to create an ethic of nonviolence, a workable, pragmatic ethic of nonviolence.

TRANSFORMING A VIOLENT LIFE

The conversion factor is the moral awareness. That is the catalyst. If there is the moral awareness, then it is possible to hold a mirror to a situation—hold a mirror to yourself and see where what you are doing is wrong or right. Ultimately it is a question of respect for life. It is a respect which we owe to others as to well as ourselves. It is a recognition, in a sense, of the divine within each one of us. Each religion is trying to approach this situation in its own way.

It is true that nonviolence has been emphasized to the point of scientific precision and awareness in Jainism. But nonviolence is, in fact, ultimately, the common thread, the golden thread, which should bind us all together.

RESOLVING HIGH POLITICAL POSITION WITH A COMMITMENT TO NONVIOLENCE

I see no contradiction. If you are able to give your time without self-seeking, without selfish aims, then you are doing precisely what the Jain tradition mandates.

I think it is also important to remember that the Jains had, in historical times, been rulers. They have also been generals in the army. They have been prime ministers, they have been wealthy

Jains in India

Although the seven to ten million Jains estimated to live in modern India constitute a tiny fraction of its population, the message and motifs of the Jain perspective, its reverence for life in all its forms, its commitment to the progress of human civilization and to the preservation of the natural environment continue to have a profound and pervasive influence on Indian life and outlook.

—Singhvi

businessmen. And all these are fully compatible with the Jain perspective of life so long as the individual concerned has the moral code which guides him. So long as he can exercise maximum possible restraint in a given situation, so long as he can keep the moral codes of principles of truth and nonviolence before him.

You begin to look at a situation in a particular setting, and you always bring to bear, on any situation, your moral judgment. Take, for instance, human rights. I find human rights commitment, which I've had all my life, the most important part of my moral awareness, my moral consciousness.

Why human rights, why human obligations? Because it enables you to bring the civilizational impact of concern and consideration to other human beings.

You meditate continuously. You introspect continuously. You apply the moral judgment continuously. You never let go the caveat, the vigilance which is within you. And this helps you to make better judgments. What are good judgments, ultimately, if they do not help the humanity as a whole or the humanity with which you are concerned?

Therefore, it makes your decisions more humane. It makes your approach more compassionate. It makes your dealings more concerned and considerate.

I have tried to understand different ways of meditation. When someone comes and tells me, "This is the Jain way of meditation," I don't accept it. There are so many different ways of meditation. The Jains were a scientific and rational people. They were trying, in the earliest part of the tradition, to make sure that they do not accept just the authority of someone handing over a verdict to you. You must use your own mind.

And they realized that in meditation, as in other things, it will be different systems which suit you—different systems that suit you at different times of your life at different phases of your life. Therefore it is ultimately important to apply the inner resources of your mind, the inner resources of your soul, the inner resources of your heart to a given situation. Then you are able to manage it in the best possible way.

Meditation is not just something you do for fifteen minutes in the morning. You meditate continuously as you go through life, day after day.

A Jain Prayer

May my thoughts and feelings be such that I may always act in a simple and straightforward manner. May I ever, so far as I can, do good in this life to others.

May I always have a friendly feeling toward all living beings of the world and may the stream of compassion always flow from my heart toward distressed and afflicted living beings.

May I ever have the good company of learned ascetics and may I ever keep them in mind. May my heart be always engrossed and inclined to adopt the rules of conduct that they observe.

Interviewer: *When I first heard of Jainism it seemed portrayed to me in a sort of trivialization, "Oh, those are the people who don't step on ants."*
L. M. Singhi: *I like that. We cannot trivialize such a profound philosophy as nonviolence by paying more importance to the little things and forgetting the bigger ones.*

JAIN

THE ECOLOGICAL SOUL
Michael Tobias
(Introduction written by Jane Morrison)

Raised in a secular Jewish tradition, schooled for many years in Jainism, Michael Tobias has haunted cathedrals, temples, synagogues, and monasteries throughout the world. He has spent an equal share of his time in the wilderness, exploring mountain regions and mountain people on every continent, while systematically chronicling the devastation mankind has wreaked on the biosphere.

A student of the history of ideas, writer, filmmaker, and ecologist, he has endeavored to share his love of nature with others through his more than eighty films and some twenty books. Best known among these are his novels *Voice of the Planet* (1990), *Believe* (with William Shatner, 1992), *Deva* (1976), *Rage and Reason* (1993), *Fatal Exposure* (1991), and *A Naked Man* (1994). *A Naked Man* is based upon the life of Mahavira, the twenty-fourth tirthankara of Jainism.

Tobias's nonfiction includes his recent works *A Vision of Nature—Traces of the Original World* (1995), *World War III—Population and the Biosphere at the End of the Millennium* (1994), *The Soul of Nature* (ed., 1994), *Environmental Meditation* (1993), *Life Force—The World of Jainism* (1991), *Mountain People* (ed., 1986), *After Eden—History, Ecology & Conscience* (1985), *Deep Ecology* (ed., 1984), and *The Mountain Spirit* (ed., 1979).

In his films, which have been broadcast in more than fifty countries, Tobias has consistently called for a "new human nature," a recognition that our morals are ineluctably linked to an ecological bottom line. "Evolution neither condemns nor liberates us," says Tobias. "Only our choices can do that."

Some of his better known films include: "Voice of the Planet" (a ten-hour dramatic miniseries, TBS, 1991), "*Ahimsa*—Nonviolence" (PBS, 1987), "Black Tide" (Discovery Channel, 1990), "Antarctica—The Last Continent" (PBS, 1987), "A Day in the Life of Ireland" (PBS, 1991), "Kazantzakis" (PBS, 1985), "World War III" (1994), and the feature film "India" (1995). In addition, he directed and produced the twenty-six part PBS series "A Parliament of Souls," from which this book was adapted.

In attempting to convey the realities of ecological abuse in this generation to the young hearts and minds that will inherit their parents' global legacy, Tobias has not shied away from graphically revealing such toxic hot spots as Cubatao in Brazil, Seveso in Italy, deforestation in Nepal, rain forest devastation in the Amazon, disruption of animal populations in the Antarctic, the impact of the *Exxon Valdez* oil spill on resident Alaskan wildlife, hunger in West Africa, overpopulation in India and Bangladesh, and unsustainable consumerism in the developed countries.

Tobias obtained his Ph.D. in the History of Consciousness from the University of California at Santa Cruz. A former professor of environmental affairs and the humanities at Dartmouth College, Tobias has lectured widely in many countries and has worked to stimulate thinking and action in the animal rights communities. In pressing for innovative, nonviolent strategies that would help end the human trespasses upon nature, Tobias has drawn attention to the ecological importance of vegetarianism, one-child families, adoption, and long-term economic reforms that can engender the preconditions for steady-state communities and effective individuals.

Underlying these broad public policy thrusts, Tobias emphasizes the messages of "interdependency" and "beauty" inherent not only to biology, but also to nearly all spiritual traditions.

ON THE BRINK OF A NEW CENTURY

I am afraid that in my way of viewing the human presence on the planet, what we have made is an utter mess. Sure, we are a

Since the Industrial Revolution, human numbers have multiplied eightfold and energy use and resource consumption have risen even faster. People now consume, control, or destroy almost 40 percent of the plant energy of the land and 25 percent of all plant energy, the ultimate source of food for all animals and almost all organisms. As a result, quite unwittingly and ignorant of the consequences, we are reshaping earth, replacing forests with farmland, farmland with wasteland, filling rivers, lakes, and seas with sediments and pollutants, unbalancing the atmosphere, subtracting species and draining gene pools, changing climate. . . . We are revising creation.

—Robert Prescott-Allen,
Caring for the World

fabulous, creative, wonderful, humane, capable organism. But as a species, we have unloaded a lot of our more mysterious, unpredictable, and aggressive behavior. And it has resulted in carnage. It has resulted in bloodletting. We have done more damage, by far, than an asteroid that would collide with the earth. I mean, one could catalogue the damage. There are a number of estimates as to what kind, and how broad the scope of damage.

It is very easy to be glib on the brink, to presume that we know what is going on. But in fact, we don't know what is going on because we don't understand the creation. We don't understand biodiversity. We only know it is there. Our numbers are fraught with murkiness. We keep upgrading the amount of biodiversity which we believe to be out there, all around us. So ascertaining the extent of our damage is plagued by our ignorance. And everyday natural science reveals new domains, new dimensions of creation which in turn imply that our projections have to be revised. The best example of this is, I suppose, the number of known species on the planet. This is perhaps the biological benchmark of our success or failure as a species. Extinction, at its current pace, is the result of human behavior. There is no mystery to this. The natural background rate of extinction on planet earth is known to be approximately three hundred species that go extinct every million years. Since about the turn of this century we have been driving to extinction anywhere between 75 and 780 species every day.

The discrepancy in those two numbers—seventy-five, seven hundred and eighty—is extraordinary, because it reflects upon our ignorance scientifically. But even more incredibly, 300 species in a million years versus 780 species in a single day.

We've already lost millions of species. The rhinos, the gorillas, the chimpanzees, the tigers are down almost to the point of extinction. It is happening right now as we speak. The level of carnage, the level of brutality, the level of ignorance of these trends is astonishing, but not surprising, because when a rare tarantula goes extinct on a remote mountain ridge in Angola, it's imperceptible to the world. This once-in-a-creation creature that knew only freedom and innocence and joy vanishes without a trace. It never existed, for all we know.

That's what's happening. It's a sordid war of incremental disasters that we don't even know about. And in our best, most earnest effort to find out, we're behind the eight ball. It's happening too fast for scientists to catch up. We're losing with every skyscraper. We're losing with every new parking garage. We're losing it so fast, before we have a chance to understand. I consider it *the* tragedy, the issue of the century.

There are those who would hold that the Second Coming, that Armageddon, the end of the world, is upon us. Most recently, twenty-one years ago at the Club of Rome, a group of well-meaning businessmen, world health authorities, scientists, demographers, and statisticians came together and examined a number of crucial criteria with regard to energy extraction, the global greenhouse effect, the population boom, and the nonrenewable resources downturn. They tried to ascertain our future, and thus initiated a whole generation of futurist studies that were solely concerned with projecting ten years, twenty years, thirty years out, in an effort to combat what is, in essence, and has been for thousands of years, a short-term motivation on the part of human behavior, whether you are speaking economically or of other forms of gratification.

Now, as we begin to project the damage that we are wreaking, we are absolutely in the dark. We are at a point where evolution no longer dictates who we are, what we are, how we behave. Choices dictate. We are now given the opportunity to be moral beings and to reform our presence on the planet morally, spiritually. And so it's hard to predict.

Living Species

The irreversible loss of species, which by 2100 may reach one third of all species now living, is especially serious. WE are losing the potential they hold for providing medicinal and other benefits, that contribute to the genetic diversity of life forms making for the robustness of the world's biological systems. . . . Our massive tampering with the world's interdependent web of life— coupled with the environmental damage inflicted by deforestation, species loss and climate change—could trigger widespread adverse effects, including unpredictable collapses of critical biological systems whose interactions and dynamics we only imperfectly understand.

THE EFFECT OF SPIRITUAL REFORM ON THE ENVIRONMENT

Many religious traditions have argued, I believe correctly, that the worst form of pollution is in the mind. And if you reform thinking, you will innately cause to be reformed the environment around you.

All religions, that I am aware of, revere nature. Our language, our imaginative ordeals, our creative possibilities seem to be guided, shaped, nurtured by the metaphors we feel for nature. As a Creation, as a Mother, as an Earth Spirit, as our soul's sustenance.

"We've come from the earth, we will return to the earth," said Aristotle. In the Greek tragedies, Gaia, the earth Goddess, held sway over all other deities at the Oracle of Delphi. Gaia was the first to be worshiped. In most cultures, the Earth Goddess represents that full spectrum of forces that we can depend upon.

I think there is an innate recognition that we are nurtured by the earth. However we define the cosmos, it is the earth that is precious, and unbelievable. It is a miracle that we can scarcely come to terms with. And we know it, and while our language isn't quite capable of touching it, the mystery is there.

But recognition of the environment on the level of policy, of economic transition, of international alliances and treaties, is a new thing. The Environmental Protection Agency is scarcely two decades old.

TRANSFORMATION INTO ACTION

This, of course, leads to the burning issue—how does awareness transform into social action? I don't know. There are any number of ways.

We tried to get a modest gasoline tax increase, and American culture, which is the most culpable in that respect, has basically rejected it. It is very difficult. Recent political administrations in China have tried to engender a sense of self-restraint with regard to the population crisis.

Given the current global total fertility rate, it is possible that by the year 2100 there could be eighteen or twenty billion people on the planet, if we continue current practices.

We can make a choice to change. Hunter-gathering, the method by which our ancestors culled their food, was, according to most anthropologists, the woman's domain. It was not hunting, it was gathering. We are created not as carnivores, but as herbivores.

The first thing that I would suggest is that you begin around the dinner table. This is an opinion, but is born of meditation and deep reflection over half a lifetime. If we are not capable of restraining our dietary habits to the extent that we exploit the bounty of twentieth-century produce—namely vegetarianism—we're already, in my estimation, losing it.

There are a number of very practical reasons that have nothing to do with opinion or morality or tastes. We are losing the fresh water reserves. The aquifers from the Ogallala to the San Joaquin Valley in California are disappearing. The disappearing water resources, by the way, go principally for grain and alfalfa to feed cattle. In Saudi Arabia they are going to suffer severe water shortages by the year 2010 because they are overproducing foodstuffs. In Southern India they've lost most of their water resources, as well.

The ecological damage by cattle which are raised specifically for meat culture is devastating. We are reaching agricultural crises because of meat-eating, because of the cattle industry.

But, of course, the larger issue here is global distribution, equitable distribution. We have over a billion people literally starving to death on the planet right now, with 5.6 billion on the planet. What's going to happen when we have 12 billion, which is a most conservative estimate that the United Nations and the World Bank both offer? We can't afford the American way of life, which is a meat-eating style of living.

So if we give up meat-eating, what is that going to do for the starving somewhere else? Oh, it will do a tremendous amount. First of all, it will liberate a lot of grain supplies which are badly needed in parts of Sub-Saharan Africa and in many other corners of the world where malnutrition is a chronic problem.

Number two, it will redirect our economic systems in such a manner that we will, hopefully, be able to engender an effect in Europe, an effect in Argentina, Brazil, Australia, China, Germany, Canada—other countries that are enormous meat-consuming nations.

It would lift a colossal burden—a spiritual burden—from the planet. Never mind the economics of it, which are satisfied by a vegetarian culture. To live in a vegetarian culture is to have demonstrably less impact on the natural resources around us.

> **Meat Eating and Ecological Destruction**
>
> *It is estimated that for every quarter-pound hamburger that comes from a steer raised in Central and South America, it is necessary to destroy approximately 165 pounds of living matter including some twenty to thirty different plant species, perhaps one hundred insect species, and dozens of bird, mammal, and reptile species.*
>
> *Today, the average American consumes 65 pounds of beef per year.*
>
> (Rifkin)

CHOICE AND CONSCIENCE

This is where I believe the future of spirituality must be headed: how to make decisive choices in an era of environmental collapse, how to transform awareness that is fraught with indeci-

Gaia: an ancient pre-Hellenic goddess, the archetypal earth mother, the primordial essence of the earth. Revered as a gentle and benign goddess, her oracle at Delphi predated that of Apollo. In Hellenic times she became Da-meter or Demeter, the grain mother whose daughter is Kore, the grain spirit.

siveness and with turmoil into a focused, positive direction. I think that the religions of the world, the spiritual and indigenous tribal aboriginal traditions, all of which have focused on God, all of which have been focused and humbled by the Creation, stand poised at the end of this millennium to redress the wrongs that our species have committed unwittingly for tens of thousands of years.

Globally, there is no question that if you were to take a poll—"Do you subscribe to the environmental doctrine?"—most human beings would say, "absolutely." It is perhaps the most significant crisis in human history. We've had wars before. Now we are in a state of what I call World War III, where the biological bottom line has risen to the surface of all of our public and spiritual affairs. The biological bottom line being that vast litany of injury that we have unleashed upon Mother Earth.

So the choice is there to be made. It's either more violence, continued runaway fertility, lack of restraint, lack of caring, lack of thoughtfulness, lack of mindfulness, or a world in which the empowerment of women, the respect of children, the adoration of our elders, and the total recognition by all people that the world is paradise—that we live in paradise here and now—comes about. Until we come to humbly absorb that simple message, which any child can grasp instantly and knows to be true, we'll act like idiots and like oil spills. We'll blunder our way forward into some unimaginably desolate, bereft, near future, in which the tiger is gone, the rhino is gone, the gorilla is gone and billions of children are living in squalor. Seventy-five percent of the world will be in city slums, cities with forty and fifty million people in them. Calcutta currently has sufficient sanitation facilities for six hundred thousand people, yet there are nearly ten million people in the city.

That's just the tip of the iceberg—if we don't begin now to radically reform everything we know about the world and to accept the recognition that we are a global community.

We are all experts in giving. Every love affair is give and take. Every marriage is a question of ceding certain things to your partner. A marriage has taught us how to be in partnership. That is the best metaphor I know as a working model for behaving on this planet.

WE HAVE TO LEARN FROM EACH OTHER

Certain countries, both historically and today, have enshrined into law codes of behavior that have effectively transformed those places into relatively steady-state communities.

I speak of Bhutan, in the Himalayas. A small kingdom of about 1.3 million people that endorsed E. F. Schumacher's phrase, "small is beautiful," into their constitution. Look into Bhutan—a fascinating glimpse into a potential future for the whole planet.

I would also cite, for example, a small community in the deserts of Rajasthan, in India, the Bishnoi—about a million of them. At a time when the worst drought of the century was afflicting India, the Bishnoi, living in their desert huts, were fine. Why? For five hundred years they have worshiped an ecological saint who taught them to hug the trees to protect them from encroachment, to never harm a living being, to be vegetarians, to carefully nurture their scarce water supplies. They even harvest the dew drops in the morning off leaves high in protein, which they cut partially so as not to injure the plant, to feed animals, which are not allowed to run amuck in terms of any grazing behavior. A remarkable testimony, not only to endurance, but to foresight.

Three hundred Bishnoi were killed back in the 1700s by some mogul who wanted the forests in Rajasthan, low desert shrubs. The Bishnoi protected them, and they were massacred. And today they have become the first ecological heroes, commemorated as such, in India.

I would certainly cite the Jains, of which there are nearly ten million on the planet now. Again one of the oldest religions in the world out of India—strict vegetarians. They have embraced nonviolence to the extent of psychoanalyzing our daily behavior. To the point that the Jain community has figured out how to walk softly on this earth—how to restrict its professions to only nonviolent ones. I have embraced Jainism.

The Taoist community, traditionally, has always revered nature and that has been the mystical source of its art, of its behavior. In the Sung dynasty, the Taoist communities were absolutely peaceful, were absolutely passive. And amazingly, even in Japan, at the height of what we assume were the wars

We who have lost our sense and our senses—our touch, our smell, our vision of who we are; we who frantically force and press all things; without rest for body or spirit, hurting our earth and injuring ourselves: we call a halt.

We want to rest. We need to rest and allow the earth to rest. We need to reflect and to rediscover the mystery that lives in us, that is the ground of every unique expression of life, the source of the fascination that calls all things to communion.

We declare a Sabbath, a space of quiet: for simply being and letting be; for recovering the great, forgotten truths; for learning how to live again.

(United Nations Environmental Sabbath Program)

The U.S. Presidential Global 2000 Report, issued by the Carter administration (1976–1980) to assess the world environmental situation, estimated that 2 million species of plants and animals will become extinct and that 5 billion new acres of desert will have been created in twenty years' time.

between the shogunates and the feudal masters—in fact, for over two hundred years under the Tokugawas, from about 1620 to nearly the 1850s—the Japanese sustained what has been called by historians the most incredibly perfect period of peace in human history. So there are examples.

We can learn from the Amazon indigenous groups who have known for thousands of years how to take only enough fruit to survive happily without injuring the tree. And today's indigenous rubber tappers, unlike the multinational conglomerates, know exactly how to do that. We have to learn from each other.

We are the most presumptuous species. I mean beavers don't do this. Mice don't do this. Zebras don't do this. We are a strange combination. We are loving; we are caring. We have the gift of laughter. Zarathustra says that the first miracle of any human being is to laugh. Other species laugh but we laugh a lot. We love a lot. We shed tears that have the same salinity as the ocean water. So we are totally connected to the planet. We are of stellar dust. We have every experience in biological history right up our backbone, in our brains. We have it all, we simply have to come to the recognition that humanity is about being humane. Period. End of story.

Thou shalt not kill. It is very simple. It is the simplest thing. I often am totally mystified by why, when we've got the Golden Rule, the Ten Commandments, the edicts of Ashoka, and so many religious testimonies to the simplicity of nonviolence, why do we make it so difficult? Why are there more wars at this time in human history than there have ever been before? Why in this century have we killed one hundred and twenty million of our fellow beings, not to mention a trillion animals? I don't understand.

But I believe fiercely that we are going to change because awareness has always led to change. And finally, the whole population of homo sapiens—which means, of course, to be knowledgeable—is aware. And so I foresee great, *great* hope.

BUDDHIST BRAHMA KUMARIS JEWISH
JAIN NATIVE AMERICAN SUFI HINDU
CHRISTIAN ROMAN CATHOLIC MUSLIM
SIKH BAHA'I JEWISH ZOROASTRIAN

JEWISH

ROMAN CATHOLIC TAOIST BUDDHIST
ZOROASTRIAN PROTESTANT CHRISTIAN
HINDU MUSLIM JAIN ROMAN CATHOLIC
TAOIST BAHA'I BUDDHIST SIKH SUFI
NATIVE AMERICAN BRAHMA KUMARIS
JEWISH PROTESTANT CHRISTIAN TAOIST
BUDDHIST HINDU ZOROASTRIAN JAIN
ROMAN CATHOLIC BAHA'I PROTESTANT
TAOIST HINDU SUFI NATIVE AMERICAN
MUSLIM BRAHMA KUMARIS BUDDHIST
SIKH SUFI JEWISH MUSLIM TAOIST
ZOROASTRIAN CHRISTIAN BAHA'I HINDU

JEWISH

RESISTING EVIL

Professor Rabbi Emil Fackenheim

Born in Germany, Professor Emil Ludwig Fackenheim was ordained as a rabbi at the Hochschule für die Wissenschaft des Dudentums in Berlin in 1939. One year later, he fled his home for Canada, where he was to become a professor at the University of Toronto, contributing significantly to scholarship concerning German idealism. But it was the unprecedented evil of the Holocaust that came to shape all of his thinking. At the core of his thought was the realization that Hitler must be destroyed posthumously.

Recently, Fackenheim moved to Jerusalem, where he teaches and writes. His many books have been celebrated for the range and depth of his compassion and lucidity. *God's Presence in History: Jewish Affirmations and Philosophical Reflections* (1972) has been called "the most important statement of the leading Holocaust theologian in Reform Judaism" (*The Reader's Adviser*). His research into the impact of Kant, Hegel, Sartre, and Heidegger on Jewish thinking was published under the name *Encounters Between Judaism and Modern Philosophy: A Preface to Future Jewish Thought* (1973). And his post-Holocaust theology, which champions the remarkable tenacity of the Jewish people, has been expounded in his work *To Mend the World: Foundations of Future Jewish Thought* (1982).

Fackenheim's other books include: *Paths to Jewish Belief* (1960), *The Religious Dimension in Hegel's Thought* (1968), *Quest for Past and Future: Essays in Jewish Theology* (1968), and *The Jewish Bible after the Holocaust* (1990).

Reform Judaism

*The new wave of immi-
grants to America in the
mid-nineteenth century
were heirs of a liberalizing
influence that had grown
among German syna-
gogues. Reformers consid-
ered the ethical teachings of
the prophets more central
to the Jewish faith than traditional ritual practices,
such as dietary laws and
strict Sabbath observance,
which they considered out-
moded. The statement of
Reform principles adopted
in 1885 rejected the vast
body of Mosaic and rab-
binic law but held to the
moral law of the Torah
and expressed a commit-
ment on that basis for the
struggle for equality be-
tween rich and poor. For
Reform Jews the true
essence of Judaism was the
quest for righteousness in
social relationships.Of the
85 percent of adult Jewish
population in the United
States that belong to Jewish
denominations, about 33
percent identify themselves
with Reform Judaism. In
1989, the Union of Ameri-
can Hebrew Congregations
had 804 synagogues and
1.3 million members.*

(Melton, *Creeds*)

Rabbi Fackenheim's ability to forgive, but never to forget, marks a whole new approach to understanding human nature and the philosophical avenues open to compassion and non-violence.

When we filmed the interview on which this chapter is based, several among the television crew quietly cried while Professor Fackenheim spoke.

WHAT IT MEANS TO BE A JEW IN THE LATE TWENTIETH CENTURY

The two completely unprecedented events that happened in Jewish history in this century are the Holocaust and the Jewish return to Jerusalem. I think the major thinking goes on about how to relate to those two events. Of course the return to Jerusalem is still under way. Not only that, I would say, in a sense, the Holocaust is still under way.

What the Nazis did was so unbelievable. Yet, in retrospect, it is only rational that people don't believe it ever happened. Therefore you now have Holocaust denials. I think it's quite shocking how many there are.

Now the reason why this is so terrible is, if this gets widely accepted, then it will undoubtedly bring forth a new outbreak of anti-Semitism. One anti-Semitic standard thing is the Jewish conspiracy. If indeed there was no Holocaust, then the conspiracy of the Jews must be even worse than "they" ever thought. There are people with numbers on their arms, there are Holocaust museums, all must be fictitious. Well, that's what they have to say if they say there never was a Holocaust.

HOW TO COME TO TERMS WITH THE EVIL THE HOLOCAUST REPRESENTS

This is, of course, the question one should ask: How do we come to terms with that evil? The mind boggles. I'm a professional philosopher. I wrote about how philosophers come to terms with evil in general for many years before I confronted this.

How do philosophers generally come to terms with evil? One theory says evil is ignorance; that was the Socratic philosophy. That's to say, if only people knew what they were doing they wouldn't be doing it.

Interviewer: There were Nazis skinning a rabbi alive in order to get a couple more skull pins on their collars!

Rabbi Fackenheim: Exactly! So this really doesn't hold. And not only that, some of them were Ph.D.'s So the Socratic theory has been refuted by the Holocaust. My fellow philosophers ought to be attending to this. How do we respond to this if we really want to be relevant? Because certainly you can't just let it go.

My own glimpse of a theory is, there's got to be a new category in philosophy, namely resistance. What can you do with evil? All you can do is resist it. And if you say, "I can't understand it," then you can't understand it, maybe. But you still know it is evil. And if relativists come along and say good is all relative, which I don't believe, well, you see, at least, that evil cannot be relative, it's absolute.

Today relativism is all over the place when it comes to the discussion of good because you're intolerant if somebody else's view of good differs from yours. Well, when it comes to radical evil, all you can do is be intolerant because it's radical evil.

All you can do is study the victims. And this is what I learned from victims, because to study the Holocaust is a terrible thing. But to study the victims—of course the only ones you can study are the ones who survived—can be a tremendously inspiring thing when people exposed to this managed the strength to resist it.

SURVIVAL BY RESISTANCE

One student of mine went to Auschwitz and afterward wrote a long paper because he couldn't understand how a person could survive it even a single day. Well, the only way you could survive it was by resisting it.

I'll give you a couple of examples. Actually a man, Terrence Des Pres, a professor, now dead, wrote a great book called *The Survivor.* He studied survivors. Well, you'd get very dirty, in the camps, filthy, filth everywhere. You want to wash but the water is dirty too. So what do you do? Never mind it, what's the

---

Conservative Judaism

Conservative Jews occupy a middle ground between Orthodox and Reform Jews in American society, affirming the God-given standing of the Torah but accommodating minor change in light of modern lifestyles. Conservative Judaism shares the basic assumption of the Orthodox that "Jewishness" and Judaism, the ethnic and the religious identities, cannot be separated. Conservatism fosters ordinary religion as it encourages Jewishness among American Jews who are observant or nonobservant of the 613 commandments of orthodoxy. Of the 85 percent of adult Jewish population in the United States that belong to Jewish denominations, about 42 percent identify themselves with Conservative Judaism. In 1989, the United Synagogue of America had 800 synagogues and 1.2 million members.

(Melton, *Creeds*)

bother? You give in and before you know, you're finished. But when people washed with water that didn't make them any cleaner, that was an act of resistance.

They put you into paradoxical situations and that was quite deliberate. I'm not talking about murdering, just the system by itself. For example, they say, "If you lose a button on your shirt, that will be severely punished." On the other hand there is no needle and no thread. How are you going to deal with that?

I was in a concentration camp before the war, which was mild in comparison. There was a sign, "Be clean, one louse might be your death." You were forbidden to die of lice because they wanted to murder you themselves.

I came across a piece that a survivor had written, her name was Levenska. I don't think this victim of the Holocaust was Jewish, but the reason I mention it—it makes it universal. She writes about an extreme experience, namely being driven into Auschwitz. At first she was completely overwhelmed by the filth and disorder. To give you just one example, they were given food that gives you diarrhea and then forbidden to relieve themselves. I don't have to spell it out further.

In this piece, I read something that has arrested my attention ever since: "Then I realized that this was not a case of disorder but of *order*. They wanted us to die in our own filth, and become in our own eyes the disgusting animals they thought we were." And she said, "From that moment my whole life was changed. I was under orders to live and if I did die at Auschwitz I was going to die as a human being."

Now the question is, whose orders? Of course I found subsequently many other examples of religious Jews who were under orders of a similar kind, not to despair of God and so on. But she doesn't say. So I think it might be quite possible to be under orders without knowing whose they are. The only thing you do know is that they've got to be obeyed.

LAW AND THE STRENGTH TO RESIST

Now that leads me back to something in the Jewish tradition: "If thy law had not been my delight I would have perished in my affliction." That threw a whole new light on it: Law is not an af-

The Trial of God

During the war, in one of the camps one evening, three Jews, who before the war were heads of academies, sages, learned men, and who knew the Talmud by heart, decided that the time had come to do something about it, to indict God. And they conducted a trial. I was very young then. But I remember I was there. They sat on the bed one evening and they began the trial, the trial of God, with all the arguments for and against. And it lasted a couple of days. It was very serious, very dramatic. . . . And I remember that after many days the verdict came. And the verdict was: "Guilty."

But, then, the head of the tribunal simply said: "Now let's go and pray."

—Elie Wiesel, Auschwitz survivor, from the BBC film "The Chosen People"

fliction and a nasty thing but a liberating experience and a strength-giving experience. This is actually part of the Jewish tradition.

This is where I stand, this is where I have been put. This is my post. I don't like that post. I wish I were anywhere else. I have to do it, [even if] I can't.

Sometimes in my own life when somebody says to me, "How can you do it?" I say, if you're in that situation, you've got a choice but you have no decent choice.

And I think there we could all, certainly in the Jewish and Christian heritage, go back to our traditions and say, "Why am I here? Why am I not someplace else?" When Abraham was told by God to sacrifice his son, he must have felt, "I wish I was somebody else."

My son once asked his mother, who wasn't Jewish at the time, "If God said to you to sacrifice me, what would you do?" My wife said, "I would say no."

The reason why I bring that in is—maybe sometimes even God has to be resisted, but you have to earn that. In the tradition, you have to take God seriously, with awe. Surely Abraham did that when he said to God, "Look you can't kill those innocent people in Sodom and Gomorrah, because maybe there are fifty righteous among them." So he haggled with God, but he earned that right.

Conflict can arise there. This is a deep philosophical issue, but if God seems to command something that is immoral, it's okay to argue with God.

That was the problem that the biblical Abraham must have had. It is a very central issue.

But my main point would be this: Where does the strength come from to resist evil? And that is something people nowadays don't want to hear, because everybody says, "What are my rights?" Nobody is saying, "What are my duties?"

THE RIGHT TO RESIST MUST BE EARNED

There are all sorts of Jews now who think you should protest against God. Abraham protested against God when He wanted to destroy Sodom and Gomorrah because God is supposed to be

To Mend the World

Shall we trust in God because we—though not they [the Holocaust victims]—were spared? Shall we trust in man because here and now—though not then and there—he bears traces of humanity? Shall we trust in ourselves—that we, unlike them, would resist being made into Muselmänner, *the living dead, with the divine spark within us destroyed?*

We can do none of these things; they are all insults, one hopes unwittingly, to the dead. Behind these unintended insults lies the attempt to repress the hidden dread, to deny the rupture that is a fact. . . . Philosophy and Christian theology can each find its respective salvation not by avoiding the great rupture, but only by confronting it.

(Fackenheim)

just. Now many of the young want to protest. It's great to protest against God but what I say is that protest has to be *earned*.

The protest against evil also has to be earned. In the 60s some kids protested against a university because there was a separate washroom for professors and for students, and *this* was persecution? I think that's ridiculous and was an insult. So I would say the protest against evil has also to be earned.

You earn it first of all, for instance, if you take the Holocaust as an orienting experience, which I would do. You'd say now, is what's happening here really a holocaust? I think it is widely abused. During the Lebanon War we were told by the media that Beirut was the Warsaw ghetto. It was nothing of the sort.

HOPE AS AN ELEMENT OF RESISTANCE

I don't know if I should reminisce because when I was in a concentration camp, that was before the war. And it was quite clear that the purpose was not yet to murder us but to terrorize us into leaving the country and to rob us in the process. So there was one element of resistance which was not too difficult for us to have, namely, "This can't last forever."

What boggles my mind is when, after the war had started and people could no longer have this moral reservoir because the war was going to last for a long time, even then, apparently, there were rumors all the time. "The Russians are coming, or the British are coming," and so on. But certainly hope is an extremely important element for resistance.

Hope is the crucial element. And if I had now to say, what does it mean to be a Jew today? I would say this: For the first time in Jewish history, hope was murdered in the Holocaust, which is a terrible thing for Jewish experience because hope is everything, it really is. You know, the messianic hope and so on.

FAITH AFTER HOPE WAS MURDERED

This is my starting point, and the main thing I am thinking about is: Hope was murdered in the Holocaust, but it was resurrected after the Holocaust. The image of death and resurrection does not apply in other respects. The imagery that Ezekiel uses, there's a valley of bones, a very powerful image. But there weren't any bones in Auschwitz because they ground them up and threw them into rivers. But the one thing that remains, it's the crucial thing: The people weren't resurrected, but hope was resurrected.

I think of a survivor, which I'm not, of course, because I got out beforehand, who saw every day or heard every day that children were thrown alive into the flames. He could hear those screams. That means, even if that person survived, hope died for him.

Now I ask what for me is the crucial question: What was that person doing? Surviving. Coming, let's say, to America, marrying again and having children. It's impossible to have children, except by accident, without hope. And that, I think, is the key experience that Jews ought to have.

A JEWISH RELIGIOUS RESPONSE

As a religious thinker, I have the task of trying to make sense of what happened. My first reaction, still in Germany, was there's got to be a Jewish religious response to what is happening. And that is when I went into Jewish studies as well as philosophy. I already realized that, in my view, this was without precedent.

But I was convinced that you have to go to the Jewish sources to see what you can find. Now, my first reaction until 1967 was to try to help rebuild the post-Holocaust Jewish theology but without really facing up to what had happened. And then one day I had a really traumatic experience.

My arm was twisted to get into a public discussion about the Holocaust and Jewish values. What particularly was traumatic for me is that one of the other participants was Eli Wiesel. He was at that time the only one I knew who was responding to the Holocaust and not with despair. So I had this terrible conflict: Either you are honest about the Holocaust, in which case it might destroy your faith. And that would be a posthumous victory for Hitler as far as I am concerned. If Hitler succeeds in destroying faith of the survivors, then he would be laughing in hell. On the other hand, if you save your faith, but in a comfort-

The Jewish Scriptures

The Jewish Bible is called the Tanakh, a word derived from the consonants T, N, and K, corresponding to the words Torah *(the Mosaic law),* Nevi'im *(the twenty-one books of the prophets), and* Ketuvim *(the thirteen books considered "other writings"). Additionally, there is the "oral Torah" or the Talmud, the recording of ongoing Jewish interpretation and commentary about God. For Jews, God continues to speak to human beings, whose task it is to study and discern his message.*

able way, then it would be a betrayal of the victims. Even afterward their voices aren't *heard*?

I had a terrible time. I got sick on the train from Toronto to New York. But after I delivered my speech, the sickness magically disappeared.

The Talmud, the foremost collection of classical Jewish law, legend, and philosophy, was edited in the fifth century C.E. but contains traditions from 750 years earlier. The Talmud consists of the Mishnah (written text of the oral law), the Jerusalem Talmud, and the Babylonian Talmud (compilations of rabbinic opinion since the Mishnah). Part of the essential spirit expressed in the Talmud is the recognition of study as a holy act, its faith in the importance of human response of the divine.

THE 614TH COMMANDMENT

I said on that occasion, to which I still stick today: Jews are forbidden to give Hitler posthumous victory. In Orthodox Judaism, there are 613 commandments, which all are supposed to come from Sinai. Now I'm not Orthodox, so I don't take it literally, but symbolically. It's strong enough because by this Jews have lived for thousands of years. To add one commandment and treat it as though it too had come from Sinai was my way of dealing with a really paradoxical situation—that God, so to speak, himself issues this commandment that Hitler must not be given posthumous victory.

Maybe I'm monomaniacal on this one, but I see a lot of posthumous victories for Hitler. Whether they have anything to do with what Hitler did is really quite secondary. If you talk about ethnic cleansing—that is a Hitler-like expression. Cleansing? What's this? You clean things by getting rid of *people*? That's what they said about Jews. It is a horrendous thing.

Of course, right at the beginning of scriptures that Jews and Christians share, it says a monumental thing—human beings were created in the image of God. Now you say get rid of them by cleansing the world?

THE RESURRECTION OF HOPE

Maybe hope sometimes died, too, but was resurrected. I think, by their acts, Jews are supposed to be a light unto the nations. We most of the time don't do very well at this. But what is the light today? The world that doesn't have much hope, that even fears a nuclear holocaust—well, the Jewish people already had a Holocaust and are witness to hope that died and was resurrected. That's, I think, what our post is today.

JEWISH

TAKING RESPONSIBILITY
Rabbi Irving (Yitz) Greenberg

Rabbi Irving Greenberg is the president and co-founder of The National Jewish Center for Learning and Leadership, known as CLAL. CLAL offers Jewish education for community leadership and is the leading organization in intra-Jewish dialogue designed to reduce religious polarization and seek unifying solutions to the problems that divide the community.

CLAL's basic principle is that education and renewed encounters with Jewish sources and vital Jewish experiences are the keys to personal choice and wise policy decisions. Uniquely, CLAL emphasizes that this can only be done on the basis of CLAL Yisrael—a true Jewish pluralism built on dignity and mutual respect and the ability of all groups to learn from each other.

An ordained Orthodox rabbi and Harvard Ph.D., Rabbi Greenberg has been a seminal thinker in confronting the Holocaust as a historical transforming event and Israel as the beginning of a third era in Jewish history. He has published articles and monographs on Jewish thought and religion. His book *The Jewish Way: Living the Holidays* (1988) offers a philosophy of Judaism based on an analysis of the Sabbath and holidays. Rabbi Greenberg also edited, with Alvin H. Rosenfeld, *Confronting the Holocaust: The Impact of Eli Wiesel* (1978).

In his university days, Rabbi Greenberg studied with Rabbi Joseph Soloveitchik, the premier philosopher of American mod-

Orthodox Judaism

Orthodox Judaism was born in the United States in the nineteenth century as a response to the efforts of new Jewish immigrants to revise the traditional forms of Jewish life and worship, stripping away nonessential items that tended to alienate the non-Jewish community. Jews who organized to defend the old ways became known as Orthodox Jews. The Union of Orthodox Jewish Congregations in America claim a membership of more than one million and a network of about 1,700 synagogues. About 85 percent of the adult Jewish population in the United States identify themselves with one of the three major denominations—Orthodox, Conservative, or Reform. Of that group, about 11 percent identify themselves as Orthodox.

(Melton, *Creeds*)

ern Jewish Orthodoxy. During his early years at Yeshiva University he became involved in the formation of Yavneh, the National Religious Students Association, a forerunner of the Jewish student movements of the 1960s.

In 1961 Rabbi Greenberg went to Israel on a Fulbright visiting professorship at Tel Aviv University. In seven years in the rabbinate, Greenberg helped found the Segalls Center for the Study and Advancement of Judaism, which brought together rabbis from all Jewish denominations to study together. His articulation of unresolved issues of orthodoxy, in light of the Holocaust, made him an increasingly controversial figure at Yeshiva.

He was instrumental in the pioneering of numerous organizations in American Jewish life, including Yavneh, the National Religious Students Association, the Student Struggle for Soviet Jewry, and the Association for Jewish Studies, the professional organization for Jewish studies in American universities.

In 1972, he became founding chairman of the Department of Jewish Studies at City College of the City University of New York. There, together with Eli Wiesel and Steven Shaw, he also founded the National Jewish Conference Center, which eventually evolved into CLAL.

Rabbi Greenberg is currently working on a book, *The Triumph of Life,* arguing that Judaism's central teaching is that there is a cosmic struggle between life and death and that Jews— and all humans through their own culture and religions—are called to partnership with the Divine (that is, the covenant) to work and contribute toward a final triumph of life.

THE TRIUMPH OF LIFE

I think the most remarkable, and in many ways the most heroic, affirmation of Judaism, really of biblical religion, is that life is going to triumph, that we are living in a world in which life has emerged, in which life is not only growing quantitatively with its remarkable luxuriance. It's also growing qualitatively, and it is becoming more and more like God.

When I was a teenager, I met a group of survivors who'd gone through the camps. They had an even purified—and that's what the word is—look, purged of the very kind of anger and evil sometimes you see in people. They had a remarkable spiritual quality to them that so moved me that I spontaneously decided not to go ahead with my standard education and study with them instead for four years.

I had to learn Yiddish to do this, but it was a very moving experience. I came out so deeply impressed by the power of the tradition, which they exemplified, that I was more critical of modernity and of my Americanism. On the other hand, I was so American, like all good Jewish boys in that generation, that I somehow couldn't let go of modernity either. So I ended up in life sort of torn between these paradoxes of modernity and tradition.

The full impact of reading and meeting survivors and realizing this just overwhelming cruelty and evil finally hit me in 1961. I had a sabbatical, a Fulbright teaching in Israel. I'd come to teach American history; modern religion is my field. I was just overwhelmed by this experience, and frankly, I think my faith was shattered. I guess I struggled to go on, not quite sure. I think there were days when I couldn't believe. How could one believe when the smoke, the smell of your own flesh just chokes you? I don't think one can see through it. There are times you can't see through the clouds of Auschwitz, to see heaven. I don't think it is possible.

And then, I say again, in 1961, how could I not believe? When you experience the incredible force of life. There is this hidden force field which we call God, an infinite source of life and goodness that sustains and nurtures.

Therefore the deeper truth, not to take away a minute from death, and not to take away that there are days when the death comes back and blocks my vision and blocks my faith, but the real truth, the deeper truth is that life has been growing and has been overcoming death.

Auschwitz is the German name for Oswiecim, a town in southeastern Poland where the Nazis organized a concentration camp during World War II (1939–1945). The genocidal system of Auschwitz consisted of three main and thirty forced-labor camps and is responsible for the deaths of several millions of European Jews and others. It is estimated that at Birkenau, merely one of the death camps in the Auschwitz system, 4 million prisoners, mostly Jews, were murdered.

IF GOD IS GOOD, HOW COULD THIS HAVE HAPPENED?

One of the fundamental Jewish teachings is not just about God, it's that every human being has infinite value. That's the implication of a human being in the image of God.

Yad Vashem

*Located in the city of
Jerusalem, Yad Vashem is
the world's largest memorial to the six million Jews
killed in the Holocaust,
1933–1945. It houses an
extensive archive that
serves as a worldwide re-
search center on the Nazi
crimes against the Jewish
people.*

In the course of the Holocaust they not only killed Jews en masse, but they tried to bring down the cost of killing Jews. It was a systematic policy. I came across this testimony in the Nuremberg trials. That was one of those things that killed me.

This woman testified that, to save the money it cost them to gas children—they were gassing children as well as women and men—they were given orders to throw the children directly into the burning pits, into the crematoria without gassing them first. And when the prosecutor asked her why did they do this, she said, well, they were told they have to save money.

I couldn't believe it first of all. And then when I checked it out, it turned out not only were they keeping track, but in 1944, when this happened, they had figured out that they could save money by cutting the gas supply in half. By extending the agony of the victims they could save money. And I checked the bills. The Nazis kept good records, and it turned out that you could estimate that it cost them about six dollars and seventy-five cents for a chamberload of gas, that is to say they could gas about fifteen hundred people for less than ten dollars, or roughly half a penny per person. And they saved that half a cent by not doing that.

Now, how can one go on speaking of God or the value of human life in that kind of a world? And so the honest answer is that, at first, I was shattered. Why did I go on with faith? I don't know.

Part of it, I think, was not to betray them. They had died because of this faith. Part of it was—it sounds paradoxical to say it—after the anger and the rage, I began to feel a certain pity for God, and a certain compassion that God was suffering.

What a world this was that not only humans suffer this way, but God suffers. I think that was the first step toward some form of reconciliation. The other thing that kept me going, my first child was born. My wife and I were in Israel for the first time in our lives for an extended period. I was sitting all day and reading at Yad Vashem. It was cold. It was bitter, it was bitter inside; the soul was worse than the physical thing. And I would come home and there was this little baby—three months old, five months old—growing, crying. Or I would come into Yad Veshem and would see Jerusalem pulsating with life. Fifteen years later it was the same experience when I came back in 1974 to do a year's research on the Holocaust.

I remember reading the climax of the Einsatzgruppen trials, which were the worst trials of all because these were the shooting squads. And you have to understand that people, to shoot women and children for a month, year, year-and-a-half at a time, the brutalization and the cruelty and viciousness and the boredom. The boredom that leads to more cruelty. When women don't fight back, you are bored so you look for entertainment in killing them. I still remember one of these reading days; when I came out I was literally chilled, physically and spiritually. Outside, I was struck by the warming sunlight and I swear I heard these children's voices.

At first I thought, "I'm hallucinating." The children were laughing. It was as if the children had come to life. Of course I stumbled toward the sound, toward the light, because I was blinded from the whole experience. And I looked down and realized I wasn't hallucinating at all. Yad Vashem is built right over a valley in Jerusalem. And this was a special holiday when the children of the school go up by the hundreds and the thousands and they play and they laugh and run around like little kids do. I thought, my God, the power of life.

I think most of us were raised with these images of the all-powerful, omnipotent God I've come to affirm. I think that is a correct image. I like to think of it as the image of the first stage of the divine relationship to the human. I've come to feel there are two co-elements in Judaism and Jewish faith.

One is this triumph of life—belief, affirmation that we are plugged into this infinite source of life, and it's going to grow. It's going to complete quantitatively and qualitatively, perfect itself and the world.

The other main truth, I think, is what I call covenantal, the process of perfecting the world. The world is not perfect. Now the world is ugly and evil and has many elements of cruelty and viciousness. But Judaism teaches that there is this partnership between the divine and the human. Not just with Jews, but all of humanity.

I've come to think of this all-powerful God as that first stage. Maybe since we were children, when God as a loving parent introduces God as a power that saves us, that does all the work for us, that takes care of our problems. Sometimes there is this magical thinking—if only I'll pray, God will save me. If only I bring the right sacrifice, God will take me out of slavery. There

Zionism is the Jewish yearning to return to Eretz Israel, *the biblical name of the land of the Israelites and of the Northern Kingdom and the modern Hebrew equivalent of Palestine. Zion is the ancient name for Jerusalem, but as early as biblical times it served to indicate the National Jewish homeland. The term Zionism was coined in 1885 for political efforts to restore Jews to Israel. Modern Zionism grew from the failure of Jewish emancipation and the resurgence of anti-Semitism in nineteenth-century Europe. For many Jews the modern state of Israel, established in 1948, constitutes the fulfillment of the Zionist dream and represents the end of the Diaspora, the "dispersion" of Jews outside the land of Israel dating back to the sixth century B.C.E.*

(Crim)

is an element of truth in that. There is the basic belief that there
should be goodness and there should be the triumph of good in
the world.

But I think the Bible itself gradually weans us and teaches us
to first of all face reality. Reality is full of evil and pain. Once
you admit that then you ask, "Well, where is God?" again. And
my answer is, again, I was tormented by where was God during
the Holocaust. It tormented me for years. And that was part of
the difficulty of faith. But once I had broken through and come
to realize that God, as an infinite consciousness, was suffering,
maybe suffering a lot more than I am, that's where the compassion came from.

After all, I, who have limited capacity for emotion, suffered
so much, and I suffered vicariously. I didn't even live through it.
I mean, my God, I often look back at the survivors, how they
had the strength to go on living.

Here is God, who has infinite consciousness and infinite
love. The agony must be beyond belief. It liberates you from all
kinds of unexpected things. One of them, I came to see, is that
through the covenant, God wants us to overcome that faith is
not just faith in God, it's becoming a partner. That's what the
divine notion is—partnership with God. And there is no excuse
and no answer other than correcting it.

When I started, there were philosophical answers to evil, and
there were spiritual answers to evil. There is no answer to evil,
and I came to see that the main point of the covenant was to accept no substitutes for the perfection of the world. This is God's
agony as well as humans'. Transform the world. That's, in a
sense, what we are all about.

HUMANS PARTICIPATING IN EVOLUTIONARY
PARTNERSHIP WITH GOD

Judaism is rich in details and orthodox groups. There are 613
commandments by tradition. There are thousands of practices—
but that's the details, that's the trees. The forest, I think, is this
vision of life perfected and transformed.

If every human being is in the image of God and that is, to
me, part of the perfection of life, that means every human being

has infinite value, every human being is unique. But the world isn't structured that way. If the human being has infinite value, there should be no hunger, there should be no oppression, there should be no racism, there should be no sexism.

God wishes humans to be free, to be fully dignified, to be infinitely valuable. But then they have to participate in their own liberation. The world has to be perfected. And humans have to participate in the process.

In the end, what this has led me to is a greater sense that the covenant means that no detail of life is irrelevant. Nothing in life is neutral.

LAW DIRECTS OUR PARTNERSHIP

The beauty of Judaism's affirmation of law is that it has argued all along that people don't have broad vision alone—that God is the details, if you will. What the law tries to do is direct you.

Let me give you an example. It's a trivial one but it's a good one—choosing food. Does the food affirm the value of life or not? In the biblical vision, we should all be vegetarian because no one should live by killing another animal. For that matter, the animals should be vegetarian. That's Isaiah's dream, that the lion will lie down with the lamb.

However, this is the paradox of the covenant. The world is not perfect now. How do you get there? The answer is, let your food and let your eating be a statement of respect for life. And Judaism says any vegetable is Kosher, any mineral is Kosher. But the minute you want to eat animals, we have all kinds of restrictions. That's what Kosher food is all about. Now you can get fixated on the details. Is this animal Kosher? This one? Is this order proper? Is the preparation proper? But if you do you've missed the point.

The point is, the basis of it is nonviolence and, in a paradoxical sort of way, the guilt of meat eating. And I say in a paradox because, in a way, it says, if you want to make the world perfect you don't jump directly to perfection. You've got to go in stages. The truth is, at certain stages you compromise.

The law is based upon love.

Isaiah's Dream

The wolf shall live with the lamb, the leopard shall lie down with the kid, the calf and the lion and the fatling together, and a little child shall lead them.

The cow and the bear shall graze, their young shall lie down together; and the lions shall eat straw like the ox. The nursing child shall play over the hole of the asp, and the weaned child shall put its hand on the adder's den.

They will not hurt or destroy on all my holy mountain; for the earth will be full of the knowledge of the Lord as the waters cover the sea.

(Isaiah 11:6–9)

AFFIRMATION

Rabbi Hillel was asked to answer while standing on one foot
what the Torah is, and he basically said, "Love your neighbor as
yourself," or the negative of that, "Do not do unto others what
you would not have them do unto you." In some ways, that can
be seen as the fundamental principle.

I am a wounded Orthodox rabbi. How can I have faith after
such suffering and cruelty? I was deeply turned around by
Christians who, when I challenged them in terms of Christian
responsibility for hatred—how in the name of the gospel of love
they had taught these stereotypes of degradation of Jews for
thousands of years—they recognized it.

In fact, their honesty, their self-criticism went far beyond
mine. It had a very paradoxical effect. First of all I realized that
this was a great religion. If it can generate such honesty, such integrity, such self-criticism, it's a great religion. It's the truth I
discovered later about democracies too. Democracies criticize
themselves. Dictatorships tell you everything is wonderful.

So I need this other religion, or this other viewpoint in my
own religion, to correct my own excesses. They need to go out
and explore what I cannot fully explore. Look, I can love one
person deeply, I can love a few people. But I can't love everybody equally deeply. It's just not in the cards. So it's good that
there are other people, other religions.

*Rabbi Hillel (ca. 60
B.C.E.–ca. 10 C.E.) was an
early and great scholar of
the Talmud, the Jewish library of oral law and tradition. He was committed to
helping the poor and to the
cause of social justice in his
time—"We must support
the poor of the Gentiles
with the poor of Israel,
visit the sick of the Gentiles
with the sick of Israel . . .
because of the ways of
peace" (Gittin 61a). Hillel
is remembered for his suc-
cinct interpretation of the
ethics of the Torah (the
Mosaic law of the first five
books of the Bible): "What
is hateful to yourself, do
not do to your fellowman.
That is the whole Torah
and the remainder is com-
mentary" (Shabbat 31a).*

(Crim)

THE EVOLUTION OF RELIGION

I once figured out that 30 percent of the Jews alive in 1939 were
killed by 1945, but 80 percent of the rabbis, scholars, educators,
Talmud students alive in 1939 were dead by 1945. Eighty percent. The Jews respond to this, not by quitting, but by renewing
life and renewing religion. There are more people studying the
Talmud today, there are more rabbis and scholars today than
ever before in Jewish history—including the golden age of
Spain, including the Talmud itself—because the response to
death has been an unparalleled affirmation of life.

I would argue that the miracle is that faith springs back, and
that in response to death you have this incredible outburst of

life. And in response to hatred there is a kind of human impulse to increase love.

Frankly, to me, it proves the belief that life is going to win out. To me it proves a classic Jewish belief, which is shared by Christianity and by Islam and by many religions, that love is really stronger than hatred. And life is stronger than death.

JEWISH

BREAKING THE BOUNDARIES
SUSANNAH HESCHEL

Susannah Heschel holds the Abba Hillel Silver Chair in Jewish Studies in the department of religion at Case Western Reserve University, in Cleveland, Ohio. She earned her doctorate in Religious Studies at the University of Pennsylvania with a concentration in modern Jewish thought. She is the editor of *On Being a Jewish Feminist: A Reader* and has written extensively on feminist theology, including the problem of anti-Judaism and anti-Semitism in Christian feminist theology. Most recently, she has written a book on the nineteenth-century German-Jewish theologian Abraham Geiger, who wrote extensively on the Jewish background of the origins of Christianity and the New Testament.

Currently, Professor Heschel is researching the history of anti-Semitism in Nazi Germany, sponsored by the Lutheran church. Working in newly opened archives in the former East Germany, she has gathered data enabling her to reconstruct the activities and membership of the institute, and, hence, to reveal critical insights regarding the perversion of religion, and the evolution of intolerance.

During the 1992–93 academic year, she spent a semester in Germany, where she held the Martin Buber Visiting Professorship in Jewish Religious Philosophy at the University of Frankfurt. While in Frankfurt she taught seminars on the history of Jewish-Christian relations in Germany.

During the 1993–94 academic year, Professor Heschel held a Lilly Foundation fellowship to develop a seminar on religion and the environment. She lectured on Judaism and ecology at the Rio Summit in 1992.

ON BEING A JEW AND A FEMINIST

From the time I was a small child, I felt very strongly about Jewish values and a very strong commitment to Jewish faith and Jewish religious practice. At the same time, I was constantly questioning why I couldn't be doing all the things that the little boy children were doing. Why was I excluded and why were women excluded from so much that was central in Jewish religious life in the synagogue and also outside the synagogue? For instance, why weren't women in our synagogue called to the Torah to say prayers and to lead the services? When we went to visit my uncle, who was a rabbi, he sat at his table surrounded only by his male disciples, while the women were in the kitchen preparing the food. I wanted to be at the table also, listening and discussing. Actually, I was born as a Jew and as a feminist.

I remember once going with a male friend to a synagogue on the holiday of *Simcah Torah*. My parents were there. All the men were dancing with the Torahs, and the women were standing at the side looking on. So I went over, joined the circle, and started dancing. Then some man came over to me, and said, "What are you doing here?"

I must have been fifteen or something, and I said, "Well, I want to dance with the Torah too."

Finally they said, "Who gave you permission?"

I said, "God." That answer wasn't acceptable to them, and they made me leave.

When I was growing up, the prophets were very important to me. And my reading of the prophets is also that the prophets went to the kings, and they went to the priests, and they went to the people and they said, "This isn't right. You are not really listening. You are not looking at things from God's perspective."

I took that seriously. That's how I feel, too, because it's part of a prophetic tradition, feminism. It is not a tradition that says

Simhat Torah, a Jewish holiday, celebrates the completion of the public reading of the Torah (the Mosaic law in the first five books of the Bible), which traditionally follows a one-year cycle. To show their joy in the renewal of Torah study, the faithful carry the Torah scrolls during much singing and dancing. A procession circles the synagogue seven times, during which prayers are offered.

Bat Mitzvah, *the occasion on which a girl assumes religious and legal maturity as a Jew, is usually conferred at the age of twelve. The central element of the celebration is the calling of the girl to read the Torah in the synagogue. She reads or chants the prescribed benedictions (praises to God), as well as the concluding part of the Pentateuch reading and the prophetic lesson. The* bat mitzvah *appears not to have been celebrated before the nineteenth century.*

that we want to walk away from Judaism. On the contrary, it's from within, to be more involved, to make our Jewish lives richer.

Both of my parents supported me all the time on these issues, agreed with me that these things were wrong, and also felt that things were going to change.

When I wanted to have a *bat mitzvah,* for instance, I had one. My father was the one who suggested to me that I apply to rabbinical school, even though at the time the conservative movement wasn't considering women rabbis.

A lot of people feel that since women are now ordained rabbis, the problems are resolved. And of course, that's a mistake. There are changes that need to take place in the curriculum. For example, a study was done recently that says that 70 percent of women rabbis report having been subjected to sexual harassment, which is the same percentage found in studies of Protestant women ministers in certain groups. So clearly people's attitudes also have to be changed.

We have a patriarchal religious community, as we do in all religions, all religions that I'm aware of in any event. I'm not so concerned about the question of why things developed the way they did. I'm more interested in the question of changing. We have to change for the future.

Feminist ideas are morally justified. They don't need any further justification. It is quite clear to me that women have to be treated with decency and equality and should not be exploited for the benefit of men.

THE CHARACTERIZATION OF GOD WITH MASCULINE AND FEMININE TERMS

Our language is gendered. And if we use exclusively male language, that means that, in some way, we are denying who God really is. It would be absolutely wrong theologically, from the Jewish perspective, to confine God to maleness, to male stereotypes. And luckily Jewish tradition has not done that because God has been described in female as well as male language, having female attributes as well as male attributes.

I think it would be wrong to say that caring or compassion are solely female attributes. For one thing, a man could easily say, "I don't have to be gentle and compassionate, I'm a man." Right? That would be very bad and very dangerous for our society. I wouldn't want to say that at all.

The point that I am making is that, within Jewish tradition, God is presented as having a male side and a female side.

God responds to us as human beings. It is a relationship that we have with God in the Bible. The Talmud says that when the Temple in Jerusalem went up in flames in the year 70, God cried. God sheds a tear when two people stop loving each other. God is affected by human deeds. What I do to another person affects God. If I injure someone, I hurt God. If I help someone, I give strength to God. It's a relationship.

ON JEWISH AND CHRISTIAN DIALOGUE

Most of the work that I've done has been in Germany, and there is a lot of pain there for me for personal reasons—for reasons of my family. I spent almost the whole of this past year in Germany. There are so many bad things going on there, so much anti-Semitism. Yet, at the same time, there are some extraordinary people, especially among Christian theologians, who are working on the issues of anti-Semitism and changing Christian theology and saying we can't go on with Christian theology as it's always been. We can't do that anymore.

It has to change because of a sense of responsibility and a sense that anti-Semitism is the central issue, they feel, for Christians in Germany today. They have done wonderful work on that subject, very intense work. I think it's far more sophisticated than anywhere else in the world.

Just about everybody's against anti-Semitism in Germany. For one thing, it's against the law. It's a terrible thing. And everyone will tell you, "I'm against it. I'm against it."

And then when you ask them something about Judaism, you hear all the same old stereotypes that are anti-Semitic stereotypes. So they are sort of anti-Semites against anti-Semitism. It's a very bizarre situation.

Destruction of the Temple

In 70 C.E., the Roman general Titus sacked Jerusalem and razed the Jewish temple in the course of a war begun four years earlier by Jews fighting against Roman rule in Palestine. Nothing but the western wall of the temple was left standing. That western wall is now called the "Wailing Wall" and is a symbol of Jewish exile and hope, a place of pilgrimage and prayer for Jews worldwide.

Jewish Population Statistics

United States	*5.8 million*
France	*530,000*
Great Britain	*350,000*
Israel	*4.4 million*
Former Soviet	
* Union*	*1.6 million*
Canada	*308,000*
Argentina	*233,000*
Brazil	*130,000*
South Africa	*120,000*

Interviewer: *How many women rabbis are there in the country right now?*
Professor Heschel: *There are about two hundred and fifty women rabbis, Reform, Reconstructionist, and Conservative.*
Interviewer: *How many men are there?*
Professor Heschel: *I'm not sure how many male rabbis there are in the United States, but I know that the rabbinical schools have about 50-50 men and women students.*

How can they continue with this? Today, I don't feel the pain, I don't feel in any way hurt or ashamed or feel that Judaism is the problem. The person who is saying this, that's the problem. My feeling is, in Germany, just a sense of being overwhelmed. How do you get rid of this? It's like trying to empty the ocean with a shovel. My students used to tease me about having office hours and people would come in one after the other and deal with their anti-Jewish stereotypes. It's overwhelming at times.

And I suppose I hear it and I remember that Hitler didn't come to power with weapons, with tanks and guns. Hitler came to power with propaganda, with words, with ideas. And I think, for this my family was murdered—with these words. It has to stop.

I don't know if it's coming back exactly the same way, but certainly there are certain anti-Semitic traditions that have continued. People are constantly saying, historians and so on, we're not having a rise of Nazism again. The Third Reich isn't returning in that sense. And I would agree that there are certain democratic institutions that have been set in place in Germany and in Europe.

I am concerned, though, with anti-Semitic stereotypes that continue. For example, there are some in Germany who have written that Nazism is a form of Judaism. Why? Because the Nazis had to obey the commands of Hitler, just like the Jews obey the commandments of God. So it's a morality of obedience to command. So Nazism is a form of Judaism. Can you imagine anything more perverse than to say such a thing? And what amazes me is that when I would show this statement to students or people at a lecture, they didn't understand what the problem was because they were so used to hearing comments like that. They are so used to it that they don't recognize that these are anti-Semitic comments.

TOWARD A JUST SOCIETY

We live in a society in which women are not respected in the same way as men, by and large, and not taken seriously. And some of this, of course, comes out of the religious traditions. If people think, mistakenly think, that God is male, that all of God's prophets are male, the voice of religion, the voice of authority, the voice of holiness is male, then how can they take a woman's voice seriously? Women would have to be, somehow, inferior to men. Of course, it's incorrect.

The Bible has some very sexist comments from time to time, but it also has other comments that make it clear. For example, the prophet Huldah, a woman prophet, authenticates the book of the law, that the Book of Deuteronomy is the word of God. And it's presented in a very matter-of-fact way in the Bible. I mean, as if it is a normal thing for a woman to be a prophet and decide, yes, this is the word of God. I think today we would have a much greater difficulty.

But our religious traditions through the centuries have been shaped by men. The texts that we have are male authored texts, and although they speak to me and I find them often deeply moving texts, I am still aware that they are exclusively male voices in these texts. Then I have to ask, how can I accept them as authoritative in my life when they haven't given me a voice, when they haven't listened to me?

There are Jewish women who want to express their Jewishness in lots of different kinds of settings and that's important. At the same time, what I would like to see is an end to the sense that women have of being inferior, or feeling excluded, or somehow, not even being aware, often, that we are excluded from certain things, not being aware of the discrimination. And so feeling, somehow, that something's wrong but not even knowing what it is.

I want women to feel free to make certain decisions about their religious spiritual life and intellectual life without fear of recrimination, without the feeling that so many generations of women have, that if you are too smart, men won't like you. That kind of thing. I don't want that sense of recrimination for the future. That's the sense of freedom.

I grew up very deeply immersed, and I am very grateful for the immersion that I had in Jewish religious life. I also feel that we've gone through a horrendous loss in this century. We lost the greatest sources of Jewish spirituality that we had. Eastern

Huldah, a Jerusalemite prophetess, was the wife of Shallum, keeper of the king's wardrobes during the reign of Josiah (639–609 B.C.E.). Huldah was consulted by the king's officials after the discovery in the temple of a "scroll of Moses"—a document some modern scholars have surmised is some form of the Book of Deuteronomy. Her prophecy, that Jerusalem would be destroyed, helped spur the king to initiate widespread religious reforms. Israel was conquered by the Babylonians and its Jewish population was exiled for about fifty years beginning in 597 B.C.E.

European Judaism was wiped out. And that's a terrible tragedy, a terrible, terrible thing. I feel that loss very strongly, and I want to hold on to something that I do feel is beautiful and wonderful and that speaks to me very deeply. It speaks out of my heart.

BUDDHIST BRAHMA KUMARIS JEWISH
IN NATIVE AMERICAN SUFI HINDU
RISTIAN ROMAN CATHOLIC MUSLIM
KH BAHA'I JEWISH ZOROASTRIAN

MUSLIM

MAN CATHOLIC TAOIST
ROASTRIAN PROTESTANT

NDU MUSLIM JAIN ROMAN CATHOLIC
OIST BAHA'I BUDDHIST SIKH SUFI
TIVE AMERICAN BRAHMA KUMARIS
WISH PROTESTANT CHRISTIAN TAOIST

DDHIST HINDU ZOROASTRIAN JAIN
MAN CATHOLIC BAHA'I PROTESTANT
OIST HINDU SUFI NATIVE AMERICAN
SLIM BRAHMA KUMARIS BUDDHIST
KH SUFI JEWISH MUSLIM TAOIST
ROASTRIAN CHRISTIAN BAHA'I HINDU

MUSLIM

REMEMBERING THE PROPHET
Dr. Azizah Y. Al-Hibri

Dr. Azizah Al-Hibri is professor of Islamic jurisprudence and corporate law at the University of Richmond and founder of the Muslim American Bar Association. President of the Parliament of the World's Religions from 1993 to 1995 and founder and president of the Muslim Women Lawyers Committee for Human Rights in 1994, she is an outspoken Muslim feminist. Her four books are: *Hypatia Reborn: Essays in Feminist Philosophy,* (ed., 1990), *Women and Islam* (ed., 1982), *Technology and Human Affairs* (ed., 1981), and *Deontic Logic: A Comprehensive Appraisal and a New Proposal* (1978).

Dr. Al-Hibri has presented wide-ranging lectures on the topics of discrimination against American Muslims, U.S. policy and Islamic reawakening, Islamic law, women and Islam, women and Shari'ah, and Islam and human rights.

Dr. Al-Hibri neither dresses nor speaks anything like the stereotyped image many Westerners harbor of Islamic woman. Her knowledge of Islam, Islamic history, philosophy, and the religious texts and commentaries, as well as the profound legalistic insights she brings to bear on questions most relevant to Islamic women today, give her a particularly unique vantage point on the diverse world of Islam. A frequent panelist, Al-Hibri participates in interviews, interfaith dialogues, and conferences concerned with law and human rights that have duly earned her a remarkable reputation as one who truly speaks on behalf of Islam and humanity. In one of her recent articles, "Symposium on Religious Law: Roman Catholic, Islamic, and Jewish Treatment of Family Matters, Including Education, Abortion, In Vitro Fertilization, Prenuptial Agreement, Contraception, and Marital Fraud," she addressed the kinds of compelling, contemporary issues that are her hallmark as a scholar, a feminist/humanist, and a true Muslim.

INDEPENDENT REASON IN ISLAM

You see, the Qur'ān, we believe, is a holy revelation from God. And to that extent, the message of the Qur'ān is eternal. God did not change his mind. Whatever truths are there are good for Muslims in all times and in all places. There's another dimension to the Qur'ān, though, that sometimes gets confused with the first. Namely that many of the *ayahs* were revealed in a specific context, in a specific society and a specific historical era. So they address some of that specificity.

As a Muslim scholar, you ought to be able to disengage these various elements and figure out what is the rule in that specific situation or even in the general Qur'ān; principles that are relevant to your time and place. Every law in the Qur'ān is relevant to your time and place, but where the principles are general, you have to supplement them with your own *ijtihād*, with your own understanding of how could they be made more specific to your context.

That means, if you have Islamic cultures that are quite diverse, all the way, say, from Pakistan to Iran to Morocco, these cultural factors are going to reflect themselves in those elements that supplement the Qur'ānic rules. All right. And that's acceptable.

In fact the Prophet encouraged people to engage in *ijtihād*. And they were afraid because they thought, after the Prophet's death, the revelation will stop and the Prophet will not be there to tell them what is right in certain circumstances they never saw before his death.

So what are they going to do? What if they engage in *ijtihād* and it turns out they're wrong? The price is high. You might end up in hell. Right, and nobody wants that, especially if they are believers. Well, the Prophet addressed that issue in his life-time. And he said, if you engage in *ijtihād* and you are right, you get two rewards from God. If you engage in *ijtihād* and you are wrong, you get one. And the people said, why do I get one at all?

You get one for the effort because in Islam it's better to think and be wrong than not to use your head at all. God gave you that head and because part of the responsibility you are going to be faced with is individual, if you do the wrong thing tomorrow and then you face your Creator and your Creator says, "Why did you do this wrong?" you can't say, "Because my teacher told me, or my father told me, or my sister or even my ruler told me," because you have moral responsibility, you have your mind. God did not give us a collective mind, although God gave us a collective responsibility in a society to advise each other and try to lead each other the right way.

But in the final analysis what you do is your moral responsibility. If you don't engage in *ijtihād*, if you are a mere follower, you're still responsible for these strong acts you make. And most of all you are responsible for not having thought, for not having made that effort.

It's not just independent thinking. It's rational analysis. It's almost like philosophical analysis of the text, of the circumstances, of the overall situation to come up with the right rule for your situation, for your context. Independence is one element of it, although it's not a bad idea, if you're trying to reach your opinion and you're not sure, to consult others because others tend to enlighten your thinking. It's at the heart of Islam and Islamic democracy, and even the Prophet engaged in it.

At heart, Islam is a democratic religion. Forget about what you see in terms of historical manifestations—we're talking religion. And the democracy derives from the very basic principles I'm telling you about. I gave you only one of them now, namely that you are responsible for your own thoughts.

Somebody else might disagree with me, for example, on the question of the *chodor*, that I should be putting on some headdress, but let me face that responsibility with God. Now if I'm doing something terribly wrong and immoral and causing corruption to society, then society as a group will have to do something about that.

Ijtihād

The term Ijtihād comes from a Hadith (deeds or utterances of the Prophet as recounted by his Companions) in which the Prophet asked one of his delegates, Muàz, by what criteria he would administer the regions under his control. "The Qur'ān," the man replied:

"And then what?" the Prophet asked.

"The Sunnah [or example of the Prophet]."

"And then what?"

"Then I will make a personal effort [ijtihād] and act according to that."

And this the Prophet approved.

Ijtihād is applied to those questions which are not covered by the Qur'ān or Sunnah, that is by established precedent, nor by direct analogy from known laws. . . .

(Glasse)

THE WEAKENING OF *IJTIHĀD*

Why did *ijtihād* weaken so much in Islam? Historically, there is a term, the closing of the doors of *ijtihād*, which happened around the tenth century and thereafter.

For the longest time Muslim scholars were engaging in this thinking and saying this is how the rule of Islam applies to this situation in our land, or to that other one. Well, as the religion spread all over the globe, then a lot of people were engaging in *ijtihād* without adequate foundation. So the religious scholars were concerned about that and started specifying certain requirements for *ijtihād* to make sure that people are not doing it without doing it properly.

But then, I think, this began to interact with the political demands of the time. And political leaders thought that might not be a bad idea—not allowing too many people to engage in *ijtihād*, under, maybe, the guise of *kof'r* or saying the wrong thing, totally unacceptable from an Islamic point of view. And we know that, in some cases, some of the major Islamic scholars that today are followed in various parts of the Muslim world were tortured for their views.

The Muslim scholar was tortured because he refused to say what the political leader wanted him to say to legitimize his rule over the Muslim people.

WOMEN AND ISLAM

Some of the most independent women in history have been Muslim women. Look at Khadīja, the first wife of the Prophet. She was fifteen years his senior. She was a businesswoman. She had hired him to help her with the business. She liked him. She proposed marriage to him, and he said yes.

Look at ʿĀʾisha, the woman the Prophet married later. She was involved in every aspect of the Muslim society, and she was a leader. A lot of the *ḥadīth*, the statements reported about the Prophet, come from her, and many other women. There were a lot of images, strong images of Muslim women that no one talks about.

Women's Rights in Islam

In ancient Arab society, the coming of Islam brought women's rights where they had none, or few, before. "You have rights over your women," says a hadīth, "and your women have rights over you." These rights were conferred as an integral part of Divine legislation without being demanded; that is to say, there is no evidence that they were the result of any struggle on the part of Arab women. A spirit of freedom under early Islam may in fact have been curtailed later, under the Abbasids (ca. eighth to thirteenth century dynasty).

(Glasse)

I must throw this in because of the discussion in Kuwait—whether women should vote or not vote. Well, I mean, how could it be a question? Please! If you open the Qur'ān it says right there that when the Prophet was being elected as a head of state in his time—because he was elected; he didn't say, "I'm the Prophet, follow me"—women voted. People actually chose him through a form of election called *el baya* where they come and shake his hand and say, "You're the leader." If enough of them do it, then he is. Well, the women came to the Prophet, as a women's delegation, to give the *baya* to the Prophet. It is in the Qur'ān.

He didn't tell them, "What are you doing here? . . . ha, ha, ha? Go back home, this is none of your business." Not at all. He had a discussion with them. And women have played a big role. If you read the Qur'ān there was a woman who came to the Prophet and argued with him about religion. There is a whole *sura* about her called "the woman who argued."

In my view, with the closing of the door of *ijtihād*, and the rise of dictatorial centralized power, patriarchy became more and more intense in the Muslim societies, not only vis-à-vis women, but even vis-à-vis the concept of democracy in society where democracy was on the ebb. When all that happened, women suffered in such an atmosphere more than any other individuals in society.

As Islam spread all over, fewer and fewer people, including, for example, Muslim Americans, can read the Qur'ān, itself. They rely on translations, or commentary, and there's no such thing as objectivity. These always reflect the view of the commentator or the translator, even unconsciously. Then you get certain patriarchal views, certain translations. Now you are being told, "This is what God wants for you." And if you are a religious woman, you don't want to go against God.

Except it has come through a translator and a whole system of patriarchy and a lot of culture facts. If you look now at Islam and you compare the understanding of Islam in Pakistan, versus Morocco, versus Iran, versus Lebanon, they are all different.

The Prophet said that you must educate your children, male and female. There is absolutely no difference in Islam. Both must be educated. So if women are not being educated in favor

The Qur'ān in English?

The Qur'ān, the scripture that sets forth a series of divine revelations given to the Prophet Muhammad through an angel, is written in Arabic. Like the Hebrew for the Jewish Bible and the Sanskrit of the Hindu Vedas, the Arabic of the Qur'ān is sacrosanct. Unlike the Bible or the Vedas, the Arabic of the Qur'ān is considered so holy that Muslims forbid any translations into foreign languages. It can be "interpreted" or "paraphrased," as it has been into English, but it can never be authentically translated.

Veil

The covering of the face is usually referred to by the general term hijab; *it is called* purdah *in the Indo-Persian countries; in Iran* chador *is the word for the tent-like black cloak worn by many women in the Middle East.*

Use of the veil to cover the face did not appear until Abbasid times (ca. eighth century). None of the Muslim legal systems actually prescribe that women must wear a veil, although they do prescribe covering the body in public, to the neck, the ankles, and below the elbow. While modesty is a religious prescription, the wearing of a veil is not a religious requirement of Islam, but a matter of cultural milieu.

(Glasse)

of males, then the analysis must come from a system which is not Islamic, but from extra elements, external to Islam, cultural perhaps that are influencing the decisions of people in those countries. And very often they don't tell you this is extra-religious because then it doesn't have the same weight.

So what they would do, they would find a religious support for it, some kind of an explanation to say, "But this is really Islam, and you have to follow it." That's where we now need what I call new jurisprudence for a new world.

I teach corporate law and I teach Islamic jurisprudence, and I am now involved in a project that I hope, through it, to present that new jurisprudence. I want to go back to the roots of Islam, to the life of the Prophet, to the *ḥadīth* and find out what are the women's rights under those conditions. They have a lot of rights that Islam has given them, and somehow they have been taken away. Even men, Muslim men nowadays are writing books saying, "Why are our women kept in this state?" Not all the men, but some of them, and very important scholars at that.

ISLAM IN NORTH AMERICA

This is a very exciting period in the history of Islam and, in particular, in the history of American Islam. Because of all the Islam around the world, all the countries that are Muslim, this is the only country where we can actually go back to the real *ijtihād* without having our arm twisted, or taken out of its socket, or tortured because the ruler does not like what we have to say. So I can really think about things and be my own conscientious scholar and put ideas out that I think are truly Islamic and get responses from the other Muslims in this country and other countries about that point of view.

FAMILY PLANNING, THE EARTH'S RESOURCES, AND THE RIGHTS OF WOMEN

The whole issue of family planning is a very important one, because you can approach it from a variety of ways. On the one hand, there is a lot of concern in Third World countries that much of the discussion about population control is really motivated not by considerations about the well-being of the planet but rather about racism.

Having said that, now I can tell you a little bit about the Islamic position on family planning. The Muslim woman in the family has a very important basic right for sexual enjoyment. In fact, under certain conditions specified by the scholars of the past, even though they were patriarchal, she could get a divorce with no problem if the husband is not satisfying, fulfilling this right. This is something many Muslim women don't know. Divorce is permissible in Islam but it is not, of course, encouraged.

It is understood by Muslim scholars that it would be unfair to ask the Muslim wife to be faithful when she is not getting satisfaction from her husband. And the Prophet himself had statements about how the Muslim husband is responsible in certain ways toward his wife in this area.

Now, one of the ways that Muslim scholars thought detracts from the sexual enjoyment of the wife is practicing *coitus interruptus*. And therefore a Muslim may not engage in this practice without first getting his wife's consent. She also has a right to procreation. That's part of her entering the marriage. The husband has to get her permission to engage in *coitus interruptus* or some other form of contraception. Yes, and also he has rights. You cannot spring on him in the marriage, "I don't want to have kids anymore."

The woman has her rights, and so does the man. But the problem has not been that the men have been denied their rights. The problem has been on the other side.

Now also, once the woman is pregnant, depending on the stage of pregnancy, and on certain other considerations, she might be able to terminate her pregnancy. It's very much, in many ways, similar to the *Roe vs. Wade* decision, believe it or not. It is a three-stage analysis. Really, you may not abort at the advanced stages when there is a *ruha* or spirit, a soul, when the baby has become a *nuffs*, the embryo has become a *nuffs*. At that point you cannot abort the child unless, for example, the life of the mother is endangered.

But before that, there are degrees. As you approach the *nuffs* stage it becomes more and more difficult to abort. Within the earlier stages it is much more easy to do so. And that is very much similar to the Supreme Court analysis.

Women and Men in Islam

Islam views men and women as equals before God. The Qur'ān says that man and woman were "created of a single soul" (4:1; 39:6). The identity between man and woman is affirmed by the capacity of woman to perform all rites; the sacerdotal function in Islam is as much woman's as it is man's.

The Middle Eastern norm for relationships between the sexes is by no means the only one possible for Islamic societies everywhere, nor is it appropriate for all cultures. It does not exhaust the possibilities allowed within the framework of the Qur'ān and Sunnah and is neither feasible nor desirable as a model for European or North American Islam.

(Glasse)

THE PROBLEM OF PERCEPTIONS, AS A WOMAN
AND A MUSLIM

Statistics on Islam in
the 1990s

Worldwide
Islam is the second largest
(behind Christianity) and
fastest growing religion in
the world. It is estimated
there are 924 million Mus-
lims worldwide, or nearly
18 percent of the total
world population

The Middle East
Although the vast majority
of Arabs are Muslim (about
200 million spread out
from Mauritania in West
Africa to Iraq in the Middle
East), Arabs compose less
than one-fifth of the world
Muslim population.

Indian Subcontinent
The largest single ethnic
group of followers of Islam
is found on the Indian sub-
continent: 350 million in
Pakistan, Bangladesh,
India, Sri Lanka, and
Nepal. The 100 million
Muslims living in India are
the largest single minority
in the world.

Well, as a woman, anyway, there is always a problem of perception. When I walk into the class and I'm teaching securities reg-
ulation or corporate law, I mean, these are male provinces!
Right?

Not so! We do very well in those areas, but you constantly
have to prove yourself. You constantly have to establish yourself as an authority and an expert. And then there are the elements when you are a Muslim woman. It is hard to separate. Is
the reaction because I'm a woman or a Muslim?

I would be incorrect to say that I am acceptable to all Muslims the way I am. Let me say that as far as my clothing, it
should be acceptable. There is no problem with that. The question arises usually as to why I am not wearing a headdress. I
have my own answers for that, when I'm asked. I believe I am
doing the right thing, but that's all really in the area of *ijtihād* or
reasoning on the basis of the holy text of the Qur'ān and then
the tradition of the Prophet.

PERSONAL FAITH AND THE NATURE OF GOD

I was raised as a Muslim, and then I became an atheist for quite
a few years. And then it really is for me a personal journey. I did
not become a Muslim for an objective, external reason. I have
my own conviction through my own *ijtihād,* my own leap of
faith, my own experience.

Very often women refer to a hole, an emptiness, something
missing. And I had that feeling, and I didn't know what was
missing. I was very happy and successful in my life. And then I
had some problems, like everybody else. You go through difficult periods and easy periods in your life. And I had to face myself at one point, and ask myself through a very interesting
spiritual journey, "Who am I? Is there a superior being? Am I
willing to recognize that there is a being superior to me?" because I was young, and successful and arrogant. And I decided
that, having thought about it, I do believe in God.

When I decided that I believed in God, I also understood that I have to pray. The most difficult act for me was the very act of prayer, when I had to bow down to God, because that clinched it, that I was not a superior being. In fact, this arrogance is not unusual. It's unusual in people who are independent and intelligent to be willing to submit to a higher authority. I resent authority. The authority I was familiar with was patriarchy. The God that was presented to me was an angry, patriarchal God.

My God is merciful. I've decided that the image of God presented to me through the culture is erroneous. And I can know this from the very first line in the Qur'ān. The minute you open the Qur'ān, the very first verse is "*Bismillah al-rahman al-rahim*—in the name of God," and then two words, each one of them meaning merciful.

That's the God that I am worshiping. He is not an angry God, he is not an authoritarian God. He is the God who says, "Consult each other, it is better for you to talk to each other." He is the God who says, "I created you all from the same *nuffs*," *nuffs* being a soul, in Arabic, a female gender word. "I created you from the same *nuffs*, male and female, and I made for that *nuffs*, its mate, so that they can have tranquillity. And I brought amongst them love and mercy."

This is the main theme of relationships. There is no rib; there is no Adam. We are created, male and female, so that we might have tranquillity with each other and have love and mercy, not conflict, not confrontation, not subjugation, none of that.

And in another part of the Qur'ān it says, "I created you from the same *nuffs*, male and female, nations and tribes." So it's not only gender, it's culture, it's also races, it goes on— classes. But why? Why did God create in us a difference—so that we can shoot at each other?

That's not what the *ayah* says. It says that we get to know each other. God wants us to get to know each other, to enjoy diversity, to celebrate diversity. That's why God created us. And there is no *one* better than the other.

Belhid means there is only one God, and all of us submit to that one God. If anyone comes to you and says, submit to me, you don't, if you're a Muslim. You only submit to God. Now,

Africa
There are more than 100 million black African Muslims, distinct from the Arab and Berber North Africans.

Southeast Asia
The country with the largest Muslim population is Indonesia. More than 180 million Muslims live in the region that includes Malaysia, Brunei, the southern Philippines, and parts of Thailand, Cambodia (Kampucha), and Singapore.

China
The number of Muslims in China are not well documented but have been estimated at anywhere from 30 to 100 million.

Interviewer: *Are women spiritual equals?*
Dr. Al-Hibri: *Absolutely. Absolutely. They're all created by the same God. What would ever give anybody the idea that women are not!*

Islam and the Environment

*Muslims believe that every-
thing was created by Allah
(God) and therefore everything is sacred, useful, and
has its place in the general
scheme of things and in the
interest of man.*

*Islam is a religion which
started in the deserts of
Arabia with a universal
message. Its concern for the
environment is a universal
concern, cutting across national, religious and geographical barriers. Its
major commandments are
directed, not to the Mus-
lims, but to the human
race. Hence its call upon
"people" (not the Arabs
nor the Muslims) to con-
serve the natural resources
which are God's gift to
mankind.*

*There are many verses
from the Holy Qur'ān and
Hadīth (statements by the
Prophet) urging people to
be kind to the land, to the
rivers, to the air and not to
abuse the fertile valleys.
Kindness to "those who
cannot speak" (animals) is
urged by the Prophet again
and again.*

—Dr. Mohammed Mehdi
(SourceBook)

that concept is very critical for women's rights and for a variety of other things.

I don't need a man. And I don't need a woman. I don't need anybody to mediate between me and God. God says, if you need something, call me.

So if I need something, I call God and ask for God's help. Everybody has his number; you just have to read the Qur'ān. So I actually sit down and read the Qur'ān and pray and I say, "God, that's what I need, and help me out." And I do get helped out. Call it faith, call it whatever you want, but it certainly has done miracles for me. I now know tranquillity, which I did not know before, to the same extent anyway.

STRENGTH IN SUBMISSION

Islam means submission. But it's a submission that makes you strong. It's that submission which frees you from anyone else's subjugation because you will only submit to one God. So if you think that because you're rich, or because you're powerful, or because you come from a certain country, or whatever, that you are better than the other person next door, you're wrong. That is not an Islamic concept. And that is where modesty comes in.

One sign of a good Muslim is humility. One sign of good humility and modesty is the way you deal with others. And God says, in the Qur'ān, the good word is like a healthy tree, deeply rooted in the earth, and its branches reach toward the heavens. So you are supposed to be a good neighbor, you are supposed to treat everybody nicely, and be a good example so that when people see you they will say Muslims are good people.

If there is somebody who doesn't believe in God at all, it's okay if you try to mention God to them. But you should not feel superior because we all are God's creatures, and because whatever God gave us in terms of rewards or benefits, whether they are intellectual or spiritual or all that then we should be thankful for and not use them as tools or weapons against others.

MUSLIM

FORGIVENESS
Imam W. D. Mohammed

Son of the Honorable Elijah Mohammed, the man commonly recognized as the "builder" of the Nation of Islam, W. D. Mohammed is a builder in his own right. For many years now, he has sought to create positive bridges between Islam and other faiths, while bringing African Americans to the gates of Orthodox Sunni Islam. He was the first Muslim to offer prayers before the U.S. Senate, in which he stated, "Bless our homes and our schools. Bless the parents, our troubled youth, our burdened inner cities to never be without hope or direction. Bless Americans to keep to the best of our ways."

It is such feeling that impelled Joshua Haberman, Senior Rabbi Emeritus of the Washington Hebrew Congregation, to write, "Imam W. D. Mohammed is one of the most enlightened religious leaders in our world today. . . . I am deeply impressed by his spiritual leadership and pray for God's blessings upon his good work."

Mohammed has represented American Muslims throughout the Middle East and North Africa. He has given love and support to the oppressed throughout the world, whether Kuwaiti refugees, the Muslims of Bosnia-Herzegovina, the cause of the suffering people of Somalia, the Afghan *mujahiddin,* and Muslims against Apartheid. His publications include *Prayer and Al-Islam, Focus on Al-Islam,* and *Al-Islam, Unity and Leadership.*

In his efforts to transform the early conservatism of his father's Nation into a far more tolerant, depoliticized spiritual

American Muslim Mission

*In 1985 W. D. Mohammed
resigned his position as
leader of the American
Muslim Mission and dis-
banded the movement's na-
tional structure. This move
is meant to establish a fully
congregational polity by
the Muslims whose local
centers are now under the
guidance of imams rather
than the control of the
Chicago headquarters.
W. D. now operates as an
independent Muslim lec-
turer and member of the
World Council of Masajid,
headquartered in Mecca,
Saudi Arabia.*

(Melton, *Creeds*)

community, Mohammed has suffered criticism from those who feel threatened by his very compassion and wit. Some have even argued that he has "sold out" to the whites.

Mohammed does not call himself a supreme minister, but rather, an Imam, or model. Since assuming leadership of his father's Nation in 1975, he has argued for justice based upon religious compassion, consistency, and integrity, not race. He has liberalized traditional strictures with regard to Islamic dress code and the freedom of individuals, both men and women. With the creation of the American Muslim Mission, Mohammed has piloted his people—hundreds of thousands of followers—to what is today a decentralized and thriving society of Muslim Americans. With mosques and schools in every major city in America, and in parts of Canada and the Caribbean, he has garnered a respect and acceptance for what he calls "proto-Islam" not known in the West before.

It has been far too easy for Americans of a countering mindset to dismiss Islam through an ignorance that is quick to fashion stereotypes and parodies. What struck me at first meeting Mohammed was his enormous gift of gab. His humor, grace, and tolerance is deeply familiar. One feels instant camaraderie with Mohammed, and, by inference, with Islam itself. And that is Mohammed's special gift, an achievement that is the quintessence of spiritual truth.

CHANGED TEACHINGS

I grew up in Chicago under the Nation of Islam or Black Muslim. My parents moved to Detroit, Michigan, around 1929, where they came in contact with a man called Fard, who was not an American, and he introduced a brand of Islam to them. In 1931 my father converted to that religion. And I was born in 1933. My mother was Sarah and my father, Elijah.

It's been twenty years since I've been relatively free as a spokesman for that leadership. In 1972 my father gave me the okay to represent him to the Nation of Islam.

It was very difficult for me to make changes, and I imagine even more difficult for many of the followers of Elijah Mohammed. We were good people, well-meaning people, but we had a kind of black nationalism and, I would say, a religion labeled Islam. But there was just a little of the spirit and ideas of Islam within that religion.

Muslim terminology, we had that, you know. "*A salaam...*, brother.*"* In the name of Allah, all praise to Allah, we had all that. But we didn't have, really, the idea of God, of man, of the world that we live in, the universe that we live in. We didn't have that as it is in the Koran, in the holy book of all Muslims. But we had the holy book, strangely enough.

Our language was a language of, I would say, condemnation. We were condemning the white race for the evils against blacks, you know, the evils that blacks suffered in the world. And that became even, I would say, basic and essential to the religion as we understood it. Our religion started with the black man being God, nothing but black people being in existence.

Before I go too far with this, I would like to say that I believe, I can't prove it, but I believe that the language that Fard gave my father was allegorical, metaphorical language, a kind of a bitter satire on the evils of the white man with regard to the treatment of the black people, the black race beginning in Africa and on to America. I want to make that clear before going any further with this.

Religion for us was to believe that black man was God, and that man only was God—that before man existed in the flesh body, he was existing in space, as a some nonmaterial entity, and then he, of his own willpower, he made himself material. And that was the black man, we were told. We were never told how he created the black woman, though.

That religion had to be—well, I don't want to say condemned—but it had to be rejected in order for us to continue to be comfortable calling ourselves Muslims. When the real, ugly circumstances in the life of America were against us and the government was supporting it, there was a place for that kind of teaching, though not a justification. Southern laws were allowed to be executed on blacks that were really abhorred by many decent whites, in the South and in the North, but that was allowed. In my opinion, there is never a justification to do wrong or to speak untruth.

Islam in North America

Four to five million Muslims live in North America, mainly African Americans and immigrant groups— Arabs, Persians, Turks, and people from the Indian subcontinent. About one half of American Muslims live in metropolitan areas: New York City, Los Angeles, Chicago, Detroit, Houston, Washington.

(Sharma)

Sunni Islam

More than 90 percent of the Muslims in the world identify themselves with the term Ahl-al-Sunnah wa al-Jama'ah, *or People of the Tradition and the Community, commonly known as Sunni Muslims, distinct from unorthodox sects or groups, such as Shi'ite Muslims. Sunni Muslims recognize the succession of the first four Caliphs, beginning with Abu Bakr, against the Shi'ites (Shi'ah, "partisans") who follow a succession of the Prophet's leadership through his son-in-law, Ali ibn Abi Talib. From the Sunni point of view, Shi'ites are Muslims because their doctrines coincide for the most part with orthodox Islam.*

(Glasse)

Nonviolence in Islam

"Shall I inform you of a better act than fasting, alms, and prayers? Making peace between one another: enmity and malice tear up heavenly rewards by the roots."

(Sayings of Muhammed 117–18)

In my opinion (that means I'm not speaking for even all Muslims) there is never a justification to do wrong or speak what is untrue. But I can understand it. After this country used its military force and other forces to bring about acceptance of blacks as citizens, as equal citizens in this country, then I think that old religion that Fard put together to attract blacks was antiquated.

The religion has to be Islam as all Muslims understand that religion. That's what it has to be.

ISLAM MEANS PEACE

Islam. Actually the word derives from the root word meaning "peace," peace. And it is a verb. It is a verb meaning to bring yourself to conform, to conform peacefully.

When we accept to be obedient, peaceful slaves to God—and what God wills—then we really have freedom and we have dignity and we have independence. When we become the slave of God we're independent of all other masters. And God is not a master—of that type.

We hope that as African American Muslims our light will send a message to the whole of America that this religion—a belief in God, a willingness to make God the authority in our life over all other authorities—was the factor which brought us from an extreme kind of black reverse supremacy to join what is worldwide Islam, and practice that religion and live that religion just as all Muslims are required to practice it and live it. And to become, ourselves, a force for healing the racial wounds in the black man and also, I hope, in America.

You know the Nation of Islam, the followers of Elijah Mohammed, my late father, those men and women, they were not cowards. Most of them were told to be brave, fearless. If you were to differ at all with Elijah Mohammed, you were in serious trouble, and I knew that. And I differed. I differed drastically with the old teachings of Elijah Mohammed.

But you know, I had faith that I was right and innocent and God was with me. So I told him, bluffing a bit, "Look, you think you're tough? The worst man that you can meet in battle is a man that believes in God and has surrendered his whole life to God. A man of peace is a man that can really war with you!"

What I am saying is this—that we have to be people of peace to be Muslims. Sadam, for example—his conduct and his aggression on Kuwait was, to me, very un-Islamic. It was savage. We can't do that.

We're people of peace but we also have to be ready to go to war.

ISLAM AND THE SUBMISSION OF WOMEN

In our religion, the first and most cherished obligation that the woman has is the obligation to aspire for motherhood, to one day have a husband and, hopefully, with God's blessing, have children and to raise a family that will be a wholesome contribution to the society for the Muslim and to the society of mankind. This is the most sacred ambition, I think, for a Muslim woman.

But if we study the early history of Islam in Arabia, we find that the Prophet himself was seen as a man giving women more freedom, liberating women. During that time, the woman was looked upon as, really, property and inferior to man, and that she should accept to please him. Polygamy was not restricted.

It was the habit of non-Muslims, the ignorant people in that age, some of them, to bury the female child alive.

I think we bury our females alive still when we deny them opportunity to go to or qualify for any college institution, to choose a profession and be successful in the world, to be wealthy, to have a voice in public affairs. I think when we deny women that, we're burying our females alive.

What a loss—a great loss—all of us suffer.

I think that a change is coming. More and more scholars are coming out and addressing these issues—the rights of women. But still they are very hesitant to do that. I find that most of them seem to be pleased with me doing it. And I would say to the whole Islamic world that we have to address this issue of equality, sexual equality. Because in my opinion, Islam is a religion that would invite people to respect the equality of the sexes.

The Rights of Women

The rights of women are sacred. See that women are maintained in the rights assigned to them.

Allah enjoins you to treat women well, for they are your mothers, daughters, and aunts.

Whoever hath a daughter, and doth not bury her alive, or scold her, or prefer his male children to her, may God bring him into Paradise.

(Sayings of Muhammed, 117–18)

COMING TOGETHER AS A NATION: DEALING WITH RACISM

You know, we want the heaven that God promised us after this is all over. And we're not going to have that. Not on this earth. So we have to accept human weaknesses, we have to have patience and tolerate each other. We have to forbear. We have to excuse each other. We have to give to each other. And we have to stop identifying every friction that we have with a member of another race as racism, because most of the time it's not racism. It's just the human weakness.

I believe that when it comes to white and black, the problem of white and black racism, it's mostly ignorance still. Although a lot of education has been given since the beginning of Dr. King's movement—I won't say the Civil Rights movement, I have to say Dr. King's movement—a lot of education has been put out in the air, but I think that the problem is still education. And I don't think the answer is education, though.

The answer is a model people. We have to have model people, and blacks are in need of a model people more than any other. I think we tend to be spiritualized and just move with the spirit of our race, you know. We're not concentrating on building a social example. And that's what we need. We need a social community of black people that sets an example to other people. With integrity as a black race. You have to have that.

PERSONAL MISREPRESENTATION

I've been misrepresented as a Muslim. I think the problem is because of the image that we have to change and come away from as Muslims in America. It is also owing a lot to a tendency on the part of immigrant Muslims, and also Muslims of the international world, who can't believe that now a black man is Muslim and he doesn't want to open up the case of racism or charge of racism and have that court continue. They can't believe that we're Muslims and we are not angry with the white man anymore. We still should be angry with America, in their view. Maybe it's because we would make a convenient instrument for

The First Black Muslim

Bilal, a black slave from Abyssinia, was an early convert to Islam and was severely mistreated by his master for that reason. Bilal was ransomed and freed by his fellow convert Abu Bakr, the First Caliph and successor to the Prophet. He was the first muezzin or caller to prayer, chosen because of his fine voice. He made the call to prayer from the top of the holy sanctuary (Ka'bah) in the center of the Grand Mosque when the Prophet entered Mecca on pilgrimage in 629 C.E. Some orthodox Black Muslims take inspiration from his life and proudly call themselves Bilalians.

(Glasse)

them if we were angry—for some of them, not all of them.

Many of them feel very much like I do. They're very happy. In fact they applaud my attitude toward the white race. For example, Sheik Abdullah Turkey, who is over the higher education of the kingdom of Saudi Arabia, Dr. Naseef, who used to be the Secretary General of the Muslum World League, and many others I could name. They applaud my position or my attitude regarding how we should deal with questions of race. But the great majority think we're supposed to be angry. And because of that they want to dig up things that I have said that now I don't include in my talks because it does confuse what is really Islam. They want to dig up those things and say, "Look what you said in 1975. Look what you said in 1980. If you said that, then how are we to believe you now? If you lied then, how do we know if you're telling the truth now?"

They don't realize that I had a strategy to wean my community off of those things that were un-Islamic, that to them were Islamic. I'll accept my day in court with God. I'll answer to God and I think God is going to be more understanding than these people who accuse me of being wrong.

Sunni Islam in the
United States

The Sunni Muslim presence in the United States is symbolically centered at the Islamic Center in Washington, D.C., officially opened in 1957. Sunni Islam is decentralized in character and organized into autonomous centers around the country. The mosque, headed by the imam *(minister-teacher), is the basic center of Islam. There are approximately 400 mosques in the United States.*

(Melton, *Creeds*)

FORGIVING AND GOING ON

That we have to do. That's the way, that's the only way. Until we do that we're just going to prevent our own life coming into a good situation. Also I find that as a member of my race, as a black person, most people, even Muslims, people of my own faith, they tend to stereotype us. We're not all the same. The great majority of us are not given to extremes anymore of, I would say, hate and love. There was a time when the majority of us were given to both extremes. We either had to all love the white man and be Jesus Christ ourselves, peace be upon Christ Jesus. Or we had to be angry Black Muslims or something. The great majority of us can't be stereotyped that way. The great majority of us are not so sentimental that we have to have all restaurants black and white, all hotels black and white, you know, all beaches black and white. Most of us are not wanting that kind of extreme. And most of us are not expecting white people to be angels and to never hurt our feelings. And again, most of us are not so hung up on racial identity that we can't be comfortable with a member of another race and relate to them and enjoy their company. We can be as peaceful with members of another race as we can be with a member of our own race.

NATIVE AMERICAN

NATIVE AMERICAN

PROPHECY

THOMAS BANYACYA

Eighty-five-year-old renowned elder, spokesperson, and interpreter for Hopi traditional spiritual leaders, Thomas Banyacya hails from the Second Mesa village of Moencopi. Refusing to register for the draft in 1941, on the grounds of Hopi principles that forbid the bearing of arms, he was arrested and imprisoned. Since 1948, beginning at the age of thirty-nine, he has represented as interpreter and spokesman the *Kikmongwis,* or spiritual leaders of the Hopi.

His charge was to convey to a global community the Hopi prophecy and its tenets of ancient wisdom as handed down in oral tradition. To this end, he has traveled the globe carrying the Hopi message of peace and concern for the environment, the necessity of waking up and recognizing the interrelatedness of all life. The cataclysmic forces of Mother Earth lately seen unleashed are her understandable and predicted reaction to the imbalances created by unchecked and irresponsible industrial activity motivated by human greed. Nature warns us to do the right thing.

Banyacya obeyed the *Kikmongwis* by expressing Hopi concerns to the "Great House of Mica," the United Nations. More recently, in addition to attending the Parliament of the World's Religions in Chicago in the fall of 1993, Banyacya participated in the Global Forum for Environment and Development in Moscow in January of 1990. And he returned to Washington, D.C., for a peace rally in October of 1994. In accordance with

Hopi teachings and the Hopi life plan, Banyacya has delivered the message of ancient Hopi prophecy to the four corners of the earth, warning the people of the need to return to a peaceful existence.

Profiled in books, films, journals, and on television, Thomas Banyacya is the recipient of numerous awards and was a nominee for the 1994 Fulbright Peace Award.

MY WORK

Since 1948 I've been on the road trying to bring ancient traditional knowledge, prophecies, warnings, spiritual instructions to the world. That's what they told me. I must do everything to bring this message to the world, because someday the terrible problem is going to be so great, it will affect every human race on this Mother Earth. This land is considered a mother because everything came from there. We are part of it. When this body dies, your body goes back to Mother Earth. We have many, many elders who are religious leaders in the Hopi country. Right now we have eleven pueblos, and each pueblo has its own spiritual leaders today.

They used to have black bear *Kikmongwis,* high spiritual leaders, like the Catholics have a pope and Tibetan people have Dalai Lama as a leader. And that's the way the Hopis were. *Kikmo* were our spiritual leaders. And they are in charge of the affairs in the villages or pueblos.

RETURN OF THE HOPI TO THE TRADITIONAL TEACHINGS

I believe there are some young people now coming back to learn their spiritual ways because most all the Hopi pueblos were able to carry on their ceremonies in their own ways. Every year they have certain ceremonies. From the first of the year, January, February, March, they have a ceremony called the Kachina societies. They put on ceremonies, night dances in the Kiva, an underground chamber. And in February they have initiations for younger children. You see hundreds, both boys and girls, being initiated in the Kachina society.

Fourth World is a term used by the World Council of Indigenous Peoples to distinguish the way of life of indigenous peoples from those of the First (highly industrialized), Second (Socialist bloc), and Third (developing) Worlds. The First, Second, and Third Worlds believe that "the land belongs to the people"; the Fourth World believes that "the people belong to the land."

—Julian Burger, *The Gaia Atlas of the First Peoples*

FORCED EDUCATION

During the early years, in my time, the government of the United States put out sort of a forced education and sent us out to different district schools. The family didn't have much say, you just had to go. They tried to make it so that the children would not be able to keep in touch with their families, or societies, or their culture because they sent us out to do away with our culture, religion, languages, and ceremonies. And they tried to make us feel like we are no longer part of our own system, culture.

In government school, we were forced to read a lot of Bible verses. They separated us—some to Catholic church, some to Protestant church. I finished high school there, but after I came home, somebody gave me a two-year scholarship to the first all-Indian college set up by the Southern Baptist church members, in Oklahoma. There again we were given a chance to learn a lot of Bible verses, hoping that those that attended that school would be missionaries or something. But I turned to teaching.

Some did stay in cities and towns because they were, so we say, brainwashed. They want to live in the city, liked all these conveniences. But some of them try to come back, because we're all made in such a way that when you're born in that area, certain ceremonies take place and certain things there draw you back.

When you get back into the pueblos, then naturally when you hear singing, ceremonies that take place, you sort of feel different. But eventually you get into it, and that's why a lot of young people begin to become initiated into the societies.

Man is an aspect of nature, and nature itself is a manifestation of primordial religion. Even the word 'religion' makes an unnecessary separation, and there is no word for it in the Indian tongues. Nature is the "Great Mysterious," the "religion before religion," the profound intuitive apprehension of the true nature of existence attained by sages of all epochs, everywhere on Earth; the whole universe is sacred, man is the whole universe, and the religious ceremony is life itself, the common acts of every day.

—Peter Matthiessen

WORKING FOR PEACE

The *Hopi* word itself means peace, kindness, gentleness—truthful person, humble person. That's a real peace. We can tell. A man can walk in there because his actions, his words or movement tells you that he's a peaceful person. He knows about stars and the moon and many other things in the universe.

Those are the high spiritual leaders now in the different Kivas, taking charge of the ceremonial thing. And they advise the younger people how to go through the ceremony in the right manner.

It has to come from the heart of a person. You feel that you need to sit down, you need to pray, you need to smoke your pipe, you need to say something, or you need to sing, dance, all that. You learn to do it because it's from the heart. In the western hemisphere we, the Hopi and Native people in this hemisphere, are still going through a prayer, a medicine ceremony to keep this land in balance.

SURVIVAL OF THE EARTH

The message is that the human being was given special instruction, warning. We look at the Bible that has contained many things that the white man was supposed to follow. Buddhist people have something. African religion has something, and other nations have that. And the Hopi have that. Native people have that.

So now we seem to turn away from that spiritual instruction and do things our own way. If we don't stop it, we are going to bring total destruction to ourselves. And this is the message the Hopi say. The first World War, a lot of people die from that and then it stopped for a while. The Second World War starts, that's when they make this atom bomb and killed thousands of people in a few seconds. The Hopi knew that it might happen by white brothers, and that's what they did.

Now we have entered most difficult period. From now on everything's going to go fast. Nature's going to warn us much more—earthquake, flooding, destruction by nature more and more, tornadoes, volcanic eruptions, the seasons changing so much that there will be hail, storms with hail going to get bigger and bigger, as big as baseballs one of these days.

It's going to be very destructive, because we are creating unbalanced life on this earth—manufacturing things that are not in line with the law of the Great Spirit of nature.

We have to look at what we have been doing up to this time. We know that uranium mining has created a lot of death. People work in the Navahos, in Hopi, Native peoples area. Someone took uranium out of there and made this atom bomb and they threw it on Hiroshima and Nagasaki. We want the world to know that the Hopi spiritual leaders have never had any part in permitting that kind of thing.

Universal Prayer for World Peace

Infinite Spirit, bring Peace and Good Will to all people. Direct the pathway of every Nation into unity, happiness, and prosperity. Remove the thought of fear and greed from the mind of man. Let every thought of hate be turned to love; every thought of fear be turned to faith; every thought of doubt be turned to certainty; every thought of war be turned to Peace. Heal the wounds of the world and bring Peace upon the face of the earth. And so it is.

—Given to a traveler
to the Taos Pueblo

The leaders said that Four Corners area was supposed to be the spiritual center surrounded by sacred mountains—four mountains—upon which they put shrines there to try to keep this center in a spiritual way, the songs, prayers, and ceremonies came around to keep this land and life in balance. But if we start disturbing them, then these things will develop in this way. That Four Corners area should be left in a natural state. No one should disturb anything. No one should take any metal resource out. We can use some of it but not in a destructive way and keeping it in a natural state as much as possible.

A Kachina leader, more than eighty-six years old, explained this once at four-days' meeting. He got up and says that the white brother might make this gourd full of ashes. The gourd that we use making rattles, small one, he referred with that. He went like this—gourd full of ashes so hot, so powerful, so small—if they ever allow that to fall on the earth it will just burn everything to ashes in a few seconds.

That thing was known to the Hopi a long time ago. It's known, that's prophesied, way back there some place and then carried up to that point and it actually happened. And so now we have entered the most difficult part of a life again. He said, if I go outside and pick up a rock and throw as hard as I can up to the sky, that rock will come much faster and hit that ground much harder. That's what's going to happen. If someone developed this so powerful thing then it might fall, throw it around the other side of the world, destroying other peoples' land and life over there.

We the Native people, the Hopi, the Native people in the western hemisphere have no business going around the other side of the world destroying land and life of people over there. Our religion is to take care of this, through prayer, meditate, ceremonies in humble ways and that's what we supposed to do.

RETURN TO SPIRITUAL TRADITIONS

We bring this message to the world, they should look at their spiritual ways again. Where did we turn wrong? Where did we make a mistake? Let's go back.

We're supposed to have the same spiritual instructions from the Great Spirit. He gave us that. Then we went around in the

Native Americans expressed in many ways their sense of the sacredness of matter. They saw power at work, awesomely and mysteriously, in every portion of nature. . . . The sacred beings were forms of animal and plant life which, in fact long ago, had pledged their bodies for food for Indian peoples. . . . Because nature—the material world—was sacred, [Native Americans] mostly tended to be natural ecologists in an age before the Euro-American concept was born.

(Albanese)

four directions around the earth—carried it wherever we go with this language. We're supposed to take care of it in ceremonial things. Each area is supposed to take care of it.

So I have no right to go and tear your region away because you were placed that way by the Great Spirit. And our space here, you have no right to come and destroy this, because my way is to take care of it in that area.

The Hopis—they are still holding on to this basic foundation of spiritual power and authority that was given to us from the Great Spirit. We still have it, and it was given to other nations that do the same thing, to go back to the spiritual ways.

With the Native people I talk with in United States and Canada and of the Yukon, they knew that there's no division. There's no Alaska, Canada, United States. This is one whole western hemisphere and we can move back and forth freely.

That's the way the animals and birds do it. But human, white brothers come and they draw the line, this is mine. And if you go in there, they either shoot you, or pick you up and throw you out.

We get to that point where we think we are God now. We think we have power. But what if tomorrow big earthquake starts, knocking all these buildings down—do you have power to stop that?

And the old people say, "Well, let's look at white man's Bible. They had Ten Commandments. I wonder if they will go back? Don't lie, don't steal, don't take anything that doesn't belong to you, don't do this and that."

That's all in there. The same thing that the old people teach us. Same thing that other religions talk about. Now if we can go back and really follow that I'm sure we can come back, recognize as one human beings, not because we have colors, we are all human beings, we are both subject to nature.

That will bring back the balanced life because then humanity will begin to recognize their mission in this world: that they were taking care of this land, mainly to develop full food that we share and that we should go back.

GOING TO THE UNITED NATIONS

Knock on the door once. And I did that in 1949 but they never open to the Native people to speak at the Assembly. Then later I knocked on the door again, second time. But they didn't open the door. That was around '82 or '83. Later, I knocked on the door again, third time. To the Hopis that's a sacred number. We go fast three days and then perform a ceremony on the fourth day. They didn't open it, and the elders said, "Don't give up. Knock on the door again." Fourth time, I finally delivered the message. John Washburn, who was the official under the Secretary-General, knew what I had been doing and received a message.

We waited. Then later, we received the message that the United Nations would declare Indigenous Year in 1993. That's when they sent us a letter that they would open the door to representatives of the western hemisphere. Every area of the western hemisphere came and there were about forty or fifty people in New York on December 9th [1992].

I went to the meeting, and the Native people decided that I should speak too. There were twenty speakers. I was the last one. I had a letter written but I didn't read it, I just talked from the heart. That's what the Hopis said, I must deliver from the heart.

It was getting dark in the evening, about the middle of my talk, a great wind came and almost knocked the United Nations over. A terrible storm came, three or four feet of water on New Jersey, tidal waves never had been before like that.

We formed a circle, with three or four prayer ceremonies. By noon it cleared up, sunshine came again.

That is the power that the Great Spirit helped us with because Native people had come to bring this awareness to the United Nations, to see if they can do something with their laws and regulations. And the spirit of the ancestors came with us with the power of rain, thunder, lightning, storms. That's what we need within this country. If we pray, meditate, we can keep this land alive and beautiful and clean.

So my message in the United Nations, December 10th ended up with a word I saw across the wall. Someone write it on the

Declaration on Indigenous Peoples Draft Resolution

In the last five centuries, the Indigenous Peoples of the western hemisphere, and in more recent centuries, in the eastern hemisphere, have been and still are living in oppressive conditions. Their culture and lands have been seriously damaged. They have been exposed to deadly diseases and reduced to grinding poverty.

We call upon all states with native peoples to respect their human rights, including the right of self-determination within existing national states, the right to manage their own territories, their resources and social structure, the right to form and develop their own distinctive institutions, and the right to preserve their unique way of life and culture that can teach us so much about sustainable living and about the spiritual dimension of the Earth Community.

We also urge the United Nations to recognize a special status for the indigenous populations of the world and to grant them representation in that global forum as well as in all of its specialized agencies.

wall there, quoting of a Bible verse, it says that all these instruments of warfare should turn into plowshares and study war no more. Let's do that!

Respect one another as human brothers and sisters. That's the way we will survive.

FINAL MESSAGE

If we clean up this mess, the Great Spirit is going to come back and live with us. And there will be no end to this life yet from here on.

I think eventually we can put aside all these destructive things and bring real peace and harmony and respect for one another. Then we can share this land together and bring about a balanced life for the next generation.

Native American Call
to Prayer

O Great Spirit,
Whose breath gives life to
*   the world*
and whose voice is heard in
*   the soft breeze*
We need your strength and
*   wisdom*
May we walk in beauty.

May our eyes
ever behold the red and
*   purple sunset*
Make us wise so that we
*   may understand*
what you have taught us
Help us learn the lessons
*   you have hidden*
in every leaf and rock
Make us always ready to
*   come to you*
with clean hands and
*   straight eyes*
So when life fades, as the
*   fading sunset,*
our spirits may come to
*   you without shame.*

SIKH

SIKH

INVERSION

SANT RAJINDER SINGH

Sant Rajinder Singh is the president of the World Fellowship of Religions and the spiritual head of Science of Spirituality. He is internationally recognized for his work toward human unity through spirituality, giving talks and meditation seminars all over the world. As head of Science of Spirituality, he convenes two annual international conferences in Delhi, India. He has hosted many conferences on nonviolence and interfaith dialogue, including the 1994 Seventh World Religions Conference in India, attended by more than 100,000 people.

Sant Rajinder Singh has also sponsored and participated in such interfaith activities in North America. Recognizing the transcendent oneness at the heart of all religions, he emphasizes prayer and meditation as the true building blocks for achieving peace and harmony. And to this end he has created libraries for religious and spiritual study in India and the United States.

In the field of education, Sant Rajinder Singh stresses ethical and spiritual development along with the physical. He has introduced innovative curricula stressing nonviolence into the school systems of both Colombia and India.

Born in India, Sant Rajinder Singh received his spiritual education from two of India's great spiritual teachers, Sant Kirpal Singh and Sant Darshan Singh. He took his master of science degree in Engineering in the United States and had a distinguished twenty-year career in science and communications.

Sikhism and Caste

Sikhism is founded on the principle of equality of all persons. It rejects the caste system, and inculcates in its adherents an egalitarian attitude and practice toward men and women of all races, religions, and social classes. Sikh names do not indicate gender. All Sikh men take the additional name Singh (lion) and women take the name Kaur (princess). Guru Gobind Singh (1666–1708), the tenth guru, instructed his followers to drop their last names, which indicate caste.

—Rajwant Singh & Georgia Rangel, *A Portrait of Sikhism*

His many inspiring publications include: *Peace Begins with You, Ecology of the Soul and Positive Mysticism, Education for a Peaceful World,* and in Hindi, *Spirituality in Modern Times.*

He has been honored by religious, civic, and political leaders for his work toward unity and peace. Says Sant Rajinder Singh, "It is only when each individual has achieved inner peace that we will see lasting outer peace in the world."

Sant Rajinder Singh's interview is located in this book under the religious designation of Sikh because that is his background, his starting place. In view of some traditional Sikhs, he may not exactly fit this designation. Yet, to so place him, perhaps, reflects the changing nature of religions as they move, through individuals, into a larger world context.

THE CONNECTION BETWEEN SCIENCE AND SPIRITUALITY

We live in an age which is very scientific. We're not living in an age where people believe things because of blind faith. In this day and age whatever we believe in, we need to experience. We call our organization the Science of Spirituality because we feel that spirituality also has a scientific bearing.

The method of spirituality, or the method by which we can really know ourselves, is an experiment where we rise above physical body consciousness. It can be repeated; an experiment that gives us known results when performed consistently and accurately. And that is what science does. We have an experiment, and we get the results that have been shown to us. And spirituality can be verifiable by an experimental method.

When we meditate, we are able to go within. We are able to experience divine lights and hear melodious music within ourselves. So to us this human body is a laboratory in which we experiment to find our real self, to find our soul, to know who we really are.

Humans have always tried to better themselves. This is why we have development. This is why we have science. We try to find out and understand the laws of nature. We're even trying to find out what we are made of.

Many years ago, our scientists were saying that the smallest element is the atom, and then they broke the atoms down to

Nature is not only the source of life, beauty, and power, but it is also an inspiration of strength in formulation of our character.

Man is composed of Five Elements.

According to Sikh Scripture, Guru Granth Sahib, these five elements of nature teach us valuable lessons:

Earth teaches us: Patience, Love

Air: Mobility, Liberty

Fire: Warmth, Courage

Sky: Equality, Broadmindedness

Water: Purity, Cleanliness

We have to imbibe these fine traits of Nature in our personality for fuller, happier and nobler lives.

—Guru Nanak (SourceBook)

neutrons and protons and electrons. Now they're saying that even those things have small particles in them that are moving very fast, which are called quarks. So we have a human tendency or yearning to know who we are. And human beings, right from day one, have been trying to find out who we really are. Are we this body? Or is there something beyond the body?

Spirituality is definitely not antirational. Spirituality is a logical process which can be thought of, which can be laid down, which can be proven for yourself through experimentation.

Religions are faiths which are propagated after a great saint or a mystic has come into this world and has exhorted each and every one who came to him or her to know themselves and to know God. Spirituality goes beyond religion in the sense that spirituality is a means by which we truly can understand ourselves, by which we truly can find our connection with God, with the Almighty. There might be people who are not religious who still might be spiritual. So spirituality talks about our own mystical experiences on which all religions and scriptures are based.

INVERSION

We do not believe in conversion. Instead we believe in inversion. We want to go within, because the treasure house of divinity is within ourselves.

Now to know ourselves, we need to understand who we really are. On the outside, we are this physical body. But when we see someone die, we see the body lying in front of us. And that body is exactly the same as it was before the person was dead. The arms are there; the legs are there; the eyes are there; the nose is there; the mouth is there. But neither can the person see, nor hear, nor can they talk or get up and walk.

So if we were just the human body, then what is missing from that dead body that prevents it from doing anything? What is missing, we believe, is our real self, which is our spirit or our soul, that which gives us life. And the knowledge of our self, our soul, is what we find when we invert. Each religion has two sides to it, an exoteric and an esoteric side. Now the exoteric side of our religion deals with rites and rituals and cultural differences.

From Sikh Scripture

Says Nanak:
There are many dogmas,
*   there are many systems,*
There are many spiritual
*   revelations,*
Many bonds fetter the self
*   (mind):*
But Release is attained
*   through God's grace;*
Truth is above all these,
But even higher is life lived
*   in Truth.*
All God's creatures are
*   noble,*
None are base.
One Potter has fashioned
*   all the pots,*
One Light pervades all cre-
*   ation.*
Truth is revealed through
*   Grace,*
And no one can resist
*   Grace.*

—Siri Rag, Ashtpadiyan

But when we talk about finding ourselves, and we talk about our own existence being our soul, which is a part of God, then it is the mystical, spiritual experience, the esoteric side of the religion that we're talking about.

We live in an age where we want to live in a community that is peaceful and that is in harmony. Now the esoteric side of every religion is based on the mystical, spiritual experiences of the great saints and mystics. We can go to practically any religion of the world, and when we read the scriptures, we find many mystical, spiritual experiences described in the Holy Bible. St. Paul says, "I die daily." He's not talking about physical death; he's talking about rising above physical body consciousness and experiencing the soul—the inner self.

Guru Nanak (1469–1539), the first of ten Sikh gurus, rejected asceticism, penance, and torturing the flesh as steps toward enlightenment. "Be in the world but not worldly," he said. When questioned by a group of yogis how a man could attain release from worldly attachments, he replied:

The lotus in the water is not wet
Nor the water-fowl in the stream
If a man would live, but by the world untouched,
Meditate and repeat the name of the Lord Supreme.

(Crim)

MEDITATION ON THE DIVINE LIGHT AND SOUND OF GOD

Our practice is called the meditation on the Divine Light and Sound of God. The process is a very simple one. In this form of meditation, the attention is focused at what is called the seat of the soul, which is between and behind the two eyebrows. We find a quiet place to sit, we close our eyes very gently, making sure that our eyeballs are focused straight ahead. And then we seek to withdraw our sensory currents.

When we interact in the world, we interact through one of our five senses. So for us to really invert and go within and find that divinity within ourselves, we need to withdraw our sensory currents.

As we withdraw, our sensory currents are raised to the single eye, that point which opens into other realms. These are realms which are spiritual in nature.

Similar references can be found in the scriptures of every religion. It is called the Holy Word in the Bible. It is called Naam or Shabd in the Sikh scriptures. It's called Jyoti and Sruti in the Vedas. It is called Naad in the Upanishads. It is called Kalma in the Muslim scriptures. This process of meditation enables the practitioner to verify the existence of this divine Light and Sound.

THE BENEFITS OF MEDITATION

The path of meditation that we follow is not a path of negative mysticism. In negative mysticism, you would negate the world. You would leave the world behind. You would go to the banks of a river or the tops of the mountains, and you would be cut off from people.

We do not believe in that. We believe in what our great spiritual teacher Sant Darshan Singh Ji Maharaj termed a path of positive mysticism. Ours is a path in which we fulfill our worldly obligations. We stay in our societies, we stay in our own religions, we stay in our own neighborhoods. And in addition to our day-to-day activities, we find the time for God.

We take out a couple of hours of our day-to-day time and put that toward meditation, because we find that the benefits that we receive are so tremendous that they bring peace and harmony, joy and bliss into our lives.

As we meditate, our concentration powers improve. When we are under stress, if we sit down for a few minutes and meditate, it really helps us to cope with our environment.

THE DIFFERENCE BETWEEN PRAYER AND MEDITATION

Meditation is the highest form of prayer. Generally when we pray, we pray to God for something. Prayer is when we are talking to God.

Now when we meditate, we are praying to God to please enlighten us. So it is the highest treasure that we can find. Anything that we pray for—let's say that we pray for a new house, a new car, or a promotion at work—these are all things of this world that are temporary, which we're going to leave behind the moment we physically die. But if we can gain enlightenment, if we can know who we truly are, then that gain will be with us forever. So meditation is the highest form of prayer; meditation is when we listen to God.

Sikhism in North America

There are no denominations in Sikhism, but in the United States, in particular, there is grouping along language and cultural lines. The majority [about half a million] of Sikhs in the United States are immigrants of Indian origin, speak Punjabi, and have distinct customs and dress that originate in Punjab, North India.

Since the 1960s, however, there has existed a group, generally called American Sikhs, who are easily distinguished from others by their all-white attire and turbans worn by both men and women. This group now numbers about 5,000. In 1969 the largest Sikh temple in the world was erected in Yuba City, California. In North America, Sikh congregations belong to local interfaith associations and participate fully in efforts such as environmental protection campaigns, issues affecting children, AIDS, food and other help for the homeless and displaced.

—Rajwant Singh & Georgia Rangel, *A Portrait of Sikhism*

GOD, THE CREATIVE POWER

As we go within, and as we connect with the divine Light and
Sound of God within ourselves, it transforms us. Transformed
people transform families, neighborhoods, cities, countries. And
transformed countries will transform this world. So we believe
that once we find peace for ourselves, it is definitely going to ra-
diate from us and not only will transform our immediate sur-
roundings, but will have an effect on the whole globe.

A Sikh Prayer

*May the kingdom of justice
   prevail!
May the believers be united
   in love!*

*May the hearts of the be-
   lievers
be humble, high their wisdom,
and may they be guided in
   their
wisdom by the Lord.*

*O Khalsa, say Wahiguru,
Glory be to God!*

SUFI

SUFI

THE ETERNAL FEMININE
Pir Vilayat Inayat Khan

Internationally famed leader of the Sufi movement, Pir Vilayat Khan has attracted thousands to his workshops, seminars, and retreats. Combining his expertise in advanced meditative practices with western psychology and science, he has pioneered the application of spiritual insights to overcoming life's daily challenges. His father, of Afghan origin, hailed from India. His mother, of English and Scottish descent, was born in Albuquerque, New Mexico. In 1910, his father, Hazrat Inayat Khan, brought Sufism to the West. When he died, Pir Vilayat was ten years old. The son has followed in his father's footsteps.

During World War II, Pir Vilayat served as a Royal Naval officer in mine sweeping. Pir Vilayat's fianceé died in a tragic accident, and his sister—a heroine with the Resistance Movement—was killed in a Nazi concentration camp. She played a critical role in the strategy of the D-Day landings and her story is told in the famed book *A Man Called Intrepid*.

Pir Vilayat was personal assistant to the Pakistani delegate to UN sessions in Paris in 1948. As a journalist, his reports of French atrocities in North Africa resulted in international pressures being applied through the UN.

He went on to found a self-sufficiency program, Hope Project, which provides food, education, and healthcare for New Delhi slum dwellers. Subsequently, Pir Vilayat organized numerous international interfaith conferences, bringing religious leaders together from dozens of countries.

Pir Hazrat Inayat Khan (1881–1927), an Indian-born musician, was initiated into the Nizami branch of the Chishti Order, one of the main Sufi schools in India. Originating in Persia, the Chishti school was brought to India and subsequently absorbed elements of Hindu Vedantic thought, giving it a unique position within Sufism. Inayat Khan intended to Westernize the Sufi path by bringing it to the United States in 1910. In his system, the unifying power of mysticism was emphasized over traditional Sufi doctrine.

(Melton, *Creeds*)

Ten Sufi Thoughts

There is:
one God, *the Eternal,*
the Only Being
　　one Master, *the Guiding*
Spirit of all souls
　　one Holy Book, *the sa-*
cred manuscript of nature
　　one Religion, *the*
unswerving progress in the
right direction toward the
ideal, which fulfils the life's
purpose of every soul
　　one Law, *the Law of*
Reciprocity, which can be
observed by a selfless con-
science together with a
sense of awakened justice
　　one Brotherhood, *the*
human Brotherhood,
which unites the children of
the earth indiscriminately
　　one Moral Principle, *the*
love that springs forth from
self-denial, and blooms in
deeds of beneficence
　　one Object of Praise,
the beauty that uplifts the
heart of its worshiper
through all aspects from
the seen to the unseen
　　one Truth, *the true*
knowledge of our being
within and without, which
is the essense of all wisdom
　　one Path, *the annihila-*
tion of the false ego leading
to perfection

(Melton, *Creeds*)

Pir Vilayat is fluent in five languages. His books include *Introducing Spirituality into Counseling and Therapy, The Call of the Dervish,* and *The Message in Our Time.* His message of fellowship has guided others to contribute their talents to founding food kitchens, donating services to prison inmates, establishing Amnesty International chapters, getting people off drugs, and sponsoring refugee families.

Pir Vilayat's educational background includes a French Lycée and École Normale de Musique, a Licence-des-Lettres from the Sorbonne, a Diplôme d'Études Superieures in Music and Philosophy from the Sorbonne and Oxford University. He received an honorary degree in divinity from the New Seminary in New York in 1986. He serves on the advisory boards of the International Committee for the World Peace Project, the United Nations Lumbini Project, the World Citizens Group, the Temple of Understanding, and is president of the Inter-Religious Congress in Paris.

In a personal note Pir Vilayat writes: "I attempt to integrate the knowledge gained from my Western education (in psychology, physiology, biochemistry, physics, music, and comparative religions) with the overview, intuition, and mastery developed through spiritual training (in the Sufi, Hindu, Buddhist, Judeo-Christian, and Islamic traditions). I apply this understanding to dealing with the problems arising amongst people living in our day and age and facing the challenges of our Western civilization."

WHAT DOES SUFI MEAN?

It's a very controversial word. There are three possible etymologies. One is *Sofia,* meaning knowledge, which is legitimate because when the neo-Platonic school was closed the Emasius and his brethren fled to Iran and they formed a school there. Of course that was the old tradition, of the messianic tradition married with the Greek tradition, and I think that is a very important influence in Sufism.

On the other hand, you have to account for the impact of Islam, the Iranian tradition. It is very possible the etymology of that word is linked with the word *sofa.* The Prophet Mohammed instituted an esoteric school for the masses. They met next to the mosque in a place where there were sofas, so that they were *al sofa*. A lot of Sufis claim their lineage from that school.

And the other possible etymology is the word *saffe*, which means pure.

Sufis would say, "See that which transpires behind that which appears." That which appears is the surface. It's like the tip of the iceberg, but the reality is behind it. So if you talk about God, then you can't reduce God to what appears at the surface and therefore you have to get very deep into yourself to discover something outside that is in yourself already.

Nobody in his right mind would call himself a Sufi. It's very presumptuous. It's regarded to be so very high. There are some rather famous people whom we call Sufis in the past, great dervishes and inspiring beings. But one wouldn't like to claim it for oneself.

I say I am an initiate in a Sufi lineage which originated in India. My father was the successor in the lineage of Sufis, and his teacher called him when he was about to die and asked him to come to the West and bring this tradition to the West. He was a very famous musician in India. He left everything to follow the injunctions of his teacher, started from scratch, and it grew and grew.

UNIVERSALITY AND UNITY IN SUFI

There have been a lot of influences of Buddhism on Sufism, Hinduism—a closely encountered osmosis between the Hindus and the Muslims in India. Sufism, I think, has been enriched by the interfacing with Yoga. In the desert, Sufis met the Christian monks. In fact, it is very well possible that the word Sufi originates from the word *soof*, which means "world."

The universal worship is a kind of religious ceremony that was founded by my father, in which we read texts of the different world religions and try to show the similarities and also the differences.

I organize congresses of religions in which we invite representatives of the different religions to come together. We have

---

The Universality of
Revelation

I am neither eastern nor western, neither heavenly nor earthly,

I am neither of the natural elements nor of the rotating spheres.

I am neither from India or China, from neither Bulgaria nor Tabriz,

From neither the country of Iraq nor the land of Khurasan.

My sign is without sign, my locus is without locus,

It is neither body nor soul for I am myself the Soul of souls.

Since I expelled all duality, I see the two worlds as one.

I see the One, I seek the One, I know the One, I call upon the One.

—Jalal al-Din Rumi (1207–1273),
Sufi poet (S. H. Nasr, trans.)

Sufism and Islam

Sufism is the science of the direct knowledge of God; its doctrines and methods are derived from the Qur'ān and Islamic revelation. Like exoteric Islam, Sufism freely makes use of paradigms and concepts derived from Greek and even Hindu sources. Despite any borrowings and influences from exterior sources, the essence of Sufism is purely Islamic: It does not spring from "Persian philosophy," Shi'ism, Christianity, philosophies of antiquity, or any other source. The goal of Sufism is to effect a union with God or the realization of the Oneness of God.

(Glasse)

dialogues where we can see very severe differences. If you study the dogmas of the different religions, then the differences are enormous. For example, a Christian would say that God had a son, that Christ was the son of God. The Muslims would say, "God can't have a son." Right away you've got conflict. Is there any way of reconciling these two? Of course there is.

My father said, "If you can recognize the features of your father or your mother in you, you can claim to be his or her son or daughter. So Jesus was able to recognize in himself features of what one ascribes to God and therefore he could claim that." But then Christ also said, "Be ye perfect, as your Father." And by saying that he means that he is not the only one. He is advising people to try and recognize those qualities in themselves.

REAL EXPERIENCES IN RELIGION

I find that the reality behind religion is real experience. That's what meditation is about. If there is not real experience, then you are talking theories or belief systems.

But of course, it's very challenging because who can say they have an experience of God? In fact, Sufism has a lot to say about this. My father said, quite rightly again, "When we talk about God, we often don't realize that what we are talking about is our concept of God rather than our experience of God." So that experience, if we can talk about experience, is to be found amongst the mystics.

I find that what mystics are doing is making experiments in the uncharted reaches of the mind, beyond the middle range common denominator. And I think this extremely valuable.

We think in concepts, but then, the thing about the mystic is that mystics are very wary of language. They realize by the fact that we need to express or communicate what we think, we reduce what we understand. And that's one of the reasons why one of the practices that we do in our spiritual retreat is to be in silence for some time. So now the mind is not geared to expression itself in words, and then we discover a whole other dimension of understanding and of thinking.

It is time to wake up. My whole teaching is how to wake up, how to change your perspective so that you are able to see things differently. By so doing you are affirming your freedom against conditioning, which is one of the great ventures of the human spirit.

I think the real breakthrough is when one realizes that one cannot discover the software behind the hardware that we consider to be the universe because our mind is of the same nature as that software. You can't see your eyes. So the breakthrough is when one's vantage point becomes so vast that it is able to encompass more and more of the vastness of the software of the universe. That's what we call awakening or illumination.

THE FUTURE OF RELIGION, THE ETERNAL FEMININE

Where are we going? Where have we come from? That's a core issue. If we made a survey of religion in our time, one is amazed by the fact that so much of that thinking is right back in the Middle Ages—belief systems, rituals, authority figures, very little scope for people to find in their own heart a conviction that does not rest upon some kind of authority. And it doesn't seem to belong to our time.

We live in a time when people are learning to take responsibility, in other words to achieve some kind of freedom from the pressure of controlling systems. There is a whole breakthrough of what I might call "the eternal feminine" which refuses that controlling masculine power that suppresses the individual. So I think that this breakthrough is going to open up new horizons for religion in the future.

When I say eternal feminine, I don't mean women as against men. I mean the recognition of the fact that there is a kind of self-organizing power within the universe if you don't try to control it. By controlling it you reduce it to what you want it to be which can never be what it is, because it's much greater than anything that you could want it to be.

A very good example of the kind of masculine controlling factors was Nazism. My sister was beaten to death in a concentration camp in Dachau. She volunteered as a radio operator to maintain contact between the War Office in London and the French underground. That was a typical example of the way that the controlling forces are trying to kill the spirit of good-

Never, in sooth, does the lover seek without being sought by his beloved.
When the lightning of love has shot into his heart, know that there is love in that heart.
When love of God waxes in thy heart, beyond any doubt God hath love of thee.
The desire of the soul is for ascent and sublimity; the desire of the body is for self and means of self-indulgence;
And that Sublimity desires and loves the soul; mark the text: "He loves them and they love Him." (Qur'ān 5:59)

—Jalal al-Din Rumi (1207–1273), Sufi poet

Beloved Lord, Almighty
  God!
Through the rays of the
  sun,
Through the waves of the
  air,
Through the All-pervading
  Life in space,
Purify and revivify me,
  and, I pray,
Heal my body, heart, and
  soul. Amen.

—Hazrat Inayat Khan, 1881–1927

will. And, in fact, are treading upon the sacredness of the status of a human being.

Religion is about discovering the divinity of one's being. My father said, "God is hidden in his creation." That's the treasure, and one has to find it in oneself instead of seeking God up there. This is why the Sufis say, "Why are you looking for God up there?" He/She is right here, but hidden, and therefore has to be unveiled.

The meaning of the eternal feminine is very important for me because it is the unveiling. In the tradition of the Muslims, and then came the Bahā'īs, and at the time of Bahā' Ullāh, an extraordinary incident happened. There was a very famous Iranian poetess, and she unveiled her face. Immediately she was attacked by the authorities. They killed her. But that's exactly what I am talking about. The unveiling of the treasure. That is the secret behind religion.

Jesus said, "What's the use of gaining the whole world and losing your soul?" There is a very good example, an apocrypha. Jesus was walking the path and there was a dead dog, and somebody said, "Master, don't look, it's so ugly." And he looked at it, and he said, "Yes, but the teeth are so beautiful." So he saw beauty where others didn't see it.

We search for the splendor that we don't believe in anymore, the meaningfulness that we don't believe anymore. And let's forget our concepts of "God."

You have to have at least a minimum faith beyond your understanding. In fact, it's the greatest power there is in really having faith, that there is meaningfulness and beauty in life. And that's where we're challenged in our lives.

DDHIST BRAHMA KUMARIS JEWISH
AIN NATIVE AMERICAN SUFI HINDU
HRISTIAN ROMAN CATHOLIC MUSLIM
KH BAHA'I JEWISH ZOROASTRIAN

TAOIST

OMAN CATHOLIC TAOIST BUDDHIST
ROASTRIAN PROTESTANT CHRISTIAN

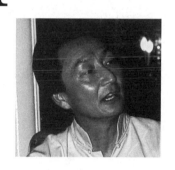

NDU MUSLIM JAIN ROMAN CATHOLIC
AOIST BAHA'I BUDDHIST SIKH SUFI
ATIVE AMERICAN BRAHMA KUMARIS
EWISH PROTESTANT CHRISTIAN TAOIST
DDHIST HINDU ZOROASTRIAN JAIN
OMAN CATHOLIC BAHA'I PROTESTANT
AOIST HINDU SUFI NATIVE AMERICAN
ISLIM BRAHMA KUMARIS BUDDHIST
KH SUFI JEWISH MUSLIM TAOIST
ROASTRIAN CHRISTIAN BAHA'I HINDU

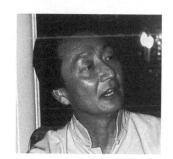

TAOIST

EMBODYING THE TAO

Chungliang Al Huang

Writer, philosopher, calligrapher, choreographer, dancer, bamboo flute player, and Tai Ji (Tai Chi) master, Chungliang Al Huang is a renaissance man and charismatic disciple of Taoism. A catalyst for the meeting of East and West, he is a Fellow of the World Academy of Arts and Science in Stockholm and an advisory board member for several foundations, including the International Transpersonal Association, the Windstar Foundation, and the Association for Humanistic Psychology.

In 1975, following a ten-year collaboration with philosopher Alan Watts, Lama Anagarika Govinda, and sinologist John Blofeld, Huang founded the Living Tao Foundation, a global network of individuals who share the belief that the way to personal and universal harmony is through creativity, compassion, and supportive human relationships. The Living Tao Foundation, based in Urbana, Illinois, is a fascinating and unique "reflection" of ancient Taoist spirituality in action. It maintains active programs throughout the world. The Foundation is working with the Chinese government to establish an international cross-cultural and interdisciplinary conference and study center in a mountainous region of China. The center will be known as the Lan Ting Institute. Huang is its international director.

Chungliang Al Huang grew up in a scholarly family, eventually coming to the United States to study architecture. He obtained his B.A. in 1960 from UCLA. Drawn to dance and theater, following study of Beijing Opera and the martial arts,

Taoism has its strongest influence in the southern rural areas of China. Outside of China, Taoist religion can be found wherever traditional Chinese culture survives—in Taiwan, Hong Kong, Singapore, Indonesia, Thailand, Hawaii, and in Western cities, such as New York, San Francisco, Vancouver, and Toronto. The strongest Taoist tradition is found in Taiwan.

(Sharma)

he eventually would perform with Sammy Davis, Jr. (the only Taoist to ever do so!) and become a featured dancer in the film "Flower Drum Song." He combined his interests in choreography with comparative religion, philosophy, and cultural anthropology and got a master's degree from Bennington College in 1963. Huang formed his own Theater Dance company in 1965, became a Ford Foundation research scholar, a visiting professor at the College of Chinese Culture, and a doctoral research fellow at the Academia Sinica in the Republic of China. He was awarded the highly prestigious Gold Medal from the Chinese Ministry of Culture and Education for his outstanding artistic achievements in 1966.

For the next twenty years, Huang was artist-in-residence at countless colleges and festivals in several countries. He collaborated in his unique form of Taoist music with such talents as Paul Horn and Paul Winter, performing, for example, "The Tao of Bach" at St. John the Divine Cathedral in New York. During this time, he taught at the Yehudi Menuhin School in England and lectured with His Holiness the Dalai Lama, Gregory Bateson, Robert Bly, Huston Smith, Karl Pribram, and Brother David Steindl-Rast.

Consistent with the "universality" of his Taoism, Huang is also an accomplished Chinese brush calligrapher-painter whose works have been exhibited at fine galleries from San Francisco to Vienna.

Chungliang Al Huang's many books include *Embrace Tiger, Return to Mountain* (1973), *Tao: The Watercourse Way* (with Alan Watts, 1975), *Living Tao: Still Visions and Dancing Brushes* (with Si Chi Ko, 1976), *Quantum Soup: Fortune Cookies in Crisis* (1983), *Tai Ji: Danse du Tao* (1986), *Tai Ji: Beginner's Tai Ji Book* (1989), *Thinking Body, Dancing Mind* (with Jerry Lynch, 1992).

THE MEANING OF TAI JI (TAI CHI)

Tai Ji is a general concept of how we learn to play with nature. Many people think Tai Ji is a form of exercise. Now all over the world in the parks you see people practice Tai Ji Chuan, which means a choreography or dance based on the Tai Ji concept. We learn to move in accordance with nature. It's a free, spontaneous dance that rekindles that wonderful ability to know that, if you are free, you are flowing with nature in your own very special way.

But Tai Ji is a philosophy of living, to learn to bring harmony with life. As a child, living in the villages, when you are close to nature, by the rice paddies, the mountains and rivers, you immediately understand why we need to learn how to move according to nature's way.

I'm simply a student of life, a student of Tai Ji. In Chinese language, it is more metaphoric and more poetic. When you say "practice," it has a totally English discipline—hard work. You knit your eyebrows and hunch your muscles. In Chinese, we would like to think of it as a play. It's like the dance of life. You play with life, you enjoy your practice. We prefer to practice life with more joy, more spontaneity.

Everybody is a dancer to begin with. We have somehow lost it along the way. The spirit embodies each person. We all have limitations and some of us can do more than the others, according to our own age and our problems or our advantages. Each person within himself and herself is a complete energy. If you're paralyzed, for instance, if you have problems you can use your Tai Ji feeling to make yourself feel whole and complete. There is no reason we all have to do Tai Ji in the same way.

I tell people I am very fortunate even though I was born during the very turbulent times, during the war with Japan and later civil war and great deal of problems internally in China, because during the war we had to run away. We were able to live in the villages amongst the farmers and people and I always consider myself very lucky.

Every Chinese would say, "May you be born in a very interesting time." It could be a curse or a blessing at the same time. And because of the good fortune of being in the villages, I was able to really learn from an early age how the Chinese practice Tai Ji, according to the way of nature.

Like many other books of the same period (fifth to third centuries B.C.E.), the Tao-te ching (literally, "the Way and its power") was compiled as a manual to instruct kings and rulers in the art of government, teaching that the state that governs least governs best. As a political work, the Tao-te ching is a failure, because its view that the king should rule by wu wei, or no-action, has never been taken seriously by any ruler in Chinese history. But as a philosophical work it has been immensely influential.

(Crim)

THE MEANING OF "JI"

The word *ji* in Chinese means breath, in a very simple way. As I breathe, I have *ji*. When I am born I have *ji*, and the sky has *ji*, the universe has *ji*.

From the Chuang Tzu

If you want to nourish a bird, you should let it live any way it chooses. Creatures differ because they have different likes and dislikes. Therefore the sages never require the same ability from all creatures. . . . The true saint leaves wisdom to the ants, takes a cue from the fishes, and leaves willfulness to the sheep. (The Chuang Tzu is the second most important book in Taoism, after the Lao Tzu.)

This room has *ji*. *Ji* is a spirit, a force of life that is intrinsic and all embracing. And *ch'i-kung* simply means how to utilize, how to find ways to create the *ji* flow—it makes you more vital—through the breath, within you, through your ability to connect with the burst of life around you.

We can feel the body breathing. Open your arms in Tai Ji. I am reaching up to the sky. The *ji* of sky funnels into my body, and I will embrace the *ji*. If I feel the earth from underneath my feet coming through my body, I bring the *ji* of the earth into my body. I can connect sky and the earth and integrate this energy together into my own sense of awareness. This is the essence of Tai Ji. When we begin to connect and we begin to dance.

There is new interest in *ch'i-kung* and practice of *ji* as a healing technique. It is a physical reality. It's the kind of meaning intrinsically in the experience. Often we separate meaning and experience because we have to describe experience and we call it meaning. In Tai Ji it's inclusive.

We call this "embrace the tiger, return to mountain." It's a wonderful metaphor. It's a wonderful feeling. You embody this tiger energy, which is a metaphor for the beauty, danger, power, fear, and all this wonderful sense of who you are. When you accept this energy, you relax. You return and you come home. We call it the mountain. When you return, you come home, you do "happy landings" [*laughs*] instead of trying to strive with higher heights.

DOES POWER LEAD TO VIOLENCE?

When I teach Tai Ji, I would say, I empower you. Or we are empowered by the spirit or by the energy we feel. So it's an inner sense of power which is inside of you. When you are content, when you are contained with the power, you are happy with yourself, therefore there is no aggression that is necessary.

But if the power is something you strive for, you try to be bigger and better and more, then you begin to invade. You begin to be aggressive and you are out of yourself. If I want to empower somebody out of aggression, or out of ego, then energy is away from me. But if I want to empower, even if I want to empower you, I want to relate to you. Therefore it is a relationship and it is a mutual containment.

It's very different than power that is, that kind of macho energy.

WHERE DOES THE POWER COME FROM?

Let's go back to the word *ji* again. We say in China, when you are born you connect the *ji* from your parents, from your ancestors, the first breath you take, and you have this *ji.* You have the power of *life.* You are given the power of life. As you grow, you are being nurtured by love, by environment, by food, also by the spirit. And we have a finite breath that's within the life span. We can also nurture ourselves by our creativity in life, the way we give and take in life.

The Chinese say that creativity is the birth of every moment. It's a way, if I feel the power within me, I go to the center of my body, this place we call *danchient.* It's the same place Japanese call *hara.* It's the gut level center. And this is my life force, right now. If I come to my own center, I know this is where I feel. That's my power. And I give this power as I speak to you. And then I receive your response and I listen to you. And we do this give-and-take Tai Ji dance as we converse. This is power, this is *ji,* this is flow. And this is what we call tao.

IS TAO GOD?

I think whatever religious background, social background, or racial background we have, we have a *big* word like "God," "Spirit." We have *big* word to describe something undefined, unknown, bigger than life that we have to pay respect, we have to bow to. In China, we use the word *Tao,* which is also bow to God. We can say God is Tao. Tao is God, but it's not defined. The Western mystic, like Meister Eckhart, used to say, "God, make me rid of 'God.'"

He actually prayed for this. The ultimate leave taking is to leave "God" for God, because the minute you say "God," it's a thing in the way you confine, define God, make him too small.

I have just three things to teach:
simplicity, patience, compassion.
These three are your greatest treasures.
Simple in actions and in thoughts,
you return to the source of being.
Patient with both friends and enemies,
you accord with the way things are.
Compassionate toward yourself,
you reconcile all beings in the world.

—Lao Tzu, #67 (Novak trans.)

Make her too small. And you see, as I do the gender dance, I don't want to say he or she, maybe it's an *it*. We don't know, but it has to be bigger than what we can utter in human terms. So we've got to learn to keep opening to a bigger concept.

In China, the word *tao* is used in many dimensions. When we say, "I know"—if I say to you, "I know, I know," I say "*tze tao, tze tao.*" You have tao in the second part. Tze simply means, "I hear the Tao, I've got the Tao." Tze is: archer hit the bull's-eye. When the archer—the knowledge, hits the center—I've got it, I tao—I understand. We say "*ji tao.*" *Ji tao* means, "I embody the tao." You can say, my body is the tao. And we use, "Tao le, tao le," means the tao fits into organic pattern—suddenly tao makes sense and we say, "*tao le, tao le*—oh! you're right, you're right, come to think about it, you're tao le." We use tao again. So we use tao in many ways.

And Confucius says, "Tao is never far away from any human." Unless you bring the tao into everyday life, it becomes too abstract, too esoteric, to "spacey." It has nothing to do with life. In my learning, I bring tao into everyday living.

I practice my Tai Ji as I talk to you. I drink tea or coffee in the morning—that's tao. Tao is in living. I created a small foundation called the Living Tao Foundation, a small network of friends all over the world who believe in using the concept of tao as an open concept to help us to learn how to live more harmoniously—with ourselves, with our fellow beings, and the world. So tao is a living process, it's a most important way to practice life.

The most wonderful metaphor to describe the tao is the flowing water. It's the water course. It's so universal because the water flows all the time, refreshes all the time, and can fit into any shape—does not have an outline—has full power and always water flows to a bigger place, more contained place and always in flux.

TEACHING OF TAO

As many people know now in the West we have so many books, *The Tao of Physics, The Tao of Love, The Tao of Leadership, The Tao of Winnie the Pooh.* Tao can apply to everything. See, compassion is a very important part. Tao sometimes translates "the way." The way of doing of things, the wisdom of being whatever you do. If you are a leader, you need to learn tao of leadership. If you are one to go into science, maybe the tao of science, the tao of relationship. And tao is everything. In the taoist sense we talk about relationship give-and-take, the coming out of your own ego center to relate to another person.

There are no moral laws or codes, or behavioral descriptions, not in a "religious" sense. An author might say, "Tao is not a religion." Sometimes people force it, confine it into a religion. There is taoist religion, a sect of taoists, they even have a priest and so-called religious leaders.

I want one to believe in a much bigger tao. My friends in the Western religious background often say to me, we believe in the bigger, the capital R, Religion, not the little r, religion. And it's the same thing. Tao cannot be confined. The tao that can be tao-ed is not the tao—the very first line of Tao Te Ching. That's the beauty of tao.

Jung called it the unconscious—something that you cannot consciously put into that place, but it's collective. In a Jungian sense, describing this kind of tao which is an unconscious, undefined way for us to relate to each other spiritually and to relate to the world spiritually, from within.

It's so simple, in the practice of Tai Ji, in the playing of the flute.

I do have my flute here. This is a simple bamboo flute, which I use to meditate, to check my own breathing. You have to focus, you have to calm down, and then you have to feel the emptiness of the instrument which relates to your own emptiness. You clean your clutter and all the chatter in your skull, all the jitters inside of you until you feel clear, and the breath is clear, and then the sound comes. [*He plays his flute.*]

And it begins to warm up, because flute is alive. It was sitting there cold, I need to warm it up. My breath has to warm it, make it living. The flute has to come alive with me. [*More playing.*]

The tone gets sweeter the second time because it is warmer. [*More playing.*] And it's something happening, something comes alive. The music happens as I breathe into this vessel. The music is everything. It's me, and the flute, and my breath, and the feeling, and the vibrations of sound that we hear.

*The highest truth cannot be put into words.
Therefore the greatest teacher has nothing to say.
He simply gives himself in service, and never worries.*

—Lao Tzu, #23 (Novak trans.)

Trees and animals, humans and insects, flowers and birds: these are active images of the subtle energies that flow from the stars throughout the universe.

Meeting and combining with each other and the elements of the Earth, they give rise to all living things. The superior person understands this, and understands that her own energies play a part in it.

Those who want to know the truth of the universe should practice . . . reverence for all life; this manifests as unconditional love and respect for oneself and all other beings.

—Lao Tzu (Brian Walker trans.)

I also say my body is my flute. This is the most clear and simple instrument. I'm simply a vehicle here. Sometimes we make a distinction between a utensil and a sacred holy vessel. If I am sitting here just being a small human being looking at my fingernails I am just a utensil, but if I sit up straight, breathe, open up to a bigger me—I am changing—I become a vessel. It is so simple, it is everyday life.

I bring the life force from the earth into my body. I breathe into my body. I let the music play me—and the tao, the universe comes into me. I change, I feel the difference in my body. I transcend the ceiling into the open sky, I transcend the limitation of the floor deep into the center of the earth. The *ji* flows from the bottom of my body all the way beyond, through me.

We find this connection, spiritually, way up there, and physically way down here, grounded, earthy, and we find the empty space. I embrace the space, I focus, I open, expand my vision, extend my horizons. I balance and I reach up to the heights, and reach down to the depths. I embody this awareness, through and through. I am the connection between heaven and earth. I wake up to this consciousness. I am awakened. Through my center, I give my life force out, to you, to the world out there. And I bring the outside back to me—from internally, where I am, to where I am out there. This simple gesture, of opening myself out to the world and letting the outside come back to me.

Everybody knows this feeling once they do it. It's not a dancing class or techniques class, it's just something you have to try to do. It's a feeling of connection. And something happens to you. You feel natural, you feel tao.

I embrace my tiger, and I return to my mountaintop.

ZOROASTRIAN

ZOROASTRIAN

THE GOOD MIND

KAIKHOSROV D. IRANI

Kaikhosrov D. Irani is Professor Emeritus of Philosophy of the City College of New York. His areas of special interest are philosophy of science, philosophy of mind, and ancient thought. Born and raised a Parsi in Bombay, and educated there at St. Xavier's School and College, he was a student of chemistry and physics. Later, he was appointed a Fellow in Physical Chemistry at St. Xavier's College, University of Bombay.

As a Parsi, Professor Irani is descended from the Zoroastrians of Iran (the Pars). They are now dispersed throughout the world, principally, as it turns out, in English-speaking lands. Professor Irani himself moved to the United States and joined the City College of New York in 1950, teaching there for forty-one years, where, he was professor and chairman of the department of philosophy before his retirement in 1991. He was also founding executive director of the program for the History and Philosophy of Science and Technology. He was for eight years director of the Academy for Humanities and Sciences of the University of New York.

Historian and philosopher, he has made a unique contribution over the past twenty-five years to the exploration of the origins of the intellectual enterprises of humanity, particularly scientific, ethical, and religious. He delivered the Government Fellowship lectures on the Emergence of Religio-Philosophic Ideas in the ancient Indo-Iranian Tradition at the Oriental Insti-

In this worldly abode of ours,
May communication drive away mis-communication
May peace drive away anarchy
May generosity drive away selfishness
May benevolence drive away hostility
May compassionate words prevail over false protestations
May truth prevail over falsehood.

—from the Dahm Afringan prayer

tute in Bombay in 1986 and has published extensively in the areas of the philosophy of mind and of science.

Professor Irani is presently president of the Zoroastrian Association of Greater New York, and is a member of the board of directors of the World Zoroastrian Organization based in London.

THE HEART OF ZOROASTRIAN TEACHING

The essence of the teaching, which comes from the Prophet Zarathustra, himself, is what one might call a reflective religion. It is a fusion of a view of the world and a way of life. The view of the world he offers is that the world was created in accordance with the principle of truth, *Asha*. It's an ideal notion. The world was supposed to be perfect, but when the material world was created, there was within the material world a spirit of opposition. This is the celebrated dualism that people talk of when they refer to Zoroastrianism.

There are not two divinities. There are two forces, vectors, within creation—one attempting to fulfill the truth, the other opposing or frustrating it. So the world is a world which was meant to be perfect, but is contaminated.

From this emerges a way of life. There is a divine attribute of the Good Mind in all of us, which enables us to do two things— to recognize the contaminated world for what it is, and to recognize the principle of truth. When one sees the disparity between the actual and the ideal, then one is inspired by a spirit that is a divine spirit, within us, the spirit to bring to fruition the perfection of the world. It is benevolence or good intention.

It is a choice. This is expressed in three or four places in the *Gathas,* the verses of Zarathustra. At all points the individual must recognize the alternatives and choose, cannot escape the choice.

The question that arose and was elaborated in the later theology was how is it that, given the Good Mind, we still make the wrong choice? There are several answers, but the most significant answer is that our Good Mind is blurred. The vision is blurred by wrong intentions within ourselves. Sometimes we act to vindicate our self-images. We act out of past frustrations and

Zoroastrian Scriptures

There are four major parts of Zoroastrian scripture, called the Avesta:
1. the Yasna, *the liturgical work that includes the* Gathas *("songs"), the oldest part of the Avesta, perhaps written by the prophet Zoroaster*
2. the Vispered, *a supplement to the* Yasna
3. the Yashts, *hymns of praise, including the* Khurda *("little")* Avesta
4. the Vivevdat, *a detailed code of ritual purification*

(Columbia)

hurts. This prevents us from seeing the world as it really is and leads to wrong choices.

One makes an effort. Zarathustra on one occasion says to God, "Make wide the vision of my mind." This has been commented on by later theologians. The reason why we see the world incorrectly is that our vision is narrow, that our personal interests force us to ignore so many things. Really there is no solution except clear and consistent thinking, and asking ourselves, how could this situation be perfected?

ZOROASTRIANISM IS NOT GNOSTICISM

Gnosticism was a doctrine which emerged quite late, actually sometime around the first century B.C. and persisted until the third century B.C. There is a very close analogy with respect to one particular aspect of Zoroastrianism. In Zoroastrianism, Ahura Mazda, that's the divinity, created an ideal world and then created the material world in which the ideals were supposed to be incorporated. So there is the doctrine of two worlds. This doctrine went into neo-Platonism where the neo-Platonists talk of the world of ideas.

Later the Gnostics made this intermediate world between the divinity and the material world a series of sixteen, sometimes sixty, sometimes six thousand worlds. And the Gnostic notion was that we are sparks of divinity that have descended through the layers. In each layer, two things happen—we forget our origin and we acquire the characteristic of that layer until finally, in this world, we have forgotten completely that we are, in essence, divine beings. And this recollection gradually takes us back through these layers to the Divinity.

The resemblance is, with Zoroastrianism, that, if we live a life of self-interest alone, then we have sacrificed the Good Mind. And to rise toward divinity we must recapture the Good Mind and begin to see the functioning of the principle of truth in this world, and then reach salvation.

Pure self-interest limits our perception of the world. It limits the functioning of the mind. You see situations through the lens of your self-interest, not as it really is. And you cannot then compare it with the ideal, as it should be. Having been an aca-

The majority of Zoroastrians, perhaps 60,000, live in India. This community, called Parsees, migrated from Persia (present-day Iran) around 936 C.E. to avoid persecution from Muslim conquerors. Those that have remained in Iran, perhaps 10,000 today, have endured severe harassment. Most of the Zoroastrians immigrating to the West settled in North America—there is a large community in Toronto, Canada. Membership in Europe in estimated at 7,000, mainly in England, with 3,000 more scattered in other parts of the world.

—Pallan R. Ichaporia, *Portrait of Zoroastrianism*

demic for twenty years, I've seen people argue things back and forth. And sometimes the argument is not with respect to what the best educational policy is, but with the interests of this particular academic or with that particular individual. Their positions have cast certain narrowing perspectives on the situation.

There is a very beautiful passage in the *Gathas*, the hymns of Zarathustra. It's sometimes been called the blessing of Zarathustra. This is how the line goes: "May we be like those who bring the world toward perfection." This is our function, to perfect this world. And we can do it in small and minor ways in this or that situation. But wherever the world has been improved, there the mind has been successful. So that's the goal and that's what we do.

AHURA MAZDA, THE CREATOR

The theology puts Ahura Mazda as the Creator, not only the creator of the ideal world of truth, the Good Mind, and so on, but the creator of the physical world. He is also completely good. No evil comes from him.

That evil arises in creation; there is no theory for why it arises. It is the voice of opposition. Later on the negativity was personalized and so we have the equivalent of Satan, the good spirit and the evil spirit. But the evil spirit—this is about eight hundred years or so after the life of the prophet—was described as the spirit having two characteristics, violence and stupidity. It cannot truly comprehend the nature of reality and attempts to break it down. Then later on some of the priests extended it by saying, well, this is what gets into human individuals. And these two spirits then have a conflict within our consciousness. But Ahura Mazda is just the Creator.

He doesn't create anything more. He continues to provide the Good Mind and inspiration for human beings. The perfection of the world is to be brought about by human beings cooperating with the divinity.

There is a guarantee that evil will ultimately be completely destroyed and the world will become perfect as it was originally meant to be. That will happen when all human beings choose only the good, because when evil is not chosen it perishes. It is

---

Zoroastrianism and Other Faiths

Some theological concepts shared by Zoroastrianism with Judaism and Christianity:

- *Belief in one supreme and loving God*
- *Heaven and Hell, and individual judgment*
- *The ultimate triumph of good over evil*
- *Strict moral and ethical codes*
- *Resurrection, final judgment, and life everlasting*
- *Satan and paradise*
- *The word* amen *is of Zoroastrian origin*

—Rohinton M. Rivetna

difficult to imagine that, and we are somewhat far from that. But I have a great feeling that such a time may come. I think, an increase in human illumination. And a social order in which no one feels forced to compromise with evil. But this is the remote future.

There is no forcing of anyone. It must come as a matter of conviction. That's a choice which each individual must make. If you avoid the choice, you've made a choice. That's the avoidance option. Yes, and it could be good or it could be bad. But often when you avoid, you are giving up the function of the Good Mind. Nor can the person avoid the responsibility for that choice.

THE TEACHINGS OF ZARATHUSTRA CONCERNING CARE OF THE WORLD

This is perhaps the major function of humanity, to care for the world. And these are the two forms. And when one perfects the world, one perfects both the natural world and the social structure. So that in the end, when perfection is achieved, there is complete harmony and no conflict. No individual human or animal needs to survive by seeking the destruction of another.

That would be the perfected state. And one should move in that direction as much as possible. To choose nonviolence over violence, which—along with stupidity—is characteristic of the Evil Mind.

So it is our chore in life, or our delight in life, to avoid violence and to become educated—and in doing that to enjoy ourselves and feel happy about what it is we are doing. So, personal enjoyment is considered to be a worthwhile thing.

One of the great high priests of Iran, during the Sasanian Empire (fourth century A.D.) wrote a series of items of advice for various people, some of his children and others, in which he told them, on this day of the month do this, on this day clean the house, on this day take care of your orchard, and on this day of the month, gather the family together and feel happy. It's an obligation to feel happy as a worthwhile thing to do.

A Zoroastrian Prayer

With bended knees,
with hands outstretched,
do I yearn for the effective
*   expression*
of the holy spirit working
*   within me:*
For this love and under-
*   standing, truth and jus-*
*   tice;*
for wisdom to know the
*   apparent*
from the real that I might
*   alleviate*
the sufferings of men on
*   earth. . . .*

—from the Avesta prayer

SOURCES

The following books are a partial listing of works used as references and for quoted material for the information that appears in the margins in this book. The notations in parentheses correspond with the citations in the text.

(Albanese)
Albanese, Catherine L. *America, Religions and Religion.* Belmont, CA: Wadsworth Publishing Co., 1981.

(Allama/Al-Mamum)
Allama, Sir Abdullah and Al-Mamum Al-Suhrawardy. *The Sayings of Muhammad.* New York: Citadel Press, 1990.

(*Almanac*)
1994 Catholic Almanac. Huntington, IN: Our Sunday Visitor, 1994.

(*SourceBook*)
Beversluis, Joel D. *A SourceBook for the Earth's Community of Religions,* (rev. ed.) Grand Rapids, MI: CoNexus Press-SourceBook Project with Global Education Associates, New York, 1995.

(Burger)
Burger, Julian. *The Gaia Atlas of the First Peoples.* New York: Doubleday, 1990.

(Campenhausen)
Campenhausen, Rufus C. *The Divine Library.* Rochester, VT: Inner Traditions International, 1992.

(Crim)
Crim, Keith, ed. *The Perennial Dictionary of World Religions*. San Francisco: HarperSanFrancisco, 1990.

(Dalai Lama)
Dalai Lama. *My Land and My People*. New York: Potala, 1983.

(Diagram)
Diagram Group. *Religions on File*. New York: Facts on File, 1990.

(*Biography*)
Dictionary of America Biography. New York: Macmillan, 1981.

(Earhart)
Earhart, H. Byron, ed. *Religious Traditions of the World*. San Francisco: HarperSanFrancisco, 1993.

(Eck)
Eck, Diana. "What Do We Mean by Dialogue?" *Current Dialogue*. 1987.

(Fackenheim)
Fackenheim, Emil L. *To Mend the World*. New York: Schocken Books, 1989.

(Glassé)
Glassé, Cyril. *The Concise Encyclopedia of Islam*. San Francisco: Harper & Row, 1989.

(Griffin)
Griffin, Albert Kirby. *Religious Proverbs*. Jefferson, NC: McFarland & Co., 1991.

(Griffiths)
Griffiths, Bede. *Return to the Centre*. London: Collins, 1976.

(Kabilsingh)
Kabilsingh, Chatsumarn. "The Future of the Bhikkuni Samgha in Thailand." In *Speaking in Faith*, edited by Diana Eck. Philadelphia, PA: New Society Publishers, 1987.

(Koszegi/Melton)
Koszegi, Michael A., and J. Gordon Melton. *Islam in North America: A Sourcebook*. New York: Garland, 1992.

(Küng)
Küng, Hans. *Global Responsibility: In Search of a New World Ethic*. New York: Crossroad, 1991.

(McBrien/*Catholicism*)
McBrien, Richard P. *Catholicism*. Rev. ed. San Francisco: Harper SanFrancisco, 1994.

(McBrien/*Encyclopedia*)
McBrien, Richard P., ed. *The HarperCollins Encyclopedia of Catholicism*. San Francisco: HarperSanFrancisco, 1995.

(Melton/*Religions*)
Melton, J. Gordon. *Encyclopedia of American Religions.* 4th ed. Detroit, MI: Gale Research, 1993.

(Melton/*Creeds*)
Melton, J. Gordon. *Encyclopedia of American Religions, Religious Creeds.* Detroit, MI: Gale Research, 1988.

(Melton/*Bodies*)
Melton, J. Gordon. *Religious Bodies in the United States: A Directory.* New York: Garland, 1992.

(Melton/*Leaders*)
Melton, J. Gordon. *Religious Leaders of America.* Detroit, MI: Gale Research, 1990.

(Muller)
Muller, Robert. *New Genesis: Shaping a Global Spirituality.* Garden City, NY: Doubleday, 1982.

(Columbia)
New Columbia Encyclopedia. 4th ed. New York: Columbia University Press, 1975.

(Novak)
Novak, Philip. *The World's Wisdom: Sacred Texts of the World's Religions.* San Francisco: HarperSanFrancisco, 1994.

(Rifkin)
Rifkin, Jeremy. *Beyond Beef: The Rise and Fall of the Cattle Culture.* New York: NAL-Dutton, 1992.

(*Earth Prayers*)
Roberts, Elizabeth, and Elias Amidon, eds. *Earth Prayers.* San Francisco: HarperSanFrancisco, 1991.

(Roof)
Roof, Wade Clark. *A Generation of Seekers.* San Francisco: HarperSanFrancisco, 1993.

(Sharma)
Sharma, Arvind, ed. *Our Religions.* San Francisco: HarperSanFrancisco, 1993.

(Smith)
Smith, Huston. *The World's Religions.* Rev. ed. San Francisco: HarperSanFrancisco, 1991.

(Snelling)
Snelling, John. *The Buddhist Handbook.* Rochester, VT: Inner Traditions International, 1991.

(Templeton)
Templeton, John. *The Humble Approach.* New York: Seabury Press, 1981.

(Tobias/*Life Force*)
Tobias, Michael. *Life Force: The World of Jainism.* Fremont, CA: Asian Humanities Press, 1991.

(Tobias/*Naked Man*)
Tobias, Michael. *A Naked Man.* Fremont, CA: Asian Humanities Press, 1994.

(Tobias/*Voice*)
Tobias, Michael. *Voice of the Planet.* New York: Bantam, 1990.

(Tobias/*WWIII*)
Tobias, Michael. *World War III: Population and the Biosphere at the End of the Millennium.* Santa Fe, NM: Bear & Co., 1994.

(Williamson)
Williamson, William B., ed. *An Encyclopedia of Religions in the United States.* New York: Crossroad, 1992.

Permission to reprint the following excerpts is gratefully acknowledged:

Quotations on pp. 25, 27, 31, 36, 57, 105, 107, 179, 228, 250 taken from *A SourceBook for Earth's Community of Religions, Revised Edition,* © 1995. Edited by Joel D. Beversluis. Published by CoNexus Press-SourceBook Project (Grand Rapid, MI) with Global Education Associates (New York). Used by permission of the publisher.

Quotations on pp. 221, 222, 224, 225, 232, 234, 260 taken from *The Concise Encyclopedia of Islam* by Cyril Glassé, © 1989. Published by HarperCollins Publishers. Reprinted with permission of the publisher.

Quotations on pp. 20, 33, 40, 41, 46, 65, 171, 194, 195, 202, 206, 230, 235, 257, 258 taken from *The Encyclopedia of American Religions: Religious Creeds, 4th Edition.* A Compilation of more than 450 creeds, confessions, statements of faith, and summaries of doctrine of religious and spiritual groups in the United States and Canada. Edited by J. Gordon Melton. Copyright © 1993 Gale Research Inc. Reprinted with permission of the publisher.

INDEX

ABOUT THE EDITORS

Michael Tobias is an internationally respected ecologist, author, and filmmaker whose prolific work has reached people in over 50 countries. Among his most prominent films and works of fiction and nonfiction are *World War III, A Vision of Nature, Black Tide, A Naked Man,* and the ten-hour dramatic television miniseries and novel *Voice of the Planet.*

Jane Morrison is a film producer, opera singer, editor, and animal activist. Her film credits include *Voice of the Planet, A Day in the Life of Ireland,* which she co-directed, and *Antarctica: The Last Continent.* Morrison and her husband Michael Tobias are frequent collaborators.

Bettina Gray is a veteran of television and radio interviews. She hosted public television's *The Creative Mind,* a series of interviews with prominent literary, visual, and performing artists, as well as the long-running radio series *Toward Better Understanding.* Gray is a founding member of the North American Interfaith Network of the United States and Canada.

Come Face to Face with Today's Most Influential Spiritual Leaders

Many of the provocative interviews from *A Parliament of Souls* are now available on home video. Sixteen interviews from across the religious spectrum offer a unique chance to hear spiritual leaders discuss the application of faith to everyday life and the individual's role in global crises.

Used as a focus for discussion or as an information resource, this two-hour video provides study groups, classes, and students of religion with a unique view of faith as it is lived.

The video includes:

Jacqueline Left Hand Bull Delahunt
Sister Jayanti
Dr. A.T. Ariyaratne
His Holiness the Dalai Lama
Dr. Chatsumarn Kabilsingh
Diana L. Eck
John Marks Templeton
Dr. Hans Küng
Robert Muller
Sri Swami Chidananda Saraswati
Dr. L.M. Singhvi
Michael Tobias
Rabbi Emil Fackenheim
Susannah Heschel
Dr. Azizah Y. Al-Hibri
Imam W.D. Mohammed

$29.95
Order by Calling 1-800-647-3600

Support your local public broadcasting station!

Every community across America is reached by one of the 346 member stations of the Public Broadcasting Service. These stations bring information, entertainment, and insight for the whole family.

Think about the programs you enjoy and remember most:
Mystery . . . Masterpiece Theatre . . . Nova . . . Nature . . . Sesame Street . . . Ghostwriter . . . Reading Rainbow . . . Baseball The Civil War . . . MacNeil/Lehrer News Hour . . . Great Performances . . . Eyes on the Prize . . . National Geographic . . . Washington Week in Review . . . and so many more.

On your local PBS station, you'll also find fascinating adult education courses, provocative documentaries, great cooking and do-it-yourself programs, and thoughtful local analysis.

Despite the generous underwriting contributions of foundations and corporations, more than half of all public television budgets come from individual member support.

For less than the cost of a night at the movies, less than a couple of months of a daily paper, less than a month of your cable TV bill, you can help make possible all the quality programming you enjoy.

Become a member of your public broadcasting station and do your part.

Public Television. You make it happen!